THE ASTROLOGY OF LOVE

The Matchmaker's Guide To The Universe

By Suzanne White

****

Published by:
Suzanne White
Copyright (c) 2012 by Suzanne White

****

All rights reserved. Without limiting the rights under copyright reserved above, no part of this publication may be reproduced, stored in or introduced into a retrieval system, or transmitted, in any form, or by any means (electronic, mechanical, photocopying, recording, or otherwise) without the prior written permission of both the copyright owner and the above publisher of this book.

****

A Savvy Blend of Chinese and Western Astrologies Uniquely Designed to Find You the Perfect Mate

Dedication

This book is dedicated to my brothers, George, Peter, and John Hoskins, and my adoptive sisters, Nicole, Tracey, and Carol Hoskins. And to my loving nephew, John Ryan, and my beloved niece, Pamela. All of you have given me the best LOVE ever!

May your tribe increase.

Love, Suzanne

Contents

Preface 1
How to use this Book 4
The Chinese Calendar 10
The Western Zodiac 15

PART ONE: Chinese Astrology Signs
    Rat.. 18
    Ox 42
    Tiger 64
    Cat/Rabbit... 84
    Dragon 103
    Snake 120
    Horse 136
    Goat 149
    Monkey 160
    Rooster.. 169
    Dog 176
    Pig 181

PART TWO: Western Astrology Signs
    Aries 186
    Taurus 211
    Gemini 235
    Cancer... 256
    Leo 276
    Virgo 293
    Libra 308
    Scorpio.. 322
    Sagittarius 334
    Capricorn 344
    Aquarius 352
    Pisces 358

Preface

Before launching into the body of this book, I'd like to tell a little story about how I got this far. Maybe autobiography decreases stage fright.

In all of my life I have but one regret: I married the wrong person. He was totally unsuitable for me. I was thoroughly wrong for him. During the initial mental-paralysis period of our romance in Paris, France, we had two children. Both in the same year. Ten months and ten days apart. One year later, when we found the time, we got married. Nine months of mental cruelty later, I walked out with a baby under each arm and headed back to Paris, where I spent much of my life wondering what had hit me. Recently, I began returning to the States periodically to see if I could fit my Frenchified self back into the American dream.

But that is another book.

The important matter here is that I am sorry my marriage did not work .I am sorry my kids had a lopsided childhood living full-time with a single mom. Of course, I am not alone. These days, family breakups are routine. Separations happen all the time. Divorce is epidemic. Kids are strewn all over creation, moved and tugged and pulled out of shape by our inability to stay together because of irreconcilable differences. Everybody is so terribly sorry. Most are still reeling. *What happened? How did I get myself (and my unsuspecting offspring) into such a mess?*

Like so many women and men today, I also rue the day I agreed to having kids with a person about whom I knew nothing. I lived in Paris. I was twenty-six. I had a good job. I thought I was intelligent.

I was an idiot.

Before taking up residence with a fellow with whom I had fallen in love in twenty-four hours' time, I ought to have found out who he really was. I should have studied his astrological portrait, his family history, and delved into his romantic past. Coldly, objectively, I ought to have taken a microscope to his character. Then (and only then) could I have made a coolheaded decision.

Today I know that I am a Scorpio—with Taurus rising, and Venus and the Moon in Scorpio. I shudder to think what I was doing back then, casting my lot with a Gemini whose rising sign I have conveniently forgotten but suspect it was something like Flibbertigibbet or Flake. Had I taken leave of my senses?

Yup.

Now that I have written umpteen books about Chinese astrology, which is a uniquely incisive system of in-depth character reading, I know as well that I am a hasty Tiger-born person. Impulsive. Daring. Risk-loving. Defiant. Willful and brazenly nonconformist. Tigers are often more courageous than intelligent. Especially swooning young female Tigers who haven't a clue how to curb their raging hormonal impetuousness.

Consequently, when I was a twenty-six-year-old, madly in love Scorpio/Tiger cub, I did no research on my prospective mate. I never asked for (nor would I have heeded) any advice on the subject of his character. I thought I knew best. I plunged blindfolded into the gorgeous pink abyss of *love* without even holding my nose, and I landed smack in hell.

My fault? Oh, certainly. Like the Katzenjammner Kids in the Sunday funnies of yore, "I brought it on myself." I made my bed and have been lying in its shredded dirty linen for the whole of my life. But never mind. None of us four Whites has yet died from the wretched mismatch. Yet, all of us have been made unhappy by it. I really should have done my homework.

Hence, this book comes to you from the pen of a woman who would like to spare you the pain of her own life-altering mismatch mistake. I am motivated by my own story. But now I am also an astrologer. More than mere regret drives me. With years of practice under my belt, I am now equipped to deliver some dead simple insights. I want to assist you in making clever choices about whom to have an affair with, live with, marry, or just keep as a good friend.

In this book, you will find out a bit more about who you actually are and why you should definitely not take up with that Leo/Pig you find so sexy, or continue to lead on the Taurus/Horse whose very soul you, as a Pisces/Snake, could devour whole in a New York millisecond. For the sake of eventual family harmony, I will also clue you into which years and signs it would be best to plan to have your children.

Before I pounce into the thick of the subject with the dense force of my four Tiger paws and the sting of my Scorpio tongue, I want to share with you a motto I first saw on a napkin as a small child in a Buffalo, New York, donut shop: "As you go through life, make this your goal: Keep your eye on the doughnut and not on the hole."

I don't know who wrote that piece of unforgettable wisdom, but I suggest you hurry up and learn it by heart, cross-stitch it on a sampler, turn it into a bumper sticker, and stamp it on all your T-shirts. Now. Before it's too late.

S. White
Paris, France / Mill Valley, California

How to Use this Book

I'll be brief. This book is exclusively about LOVE. Your LOVE.

I wrote it to help you find someone who is right for you. If you have already found someone, maybe *ASTRO LOVE* will assist you in sorting out your differences. I sincerely hope so.

Some years ago, I invented the *New Astrology*. I blended both Chinese and Western astrologies into 12 x 12, or 144 New Astrology signs. I wanted to include compatibilities in that book. But they wouldn't fit. When you match twelve Chinese animal signs with twelve Western zodiac signs, you get 156 different possible compatibility combinations. The data would fill a whole book! So I wrote one and call it *ASTRO LOVE*.

At first, it looked easy. I figured I would simply take a New Astrology sign , throw it into my mental blender with another New Astrology sign, and get a good, mediocre, or horrible couple result. But if I had done that—144 signs blended with 144 signs—the *ASTRO LOVE* would have to be about as big as New Hampshire.

So I have chosen instead to separate Chinese signs from Western signs into two distinct sections. If you don't know your Chinese or Western astrological sign, you can find them on the charts at the end of this introduction. Then you, my loyal reader, will put your mental blender to work. The final half of the *ASTRO LOVE* covers all the Chinese signs, from Rat to Pig, and discusses their relative compatibilities. The second half deals with all Zodiac signs, from Aries to Pisces, and describes their respective compatibilities. Now it's your turn.

If you are, say, a Cancer/Tiger and you want to find out how you get along with that Scorpio/Horse you are salivating over, sit down and read the chapter on Tiger/Horse to find out how the Chinese part of your couple works. In each chapter, there's a general getting along section, tips on household and money matters, maybe a juicy section about sex (if there is any). And a bit about what kind of babies you should make together, if any.

After you have read all the Chinese astrology data, your heart will be pounding. Take a deep breath and turn to the Western zodiac signs half of the book. Read the chapter on Cancer/Scorpio couples. Here, you will discover if you, Cancer, get along with Scorpios in general and in money matters, how your couple fares in bed, and what kind of kids to have or have not.

Now switch on your mental blender. Mix together the information I have given you to decide whether a Cancer/Tiger marriage to a Scorpio/Horse partner will be an absolute harmonious lifelong nirvana, a so-so fixer-upper that needs TLC, or (worst-case scenario) a disgusting, boring, yawn-city union to be avoided at any cost. If what I say about your two New Astrology signs doesn't jibe with what your heart wants, you are hereby advised to give your same two chapters another good hard read, set the mental blender on "high" for ten full minutes, and see if you don't get a clearer picture. Sometimes we manage to hide from the truth because we don't wish to face it.

Personality and *character* are words often mistakenly used interchangeably to describe human behavior. It is the rare human being who, upon first (or sometimes even forty-fifth) meeting, presents you with his or her true character up front. What we usually get to see when we meet someone is his or her personality—the facade that the conscious mind has concocted to slather over the surface of a person's face and demeanor in order to ensure that the person becomes socially acceptable and presentable to the outside world. What the subconscious mind is doing while junior is out there presenting his sunny, charming, outgoing, friendly, warmhearted, easy-to-live-with personality to the world is anybody's guess. Subconscious minds are put there by Zeus in the first place to teach every smutty thought and slimy fantasy we have ever had to live in relative harmony with our noble dreams of becoming president and saving the world. For all we know, while we care for the sick or rescue drowning kittens, our subconscious might be planning a mass murder. Or thinking up ways to explode Mexico. Or wondering how we can steal our best friend's lover before the engagement is announced. Subconscious minds are extremely unpredictable things.

Character almost always abides in the subconscious mind's basement. As I said up top, it is the rare character we see when we meet or know someone slightly. It usually takes eons of knowing someone for the subconscious mind to dare to peek out from the sub-basement's trapdoor and manifest (ta dah!) the *real* person.

Bye-bye personality. Hello character.

My mother, Elva was her name, always said that you didn't know a person until you had lived with them. I accepted Elva's live-in policy so vigorously that I lived in sin with my ex-husband for almost a year before I had our first child. Then I lived with him for ten more months before our second baby was born. In Elva's book, my unique style of living with somebody to get to know him was a bit exaggerated. But she was a good egg about it. And once she met my children's father, she certainly did not press me to marry him. Yet, despite Elva's intentional, indifference to my swashbuckling Gemini/Goat fiancé, I married him. Something about health insurance not being available to unmarried parents in those days.

Nonetheless, just as Mom had promised, I had by then gotten to know tons about this fellow's character (details of which I will spare you until my autobiography). And trust me, what I found out in the *character* days as opposed to what little I had glimpsed back in the good old *personality* days was not a pretty sight. A few months later, I ran screaming back to Paris with a child under each arm.

People can be on good behavior for a very long time. How about my friend Jim, who lived with a woman for fifteen years before he found out she was and had always been an alcoholic? (She drank at night while ironing his dress shirts.) Or my pal Marie, who lived with a guy for four years, having a perfectly marvelous "normal" sex life, when he announced that in order to be sexually satisfied he needed to be tied up and lashed with a whip—and did she mind terribly much doing him that little favor while slapping him about the head?

Or the guy who discovers his wife has had their church pastor as her lover for ten years and he never even suspected? Or the woman who marries the guy who swears he's never been married before, only to find he's been married five times before and has seven kids to support back in Nebraska?

Secrets, dirty little secrets, lurk in the dank sub-basements of the best of us, in the best of families and in all walks of life. Some of the healthier among us deal with our secrets by integrating them into our personalities and taking them out to the party with us. Our secrets and hang-ups can become our friends.

But many of us bury our sorriest attributes and leave them buried until there's a crisis. In emergencies or tight spots, the trap door of the subconscious sometimes comes unglued, allowing very unsavory bits and pieces to float out into the atmosphere and bite us on the neck. If you have ever tried living with someone or being married, you know precisely what I mean. A mere suggestion of a sore subject—about which you knew nothing two minutes before you said it—can cause a mate to fly into a rage, buy a gun, make it with the fourteen-year-old babysitter, or secretly abuse your family's pet turtle. I mean, when they are tweaked by some unpredictable stimulus or pressured by stress, people can get up to some big-time *weirdness.*

Hence my warning about keeping your eye on the donut and not on the hole. Find out the substance of the person you are in love with. Dig and delve until you know the very marrow of the guy at the office you can't resist. Not only might he be married, he might be a transvestite or play with Barbie dolls or rip off old women for their Social Security checks. Research that woman you met—the one with the long legs and the burnished amber hair—find out everything about that luscious little number you may be about to give up your freedom for. Leave no stone unturned when you go looking for any bugs that may be hidden deep in her hard drive. Marriage, remember, is forever. Kids last even longer. Take your time. Choose carefully.

Okay, I said I'd be brief. Just don't go marrying anybody's personality. Oh, and by the way, each set of signs diminishes by one as my *ASTRO LOVE* system goes along. So, if you are a Pisces, you don't necessarily want to turn to the Pisces chapter to read about yourself and some other sign. As Pisces is the final sign of the zodiac, you will find out how Pisces gets on with Aries in the Aries chapter, and Cancer with Pisces will be in the Cancer chapter. This goes for all the signs all the way through the book. If you don't find your sign matched with the one you're seeking in the chapter for your sign, go fish for your sign in the other person's chapter.

The hearts, or lack thereof, at the top of each pairing give you a general idea of what I think the relationship is worth for the long haul:

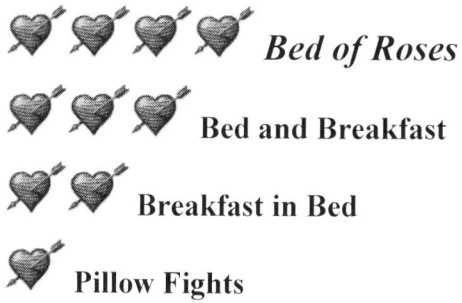

♥♥♥♥ ***Bed of Roses***

♥♥♥ **Bed and Breakfast**

♥♥ **Breakfast in Bed**

♥ **Pillow Fights**

No Hearts   Bed of Nails

If you do not agree, please take these hearts with a grain of salt and call me in the morning.

One caveat: For many years I called the fourth sign of the Chinese Zodiac "Cat" because I was taught Chinese Astrology by a Vietnamese expert in Paris. Then, I discovered that Chinese people call that sign "Rabbit". Some readers had got used to Cat.

Others still insisted on Rabbit. I could not very well go back to Cat or forward to Rabbit without warning people. Instead, in this book, I've decided to call this sign Cat/Rabbit. I hope my message reaches any and all Asian peoples who have had doubts about this issue.

Happy hunting!

The Chinese Calendar

Year | Sign | Year begins | Year ends

1900 | Rat | 01/31/1900 | 02/18/1901

1901 | Ox | 02/19/1901 | 02/07/1902

1902 | Tiger | 02/08/1902 | 01/28/1903

1903 | Cat | 01/29/1903 | 02/15/1904

1904 | Dragon | 02/16/1904 | 02/03/1905

1905 | Snake | 02/04/1905 | 01/24/1906

1906 | Horse | 01/25/1906 | 02/12/1907

1907 | Goat | 02/13/1907 | 02/01/1908

1908 | Monkey | 02/02/1908 | 01/21/1909

1909 | Rooster | 01/22/1909 | 02/09/1910

1910 | Dog | 02/10/1910 | 01/29/1911

1911 | Pig | 01/30/1911 | 02/17/1912

1912 | Rat | 02/18/1912 | 02/05/1913

1913 | Ox | 02/06/1913 | 01/25/1914

1914 | Tiger | 01/26/1914 | 02/13/1915

1915 | Cat | 02/14/1915 | 02/02/1916

1916 | Dragon | 02/03/1916 | 01/22/1917

1917 | Snake | 01/23/1917 | 02/10/1918

1918 | Horse | 02/11/1918 | 01/31/1919

1919 | Goat | 02/01/1919 | 02/19/1920
1920 | Monkey | 02/20/1920 | 02/07/1921
1921 | Rooster | 02/08/1921 | 01/27/1922
1922 | Dog | 01/28/1922 | 02/15/1923
1923 | Pig | 02/16/1923 | 02/04/1924
1924 | Rat | 02/05/1924 | 01/23/1925
1925 | Ox | 01/24/1925 | 02/12/1926
1926 | Tiger | 02/13/1926 | 02/01/1927
1927 | Cat | 02/02/1927 | 01/22/1928
1928 | Dragon | 01/23/1928 | 02/09/1929
1929 | Snake | 02/10/1929 | 01/29/1930
1930 | Horse | 01/30/1930 | 02/16/1931
1931 | Goat | 02/17/1931 | 02/05/1932
1932 | Monkey | 02/06/1932 | 01/25/1933
1933 | Rooster | 01/26/1933 | 02/13/1934
1934 | Dog | 02/14/1934 | 02/03/1935
1935 | Pig | 02/04/1935 | 01/23/1936
1936 | Rat | 01/24/1936 | 02/10/1937
1937 | Ox | 02/11/1937 | 01/30/1938
1938 | Tiger | 01/31/1938 | 02/18/1939
1939 | Cat | 02/19/1939 | 02/07/1940
1940 | Dragon | 02/08/1940 | 01/26/1941
1941 | Snake | 01/27/1941 | 02/14/1942
1942 | Horse | 02/15/1942 | 02/04/1943
1943 | Goat | 02/05/1943 | 01/24/1944
1944 | Monkey | 01/25/1944 | 02/12/1945
1945 | Rooster | 02/13/1945 | 02/01/1946

1946 | Dog | 02/02/1946 | 01/21/1947

1947 | Pig | 01/22/1947 | 02/09/1948

1948 | Rat | 02/10/1948 | 01/28/1949

1949 | Ox | 01/29/1949 | 02/16/1950

1950 | Tiger | 02/17/1950 | 02/05/1951

1951 | Cat | 02/06/1951 | 01/26/1952

1952 | Dragon | 01/27/1952 | 02/13/1953

1953 | Snake | 02/14/1953 | 02/02/1954

1954 | Horse | 02/03/1954 | 01/23/1955

1955 | Goat | 01/24/1955 | 02/11/1956

1956 | Monkey | 02/12/1956 | 01/30/1957

1957 | Rooster | 01/31/1957 | 02/17/1958

1958 | Dog | 02/18/1958 | 02/07/1959

1959 | Pig | 02/08/1959 | 01/27/1960

1960 | Rat | 01/28/1960 | 02/14/1961

1961 | Ox | 02/15/1961 | 02/04/1962

1962 | Tiger | 02/05/1962 | 01/24/1963

1963 | Cat | 01/25/1963 | 02/12/1964

1964 | Dragon | 02/13/1964 | 02/01/1965

1965 | Snake | 02/02/1965 | 01/20/1966

1966 | Horse | 01/21/1966 | 02/08/1967

1967 | Goat | 02/09/1967 | 01/29/1968

1968 | Monkey | 01/30/1968 | 02/16/1969

1969 | Rooster | 02/17/1969 | 02/05/1970

1970 | Dog | 02/06/1970 | 01/26/1971

1971 | Pig | 01/27/1971 | 02/14/1972

1972 | Rat | 02/15/1972 | 02/02/1973

1973 | Ox | 02/03/1973 | 01/22/1974
1974 | Tiger | 01/23/1974 | 02/10/1975
1975 | Cat | 02/11/1975 | 01/30/1976
1976 | Dragon | 01/31/1976 | 02/17/1977
1977 | Snake | 02/18/1977 | 02/06/1978
1978 | Horse | 02/07/1978 | 01/27/1979
1979 | Goat | 01/28/1979 | 02/15/1980
1980 | Monkey | 02/16/1980 | 02/04/1981
1981 | Rooster | 02/05/1981 | 01/24/1982
1982 | Dog | 01/25/1982 | 02/12/1983
1983 | Pig | 02/13/1983 | 02/01/1984
1984 | Rat | 02/02/1984 | 02/19/1985
1985 | Ox | 02/20/1985 | 02/08/1986
1986 | Tiger | 02/09/1986 | 01/28/1987
1987 | Cat | 01/29/1987 | 02/16/1988
1988 | Dragon | 02/17/1988 | 02/05/1989
1989 | Snake | 02/06/1989 | 01/26/1990
1990 | Horse | 01/27/1990 | 02/14/1991
1991 | Goat | 02/15/1991 | 02/03/1992
1992 | Monkey | 02/04/1992 | 01/22/1993
1993 | Rooster | 01/23/1993 | 02/09/1994
1994 | Dog | 02/10/1994 | 01/30/1995
1995 | Pig | 01/31/1995 | 02/18/1996
1996 | Rat | 02/19/1996 | 02/06/1997
1997 | Ox | 02/07/1997 | 01/27/1998
1998 | Tiger | 01/28/1998 | 02/15/1999
1999 | Cat | 02/16/1999 | 02/04/2000

2000 | Dragon | 02/05/2000 | 01/23/2001

2001 | Snake | 01/24/2001 | 02/11/2002

2002 | Horse | 02/12/2002 | 01/31/2003

2003 | Goat | 02/01/2003 | 01/21/2004

2004 | Monkey | 01/22/2004 | 02/08/2005

2005 | Rooster | 02/09/2005 | 01/28/2006

2006 | Dog | 01/29/2006 | 02/17/2007

2007 | Pig | 02/18/2007 | 02/06/2008

2008 | Rat | 02/07/2008 | 01/25/2009

2009 | Ox | 01/26/2009 | 02/13/2010

2010 | Tiger | 02/14/2010 | 02/02/2011

2011 | Cat | 02/03/2011 | 01/22/2012

2012 | Dragon | 01/23/2012 | 02/09/2013

2013 | Snake | 02/10/2013 | 01/30/2014

2014 | Horse | 01/31/2014 | 02/18/2015

2015 | Goat | 02/19/2015 | 02/07/2016

2016 | Monkey | 02/08/2016 | 01/27/2017

2017 | Rooster | 01/28/2017 | 02/15/2018

2018 | Dog | 02/16/2018 | 02/04/2019

2019 | Pig | 02/05/2019 | 01/24/2020

The Western Zodiac

DATES | SIGN
21 MARCH-19 APRIL | ARIES
20 APRIL-20 MAY | TAURUS
21 MAY621 JUNE | GEMINI
22 JUNE-22 JULY | CANCER
23 JULY-22 AUGUST | LEO
23 AUGUST-22 SEPTEMBER | VIRGO
23 SEPTEMBER-23 OCTOBER | LIBRA
24 OCTOBER-21 NOVEMBER | SCORPIO
22 NOVEMBER-21 DECEMBER | SAGITTARIUS
22 DECEMBER-19 JANUARY | CAPRICORN
20 JANUARY-18 FEBRUARY | AQUARIUS
19 FEBRUARY-20 MARCH | PISCES

PART ONE

Chinese Astrology Signs

RAT

Taken to the extreme, all of our qualities can become frailties. Some of us are generous to a fault, which may be deemed wasteful. Good communicators can also be considered blabbermouths. Well-meaning, nurturing parents can smother their children. Fortunately free will allows us to balance the positive and negative sides of our character. The Rat, a Domineering Benefactor, was born:

On the plus side | On the minus side

seductive | hustler

cautious | anxious

discreet | covert

meticulous | finicky

protective | smothering

ambitious | power-hungry

 ½ Rat with Rat

A duo to absolutely love! Rats are definitely the marrying kind. I know several Rats who are working on their fifth marriage. Rat people admire other Rat people. A pair of Rats will chatter gaily on, vividly sharing their respective difficulties, immersing themselves in myriad social events, or nervously twitching amorously entwined legs, all the while trying diligently to become the tandem presidents of the world. A Rat whose spouse is also a Rat will instinctively know how to listen for the other's needs, leap into the breach when the Rat partner is in business or career trouble, and always lend an efficient, positive, helping hand and (Rats really talk a lot!) a willing, empathetic ear.

Two Rats may be drawn together by their mutual fear of loneliness. There is a basic "aloneness" about individual Rats that belies their daytime reputation for craving society's approval. Rats are unduly sociable. But the flip side of that hail-fellow-well-met cheery rattishness is a dark tendency to conceal. You Rats are not liars, but you can b covert. Beneath a deliciously charming exterior you carry a wealth of unuttered information about which we may never know diddley squat. Rats may talk all the time, but there are certain facts about themselves that they never divulge.

This secret side of Rat life would drive most of us mad with curiosity. But one Rat partner won't even question the other about it. The other Rat has an obfuscated slag heap of his or her own to deal with and cannot be bothered prying into his or her Rat partner's mental britches. This hands-off-your-inner-soul policy suits the Rat couple's joint need for private space.

A veritable wellspring of material accumulation and showers of presents characterize your relationship. You both know how to make and invest money. So you shouldn't disagree about finances. Let the cleverest Rat handle the bank accounts. Or, why not work out household budgets together? Rats are naturally protective, nurturing creatures, so other peoples' comfort and security counts for a lot. As a couple, when you are not out buying extra gourmet food supplies to hoard, the two of you will spend many of your fidgety waking bouts considering what trinket or toy would please this family member or delight that loved one.

Not everything about this love match is perfect. The Rat's sexuality is a fierce force. Yet, for all of its intensity, the sex drive of Rat subjects suffers from unevenness. With Rats, the fiery urge is simply not always there. As a result, long fallow periods may extend longer than is desirable. One or the other Rat gets to feeling very needy in the hormone department and may begin some naughty sexual straying. If somebody *rats* on the faithless Rat partner, get ready for heavy bouts of tooth-and-claw psychodrama. To prevent the eventuality of divorce, I suggest that you two Rats promise straightaway to discuss everything about sex openly. Disclose your wildest fantasies. Then set out, as an earnest couple should, to serve each other's sexual needs till death parts you.

As a busy couple of born providers, you two should have kids who can share your enthusiasms, agree with your windy opinions, and lend an intelligent ear to your more-than-occasional blab marathons. I suggest a bustling, bright Monkey to help solve problems or a noisy, party-loving Dragon baby. You might also decide you want to hatch a lumbering, chubby little Ox, whose wise advice will guide you through many a mire. Or, the two of you could be ever so sweet as the parents of a dynamic Rooster kid, whose boundless energy and fascination with the world will delight and challenge your communal mind, lifting you to the absolute summit of parental joy.

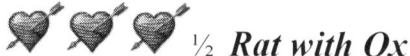 ½ **Rat with Ox**

The undisputed name of this game *is stability*. Oxen settle Rats down. Rats enliven Oxen. For a marriage, what could be better? Well, a lot of things could, but we won't go into that now. If you are a Rat seeking a partner or an Ox looking for a mate, I would suggest you do some serious prospecting here. The Rat initiates action, the Ox gives a mighty bulldozing push, and the

Rat takes the ball and runs it to the goal. It's a sound (if not hilarious) long-term commitment.

Oxen are somewhat stodgy. On the surface, they can appear charming and jolly—even amusing at times. But deep down, Oxen are steady-as-you-go hard-row hoers, whose lot it is to glue life together when its coming apart at the seams. Oxen sit a lot and ponder. They delve and dig too. They plot and plan. They organize and lift that barge and tote that bale more diligently than members of any other Chinese astrological sign group. The only entertaining thing they do is spin a mean yarn (they know how to tell intricate fibs as well). But no Ox will ever be the life of the party—unless he or she is irretrievably sloshed, which doesn't even happen all that often.

Now Rats, as we know, are talkers and doers—lively, anxious, and, for the most part, outgoing. Rats have more charm in their left pinky claw than Arnold Swashbuckler has in his whole charismatic life. Rats make delightful company, talk a mile a minute, and sometimes even rant a bit. None of this hyperactivity (Rats only look calm—they are jittery inside) offends the steady Ox. In fact, Ox is inspired by the pulsing, motor-running Rat's agitated style. Where a less vigorous character might only drag the stolid Ox deeper into the comfy safe muck, the Rat's cheerful sociability boosts the Ox over stile after stile until finally he turns around one day and notices that he is indeed having a very jolly time.

Financially, you two ought to beat the world at its own perilous game. Oxen understand travail. They endure interminable delays, ride out wild storms, and tough through lean years without a whimper. Rats are intrepid and relentless. The combination is unbeatable when it comes to making and keeping a living. Ox burns the midnight oil to pore over tax returns, budget plans, and spreadsheets. Rat appreciates this favor, as paperwork of every stripe (except writing a novel, poem or play) gives the Rat heartburn.

As a Rat/Ox couple, your sex life will be fulfilling. The Ox is mostly faithful and loyal to his cause. Rats? Well, if they aren't always completely physically faithful, their hearts are at home in bed with Oxie-poo where they belong. Rats, you must understand, have an overwhelming need for the touchy-feelies. They are demonstrative to their loved ones, always petting them and waxing romantic. For Rat people, the act of love is multifaceted—a true sharing of all the various aspects of the relationship. They coddle their sex partners.

Oxen don't mind being hovered over, but they cannot return the favor. The Ox may be sexually ardent and deeply attached to a single lover. But Oxen are neither affectionate nor demonstrative. The sex act itself is what the Ox is after—the release and subsequent relaxation are necessary to his well-being. But don't count on Mr. or Mrs. Ox for much more than a few playful fanny pinches in the foreplay department. The Rat's tender sweetness toward an Ox partner lends special dimension to an Ox's love life. Rat, in turn, feels appreciated and, best of all, needed.

Having kids is an absolute *must* for you two. Oxen love to stay at home by the cradle and the stove. Part of the time, Rats enjoy careening about, kissing all the babies, and getting themselves elected to public office. But when work is over, security beckons. You, Ratsy-pie, cannot wait to scamper home to Oxie and the little ones, chow down the latest gourmet treats, and croon rock-a-bye-baby 'til the cows come home.

Try to plan your kids in Dragon or Rooster years. The Ox has something basic in common with the Rooster—a firmness of mindset. Oxen adore Snakes too. Monkeys make good companions for both of you. Neither Rat nor Ox is annoyed by the Monkey's capers. Better not dabble in baby Goats. Neither of you has tolerance for the Goat's gossamer mind games. Leave Tiger cubs alone too. They will try to eat the pair of you in one gulp—and will get themselves devoured in the process.

 *Rat with Tiger*

This is a tough match to hold onto but worth its weight in mutual satisfaction. Two more magnetic, charismatic souls hardly exist. If you can make this sizzling marriage work, the rewards in self-awareness and sexual delight will sweep you off your collective feet. One thing is certain-- Rats who live with Tigers (and vice versa) *never* get bored.

By nature, the Tiger stalks instability. Tigers adore the prospect of a new job every year. Whether it's Paris or Rangoon, when change-of-scene beckons, Tiger packs a bag. You, brave Rat, will not always find your Tiger's inconsistencies appealing. You will jitter and fret. Your very equilibrium depends on material security. Tiger's world-hopping penchant is not your favorite sport.

Tigers don't want to give up the nomadic lifestyle. Yet, they want to maintain their exclusive relationship with you. A stay-at-home Rat may appear calm in the face of Tiger's eternal defections. But inside, the steady-loving Rat is self-shredding, ulcerating, and fuming at the injustice of it all.

The carefree Tiger is oblivious. Tiger is under the false impression that a capable Rat mate can take care of everything—the children, the accounts, *and* the leaky roof, while Tiger roams. Tiger, your whole purpose in getting into a serious relationship was to have somebody competent to minister to your illustrious needs, wasn't it now? Well, this may come as a shock to you, Tiger: Rats don't mind nurturing and taking charge of the whole world, but they do need regular, on-the-spot, hang-around-the-kitchen-and-kibitz-for-hours companionship. Rat seeks to bounce *all* their ideas off a mate. For you, Tiger dear, uninterrupted listening is a chore.

Remaining together will require true sacrifice on both sides. Forget the cute schemes you have each worked out to *cope* with the other's idiosyncrasies. Lay all the cards face up on the table. Rat gets to handle the money. Tigers accept living on a reasonable allowance. Rat, you will have to learn to get by without a full-time bed, kitchen, and TV-watching partner to yak to all the time. And Tiger, you will be obliged to give up a portion of your independence, to learn to listen up, and to accept sharing center stage with your talented Rat partner.

Both of you attract squadrons of admirers. But when it comes to charming the pants off Tigers, Rats take first prize. Rats approach the great Tiger cat hesitantly at first, snooping around for points of entry. The ever-cunning Rat may offer assistance. "Here sweetie, let me take care of that." Or "I can make that call for you, darling, you're *so* busy." A helping hand carries a lot of weight with the chronically overextended and muddle-minded Tiger, who soon falls *kerplop, blam!* into the wily Rat's trap.

The Rat/Tiger couple boasts a meltingly torrid sexuality. These two are notoriously drawn to each other's bodies via a strong meeting of the mind and spirit. Ask any Rat who lives with a Tiger (or vice versa). They will concede that although during the day they may feel like murdering their partner, as evening draws nigh, their attitude changes. Between Tiger and Rat, sex slowly creeps in and eventually takes over. Conversations become caresses. Strokes turn into embraces. Next thing either Rat or Tiger remembers is a final clink of wine grasses, bouts of luscious lovemaking, and delicious leaden sleep.

Kids? Well, this *is* tricky. You two will have plenty to do just keeping your reciprocal bodies and souls on some kind of mutual wavelength. But if children you must, then try for some who can ride out rough spots with you. Dragons will be strong enough to steal the fire of either parent whenever necessary. No supplementary Rats or Tigers please. Steer clear of Pigs and Snakes, who will have trouble shifting emotional gears. A resilient little Rooster is a good idea. Or a baby Monkey, who has more mischief up his tiny sleeve than you two can invent in a lifetime of parenting. No Goats. They require routine. You ain't got any.

Rat with Cat/Rabbit

In love, Cat and Rat are not compatible. Members of both signs cherish a good home and enjoy luxurious surroundings. Indeed, one might expect to see this jaunty couple wandering hand in hand through designer furniture outlets, hunting down antiques and collectibles, pawing over flea markets. They may be very good *friends*. But Rats and Cats do not share a common style.

The Cat fears confrontation, deplores conflict, and will do anything to escape a contentious atmosphere. The Rat is aggressive. A Rat will fight for what's best in life, insists on talking things through and, worse, is often happiest amidst the frantic, spiteful rantings of an outraged mate. Rats adore the process. A Rat in love will lose any kind of war for the luxury of hanging out with the person they adore. Cats are ponderers and often prefer to be left on their own, listening to classical jazz or baroque music in their silken drawing rooms, dreaming of the ravishingly beautiful ballets they plan to attend. Rat/Cat disharmony is basic. Each of these two signs has a visceral distaste for the *odd* ways of the other.

You are both given to acts of pure selflessness. But again, you are stylistically different. Cars are snobbish. They like to help their poor friends and deserving acquaintances by pushing a bit of food or money over the wall of the château and rushing back inside to turn up the chamber music full volume so they can't hear the rabble-rousing below. Socially conscious Rats like to give their rabble-rousing pals a hand by taking them (and, if necessary, their entire families) in to live cozily with them, sharing fancy foods and marble bathrooms in an effort to prove how democratic they can be. Cats are quite modest. They don't care if anyone ever finds out about their philanthropy. Rats want all the media to hail their great acts of charity and get them votes.

To save this couple, neither of you Rat/Cat people is prepared to make compromises. Spats are common. Spiteful remarks. Groundless comparisons. You, Cat, will sneer at the Rat's impetuous decision to buy a Christmas pudding-shaped hat for his mother and wonder why Rat was so heavy-handed with the nutmeg in the eggnog. The vengeful Rat will *tee hee* and secretly add more nutmeg. The observant Cat will notice. But rather than confront, Cat may instead grow picky and fuss over the Rat's casual appearance or feign a fainting spell or invent a migraine. In this ill-fated couple, a mere flick of a whisker and the fight is on!

You don't agree on money. Cat deems Rat wasteful. Rat thinks Cat is uptight and penny-pinching. You might find some harmony in the pursuit of cultural stimulation. Then again, as your tastes differ so, you might not. Rats love all forms of theater, poetry, and music. Cats are not so easy to please: they prefer ballet to rock, Shakespeare to Broadway, and figure skating to football. At home, the discreet and hypersensitive Cat will lean to gold-framed ancestors and quiet champagne gatherings for a few close friends. The Rat will long for a huge sleek loft space where he can throw gigantic parties for movie and rock stars complete with heavy metal bands *and* a country western singer. Once again, Rat/Cat styles just don't jibe.

Of course, sometimes opposites do attract. You two may have a brief, bristling affair. But I don't see you hanging on, long term, to a strong relationship. Then again, if you have managed to get married and stay married as a relentless Rat and a cautious Cat couple, my hat is off to you. I am, however, moved to inquire as to which one of you is on Prozac.

Children for this quarrelsome pair? I don't think so.

 ***Rat with Dragon***

You won't regret this relationship for a single second. The Rat/Dragon couple works very well—especially when the right Western signs are in play. Dragons emanate warmth, pride, and generosity of spirit. Rats are gnawingly insecure worriers. The Dragon's huge capacity for dispensing both understanding and comfort provides an insecure Rat partner with a hefty dose of constantly renewable faith in both self and mate.

Each of these partners is born with an irrepressible sense of fun. Dragons adore giving parties to celebrate holidays, birthdays, anniversaries, or whatever they can think up as a reason to open the doors and tables of their home. Rats likewise never miss a chance to throw a party. You just never know what the Rat will come up with next in the way of exotic entertainment: magicians, musicians, wandering poets, or performing ponies—nothing is too eccentric or expansive for the Rat host or hostess who wants to please guests.

So, as a team, you can expect a Rat/Dragon couple to keep an open-house policy. At any time of the day or night, you may find strangers ambling across the Rat/Dragon living room munching on a sandwich—a straggler guest from last night's shindig, or maybe a friend of one of the children who plumb forgot to go home after school. Rats love to gab. The more interlocutors they can round up in one place, the happier the Rat. Dragons are not quite so indiscriminate about whom they recruit. But they are tolerant of the Rat's social needs. Besides, while the Rat is occupied yammering to a perfect stranger, the versatile Dragon gets some time off from listening duty to run an empire, learn a new skill or take up Zen Buddhism.

As much as the Rat loves and needs to have power over others, with a Dragon as partner the fretful Rat can give up the pushy quest for dominion, relax, and let the Dragon take over the reins in both boardroom and bedroom. This fact alone is sufficient reason for the potentially neurotic Rat to take this relationship seriously and quickly marry up. The Dragon benefits as well from intimacy with a Rat. A sincere Dragon will always be understood by, a nurturing Rat partner. Dragons are proud and may shy away from exhibiting their own deep sentimentality. Not a whisper of a problem here. Rats know how to keep a secret. The Dragon's fears and weepy outbursts are safe in the hands of the compassionate Rat, whose duty it is to protect this tenderhearted loved one.

Rats will not mind staying at home with kids and the pets, cooking and tending the hearth fires, as long as their busy Dragon partners need them too. The reverse is also true. If Rat is out and about doing business and bringing home bacon, Dragon willingly stays home playing with the kids, ordering in meals, and building bigger and better home fires. There is very little ego competition between these two signs. Give-and-take comes easy because they have no axes to grind.

How's the sex? Well, it's just great, thank you very much. Although Rat is the great all-time seducer of unsuspecting folks into the bedroom, Dragon pays this fact little mind. In this couple, Dragon takes the sexual lead and inveigles the lusty Rat into some of the most imaginative sexual playacting ever! Dragon appreciates being spoiled with Rat's many compliments and caresses, whilst Rat takes enormous pleasure in providing same. You two should have lots of kids and lots of fun making them.

I strongly suggest Monkey kids for you. Monkeys are innately fun-loving and will readily take to your crowded lifestyle. Baby Oxen gain ground against their own gravity by being born into your jolly household. You might also want to clone yourselves by birthing a Rat or a Dragon child—or both. The harmony will only improve with numbers. Don't inflict yourselves on quiet-seeking Cats or Snakes. And keep your noisy house safe from Tiger cubs—too many power struggles.

Rat with Snake

Beware, devoted Rat, of the Snake's sexual sorcery. And *be-double*ware, fine Snake, of the Rat's parsimoniousness when it comes to expensive futilities and glittering accessories. As friends, you two probably form a super team. The Rat's good-natured chatter appeals to the silent Snake, who knows well how to listen and deduce the right solutions to the Rat's innumerable problems. I can almost feel how tempted you both are to go all the way, have a romantic relationship, perhaps even to marry! May I suggest you keep your friendship instead? Be pals. Help each other out when you are in need. Have dinner out every night and go to parties with each other for many years—but please…do not attempt to be lovers forever and a day. It will not work. Long term, your romance will sour, becoming a roiling mass of bitterness and acid—especially about money and secrets.

Both Rats and Snakes spend lots of time dreaming about being more secure, living in luxurious prosperity, never fearing the bill collector again. Trouble is, your individual methods of getting to this state of financial nirvana are entirely different. Rats push and elbow, mouth off, and grab at every passing opportunity. Snakes slither and slide their way into positions of power to which they aspire only mildly, but at which they often arrive simply because they are the most attractive person in the bunch.

At some point you might want to upgrade your companionable friendship into a sexual relationship. It could well happen, you know. You are *very* attractive to each other. Rat so attentive and charming, Snake. so susceptible to attention and applause. And the actual sex part in the entanglement should be sensational. I have no quarrel with it at all. So far, so good. But mark my words, as soon as one of you crawls out of bed to answer a ringing telephone, there will be trouble. The very air in the bedroom will be pregnant with an unspoken *who is that?* Each of you likes (and don't fib here, please) to keep a second, mysterious side to your love life and neither of you wants the other to so much as guess at it. Snakes always have plenty of admirers. They are too enticing not to be sought after by throngs of potential lovers. Whereas with Rats, it is the Rat's unparalleled charm that wins him or her many crushes. Rats are the seducers, the con artist we know and love— that sweet person at work who always tells us just how cute we look or how handsome our new mustache makes us. Subterfuge (a necessity between the Snake and the Rat) inevitably causes major differences, ignites jealousy wars, and eventually precipitates separations.

So please resist the tug of marital bliss. Have an affair if you must. But don't go getting all involved with sharing a future. If your passion endures (and it may) whatever you do, don't go snooping in the other guy's private life—what you find there will always hurt your most vulnerable feelings.

I cannot advocate children for you two. If you ever do manage stay together, the atmosphere in your elegantly decorated, lavishly appointed Beverly Hills townhouse or Aspen chalet mansion would undoubtedly not be conducive to raising well-balanced, stable kids with the normal dirty sneakers and holes in their jeans. Besides, while engaged in such a tense and secretive relationship as yours, neither of you would have much emotional space to spare for the children's needs.

Rat with Horse

In China, this relationship is taboo. The Horse is far too self-centered to allow for the Rat's protective, giving, dependent nature. No real tenderness exists between members of this couple. If involved at all, the Horse's motive will be purely pragmatic: money and position. The Rat, meanwhile, will skitter amiably along, trying to seduce and please the Horse. But the Horse's profound interest in hard work and self-advancement precludes taking time to deal with the myriad neurotic issues a garrulous Rat partner goes on about. Horses feel they have enough problems without putting up with the Rat's difficulties too.

The Horse, you see, is too individualistic to even consider the Rat's sensitive feelings. Horses trot arrogantly through life, wearing blinders, paying little attention to their mate's suffering. Rats are delicately strung characters whose emotional battlement may depend on or not someone says good morning. Results and tangible evidence are the Horse's main aims. On the sentimental level, Horses are anything but subtle romantics. Rats thrive on shades of meaning or bad vibes. The Rat adores lingering over seduction. The Horse finds the whole foreplay fuss futile and a waste of important work time.

Unless this Rat has truckloads of capital to spare, the Horse's interest may prove to be but a passing fancy. The Horse doesn't beat about the bush, and may actually frighten the Rat: "Where is the check for a hundred thousand you promised me for my birthday?" The Rat, all scrambled feelings and mixed emotions about absolutely everything, will be shocked by such a candid blurt and back off into a fit of anger, panic—or worse.

On the other hand, the Horse is a passionate sort of person. In fact, true love and sexual addiction to another person can be the Horse's undoing. It usually takes more than a devoted Rat to undo old Dobbin's corset laces, but if a relentless Rat sneaks under the tough skin of a Horse person's soul, the sex be fantastic! As I said above, Horses are lusty creatures. And nobody loves hearty sex more than an adoring Rat. A Horse madly in love with a very devoted Rat might get up to some epic lovemaking and a good time will be had by all. Still...

Bottom line, the self-important Horse will not feel challenged by a Rat partner. Once Horsey senses how easy it is to wound the Poor Rat's feelings, things usually heat up. Horse makes a hurtful remark. Rat shoots something back. But as Rat is less ruthlessly unkind by nature, Horse only laughs. Now Horsey will misuse his or her astute intellect to formulate ever more vicious remarks. The Rat eventually shuts down. The Horse grows to despise the Rat as weak and ineffectual. Impatient, the racy Horse will look elsewhere for pleasure and be mercilessly unfaithful to the agitated Rat. All of the negative aspects of the Horse personality will be drawn out by the Rat's frailties.

If you already have such a relationship, you know what I mean. If Horse will have it, a family with kids to shower love on may be the only thing to save Rat from total despair in this relationship. A brace of adorable children could return the once sweetie-pie Rat to his or playful, whimsical self. The Horsey, given enough time, may soften up at the appearance of a gentle Goat kid or a bouncy, irreverent Tiger child.

I do not advise marriage for you two. But if it has already happened, I can only hope that your children will teach you how to be kinder to each other.

Rat with Goat

Contradictory natures characterize these two partners. Rats appear calm on the outside, but inside they are anxious. They often have difficulty sleeping and can stay awake fretting and fussing over details of their finances or obsessing over the loss of a stock or bond, a ski pole, or a garden rake. Goats behave in a lighter-hearted, more frivolous manner. They are exceedingly creative and some even approach genius level. But Goats also enjoy being supported, sought after, and given their good old time to gid about being giddy, or working 'til all hours on unscheduled projects in an unscheduled fashion, then sleeping for thirty-six bouts nonstop. All of this Goatly uncertainty and lack of order drives the already fretful Rat bonkers.

Rats do favor marriage. If one ends in divorce, they may remarry as many as three or four times. But Rats need ambitious allies, mates who can second them in their efforts at seizing power and amassing a fortune. While they are young and full of vigor, Rats want to beat the world at its own game, grab opportunity after opportunity, and be the *best* at whatever career or profession they have chosen. But if, after the age of forty or forty-five, the Rat's ship persists in not coming in, a Rat can become discouraged, fall into desultory habits of sloth, drugs, or extreme anxiety, and may even drop out, take to his or her room to spend a bitter old age in embarrassed solitude as a social misfit.

One thing Rats don't need is a down-in-the-mouth, overly dependent Goat spouse. Goats are born pessimists Not only do Goats see the glass as half-empty, they drink it all up and wonder why someone doesn't come and fill it half full again right away. Goats need special care. They hate cleaning up their own messes. They are artistic, brilliant dreamers and have no time or talent for tending to the gearworks of everyday existence. Goats are impractical. They spend money they don't have on projects and plans that rarely work out unless they are assisted, supported, and shouldered all along the way. A Goat mate cannot tolerate being harped at, nagged, or even urged to change. The Goat doesn't want to make sweeping behavior modifications or hurry up and get with the program. Goats prefer to dream.

Rats are fusspots. They niggle over details and grow frantic when the lights flicker; for fear their computers will crash. Within this odd couple, Ratso worries insanely about the Goat's well-being, and so does Goat. This leaves nobody to be concerned about the poor, anxious Rat, which is a real disaster because protective as they are, Rats need attention—full time.

Goats are not big on assuming responsibilities alone. Goats need a push, a reminder, an emergency or a jump start before igniting into motion. The Rat, of course, is a homebody and rejoices at the opportunity to be in charge of the whole flaming household. However, the Goat's persistently languid attitudes will grate on his nerves. Also, Goats love to squander money on every last gadget—an expansive jet-propelled can opener, a remote clicker to open the garage door from the executive john. Yet, once Goats acquire these treasures, they simply don't maintain them. They may leave them out to rust, or else forget to bring clicker home from the office. Then nobody can get back into the garage. In a union of this sort, it won't be long before the Rat feels overburdened by a total lack of control and by insecurity about the future. Goat will feel pressured by the Rat's niggling about every penny spent, and the fight will be on.

Lovemaking is the one area in which the Goat will be able to take dominion over a Rat partner As the Rat is sexy yet slightly passive in bed, the Goat's unexpected prowess here will provide intermittent truces in an otherwise permanent cold war. I see your sex life as the single area in which you two can hope to find occasional true bliss.

Please, whatever you do, don't have kids.

Rat with Monkey

Just what the doctor ordered for a fun-filled life of Riley—a wily Monkey and a chatty Rat. The whole shebang looks like giggles and laughs, both at yourselves and at your unsuspecting entourage, all the rest of your days. As a couple, you will seek out amusing people, cook up new forms of family activities designed to teach as well as thrill the kids, dance until dawn, and don your Rollerblades for a spin around the park before breakfast. Lucky is the Monkey who hitches up with a Rat person—because Rats not only laugh at their Monkey's incessant jokes, they mean it. Besides, the Rat is no slouch in the silly department and will do what is necessary to keep the party rolling. Whatever you two get up to, your lives will not be dull.

The Rat and the Monkey are traditionally well-matched, as friends as well as lovers—you two understand each other. Rats are ambitions, power hungry, aggressive, and relentless about going after what they want. In fact, Rats almost never take no for an answer. Rats wants control—even emotional control—over their domain and long to appear to be running the show.

This trait of Rat character—wanting to wear the crown even if he or she is not the real ruler—suits the Monkey personality down to the ground. Monkeys do not—I repeat—do not *ever* want to be the star. They may indeed be the brains behind the top Rat, but you will not see them much in CEO jobs. Monkeys are the world's problem-solvers. They are behind-the-scenes people who gladly serve as their master's or mistress's *eminence grise*, cogitating the boss's next move, checking out each new prospect, and always finding the best solution for the nervous, anxious, fidgety Rat partner to carry out. Monkey will even give the Rat public credit for being so clever. Monkey won't greet people at the door saying, "I built this porch all by myself." The Monkey is more likely to tell friends that the Rat did it all alone and agree to receive praise only for cooking up the idea of a porch in the first place.

Of course, the proud Rat adores an agile--minded Monkey mate, and freely gives his or her nervous little heart away. The sometimes repressed or secretive Rat will trust in this relationship and may become even more of a yammering chatterbox alongside a mellow Monkey. But as the merry Monkey never tires of the clever Rat's diatribes and exposés, the pair of them goes on like a couple of walking radio talk shows day and night.

This naturally sociable pair loves to eat out or invite their friends in. They have a reputation for being generous hosts. Rats love to provide, and Monkeys like to be on stage in social settings , to amuse the gang and to tell tales ad nauseum. As they, always have a lot of people around them, home will probably not be a palace of order and luxury. Rats, of course, cherish elegant surroundings and spiffy gear. But if they see that their Monkey love is not content to save the couple's hard-earned capital until they can afford a real Van Gogh etching, the Rat knows how to back off and allow the Monkey to acquire another SPCA cat or take in a stray gerbil. Rats, remember, are marriers. The Rat will always try to keep the relationship going rather than make waves about Aubusson tapestries that practical Monkeys see no need to own.

Barring hanky-panky, the sex between you two should be dreamy. Rats rarely leave the nest for the purpose of "fooling around" with other partners. I cannot say the same for Monkeys, who, because of their diverse interests and devil-may-care approach to life, are frequently tempted away from their main squeeze. If Ratso finds out, the marriage will suffer. Although Rats love to flirt, they are devoted mates and believe so heartily in the challenge of the couple as a way of life that a mate's infidelity really hurts them. Monkeys, be discreet—don't let your Rat mate down.

Should you have children? Yes. Of course. Slews. I suggest a dauntless Dragon, a placid worker Ox, or even another Monkey or Rat person around the house. You two would also get on well with a tenacious little Tiger kid and probably enjoy the company of a jaunty Rooster as well. In fact, because

Monkeys love large families and Rats love to protect and nurture, I can see you getting along with children of almost any sign.

❤ Rat with Rooster

Pick. Pick. Pick. Here is a couple doomed to joint competition and incompatibility, no matter what! I cannot advise you to stay together unless you already have six kids, a giant mortgage, and no other way to solve the basic problem of jousting for position that invariably defeats your efforts to get along.

Rats want power. They don't even mind if the power is artificial, so long as they appear to be the head honcho wherever they live. Rat people, although utterly charming, also want to carry the scepter of authority. Rats have never been known for their unswervably upright ways. They tend to interpret every event through their own eyes, and deem that because they see it that way, it's true. They don't mean to have ulterior motives. But because of a built-in neurotic need for viewing life as they would have it rather than as it really is, they are often accused of duplicity.

Roosters are natural head honchos. They say it like it is and are almost never accused of duplicity. In fact, they have the opposite problem. Roosters are terminally blunt, straightforward and direct, without artificiality of any sort. Their word is as good as gold. Roosters hate shades of meaning and gray areas. They are short on patience with people who are not pulling their weight at all times and in all circumstances, and they can't stand crybabies.

Rats and Roosters are both jealous and possessive. The Rat might be long-suffering about feeling rejected or cheated on. But not the Rooster—one strike and you're out. Roosters are also categorical about finances. Rats take money seriously too. You might imagine this pair would at least agree to pore over their accounts, save pennies here and there, and tot up every last expense in an effort to grow rich together. But it doesn't work that way. Instead, each expects the other to be the most budget-minded and accuses his or her partner of every sort of chicanery about funds. You two will always argue over money. Roosters spend too much on appearances. Rats spend too much on champagne and caviar.

There could be a strong initial sexual draw between the two. Rats are so damned seductive and appealing that Roosters, with their flinty, upstanding, not-too-subtle character, will frankly not know what hit them when a Rat comes along. Rats are born salespeople. Rats sense what others need from them and always give the impression that they will be just the person to provide that mysterious ingredient. Roosters love to be admired, looked up to, and held in esteem. Old Rat has got the vain Rooster's number and will not hesitate to use it: "My you have a lovely head of hair" is but a mild come-on from our Rat lover-to-be. Or, "Is that an Armani suit you're wearing? It certainly is elegant. And it fits you like a glove." Rat-a-tat flattery will ensure even the most resistant Rooster an unexpectedly spicy, erotic experience. But beware: Rats are social to a fault. Roosters seize up when they see how many admirers the Rat attracts. Rooster, of course, is not only made to feel insecure by the Rat's success, but is also envious. To get his or her own back, the Rooster may either set to flirting or do an about face and refuse to be seen with the Rat in public. Rats hate to be abandoned by the ones they love, so even this mild rejection will set the Rat to whining and whimpering—which will, in turn, infuriate the Rooster. How can you two ever hope to find harmony in a love relationship? Truth is, you cannot. Rat will be misunderstood and constantly told to stop sniveling. Rooster will be considered cruel and unfeeling, refusing to even consider hearing one more syllable about Rat's eternal personal problems. Oh, it is a jolly combo.

Don't have children.

❥❥❥ Rat with Dog

With a bit of compromise, Rat and Dog can find meaningful happiness in each other's laps. Conversations will be profound, long and loaded with redeeming social value. Doggies have much to say on everything, from their beliefs about stamping out injustice to their dreams of reforming the social order. Rats simply have a great deal to say—about anything. I foresee many a white night passed neither in sleep, nor in hanky-panky, wherein you two pursue home truths and dense philosophies hitherto untrammeled by the *ordinary* human mind. If the two of you are the intellectual type, these same in-depth chats may go on all day as well.

Dogs worry a lot. They feel the necessity to be constantly on their guard, patrolling and watching for both real and imagined dangers. The Rat's innate gaiety and sensitivity to others' problems make it easier for Dog eventually to let go of the controls. Doggy learns in due time to trust in the Rat's capacity to take over the watch. Rats are naturally suspicious and can become nearly as proficient as Dogs at protecting the household.

The Rat is materialistic, the Dog an idealist. If only to be charitable, the Dog may donate all of the family money to some worthy cause, then be unable to pay for food or rent. The Dog is a true Samaritan. If someone needs an operation or a lift, a hand building a porch or birthing a baby, Doggy will be right there, loyal and true no matter what. Dogs can't resist the opportunity to rescue. Their self-respect and image demand that they be devoted to others.

Rats are, by nature, investors. They know full well that charity begins at home, and may scold and grow anxious about the Dog's precarious treasury situation. But deep down, even though they fret, Rats are giving people. A happy compromise can be achieved for the handling of your finances.

Both of you are quite sweetly romantic. Doggy prefers to unearth practical presents and lay them sheepishly at the Rat's feet. Rat is more glad-handed, always scouting and nosing about for ever-more exotic and jolly gifts to fill a shared nest. The disquieted and plainspoken Dog is reassured by his wily Rat partner's canny ability to buy at a discount, hoard cans of the best patés, stock up on vintage ports, and make certain there is enough firewood to warm the hearth.

Your sex life will be intermittently passionate. Rats are not all that likely to leave the nest for extracurricular sex, but they do have a very uneven pattern to their sexual appetites that can frustrate the eager pooch. Dogs are highly sexed creatures and have been known to stray. Yet Dogs are so loyal that committing an infidelity inflicts moral pain on their hearts. If the Dog can learn to be more patient and the Rat less skittish about sex, you will find your sexual equilibrium. If not, you may be destined to settle for a few more of those all-night chats and some lukewarm cuddle sessions. In my view, some therapy or other should be actively pursued by both parties in this combination to allay the inevitability of sexual discord.

Both of you are family types. You ought to have lots of children to love and protect, to shower with affection, and to take to Disneyland. As you both suffer from acute anxiety over everything from which teacher junior has this year to whether or not the cat has been left let out, I suggest that you have your kids in solid, independent signs such as Tiger and Dragon, Horse, and even Monkey. If your astrological configurations are harmonious and strong, I might advise you to have a creative Goat kid too. But not unless you are prepared to take care of him or her forever, as this child will require moral and financial support for much longer than the others.

💘💘💘💘 Rat with Pig

Oh joy! What a fine match this one is. Indeed, you two make marvelous mates for each other. Pigs attract wealth. Rats know how to invest money and require a feeling of profound security to warm the anguish that lives just under their skin. What could be better? A practical, cultivated, nature-loving, tolerant Pig mate for the nervous, never still, worrying Rat? Pigs don't want power. Rats do. Pigs adore conviviality. Rats adore throwing parties. Rats like to take over. Pigs love to comply.

Enjoying a safe home where they feel surrounded by love can help Rats to quiet down, still some of their fears, and keep their minds on work. As the Pig is too kindhearted, overly generous, and easygoing, business deals often go awry. Piggy probably forgot to say no to a killer clause in the contract, or was in some other way bullied. Luckily, the wily Rat mate is there to protect his or her Pig partner. The Rat/Pig combo is a good business match, unhindered by false notions of competition. So being together definitely enhances ties for both.

No doubt, as a couple you will have the reputation of having means. You enjoy spending lavishly on the best food products and will join forces to cook and prepare things just so for the guests or family members who come and share your bounty. Rat should be designated as the household manager. Pigs spend too lavishly and always want to give away their riches. The Pig partner ought to be given the opportunity to run the cultural side of this couple's life. Rats may forget to attend the opera and buy season tickets to the theater. Not the Pig. Piggy never forgets to keep the mind and soul nourished.

Where to live may pose something of a problem between the two of you, as Pigs invariably prefer the countryside to the rushing, dirty city. Of course, Pigs never mind using the facilities of a metropolis to conduct business or attend exhibitions. But when day is done and time out is at hand, the Pig will generally snuggle as closely to Mother Earth as time and proximity will allow. Rats also love the country and are particularly gifted for growing things. But Rats can opt to live in a big city and spend an odd weekend in a rural setting without suffering undue stress. Pigs cannot take too much clanging racket. Their aim is usually to be an integral part of a household where kids and relatives interact together in a family atmosphere.

If at all possible, try to make sure that the majority of Piggy's time is spent in a quiet setting. The house you share will be wonderfully comfortable—luxury-filled and yet easy to live in. Pigs and Rats are lovers and sharers of wealth and all that riches bring to a home. You may not necessarily require the latest in modern electronic equipment, but will definitely have a good source of musical enjoyment. No matter how modest your abode, the furnishings and accessories will shout quality, authenticity, and purity. Gold will be apparent in some fabric choices, as will the earthy tones of ochre and rose.

The sex? Silly question. You two are splendidly sensuous and understand the act of lovemaking. Moreover, neither of you is in a hurry to get it over with. You will surely spend eons of quality time together in bed, eating and reading and making lots of babies. The Pig takes immense pleasure in affording sexual satisfaction to a mate. The Rat does likewise—especially with the Pig, because in such kindly company Rat doesn't even feel obliged to perform. The Rat's sexual appetites are uneven—steady and intense for weeks, then flat for some more weeks. Pigs are nonjudgmental about such details and always try to bring their Rat partner around in a gentle, coaxing manner.

You both love children. Rat wants to nurture and protect, Piggy wants to smother and love with abject indulgence. Rat will pick up on the need for some order and discipline, and never hesitates to deals with the kids. Rat parents demand that their children perform the way that a chief Rat can be proud of You should try to have your young'uns in the Dragon, Goat, and Monkey years. Dragons bring pizzazz to the party. Goats need your nurturing hand and get along quite well with the Pig-parent, who supports and encourages creativity the way Goat likes it. As for Monkeys, well, they also get along well in convivial, congenial homes such as yours. Bon voyage!

Ox

Taken to the extreme, all of our qualities can become frailties. Some of us are generous, to a fault, which can be wasteful. Good communicators can also be blabbermouths. Nurturing parents can smother their children. Fortunately, free will allows us to balance the positive and negative sides of our character The Ox, a plodding tyrant, was born:

POSITIVE | NEGATIVE

knowledgeable | doctrinaire

contemplative | brooding

eloquent | repetitious

confident | despotic

industrious | zealous

steady | monotonous

💘💘💘 Ox with Ox

If life were strife-ridden, like life in pioneer days or under the iron thumb of some hard-bitten despot, then I would advise all Oxen to team up forever with one of their own kind. Under duress, in hard times, and when the proverbial porridge hits Papa Bear in the eye, this duo cannot be beat. Hard work and obstacles never dampened the diligence of a single Ox. So why would such trifles as war and famine get in the way of a pair of Oxen? Modern life, however, with its household conveniences, electronic devices, and labor smoother-outers is not quite so challenging to this couple. But even these days, I approve of this double Ox marriage. These two strugglers will persevere to make things happen for themselves and their family. If your potential Ox mate is born under a more acquiescent Zodiac sign than your own, your chances of making the marriage work are quite a bit better. Two Capricorn Oxen, for example, would surely lock step toward a very ambitions and coolheaded future. But a hyper-sensual Scorpio/Ox might be just the ticket for a dreamier Piscean or a more emotional Cancerian Ox. See the Western zodiac section for help.

Happy Oxen live mostly in the countryside. Oxen adore Nature. And nature returns the favor by endowing you all with bright green thumbs, forbearance for caring for slews of colicky, uncooperative offspring, stoicism for dealing with obstreperous weather patterns, and a heightened sense of duty to complete the perfect country-living package portrait. In the wild, two industrious people to do chores are always better than one. Besides, both of you enjoy living in relative solitude and don't mind being far away from the metropolitan horde. So if you or are an Ox couple or contemplating becoming a yoked set of Oxen for life, move away from town.

You two will undoubtedly steam up over almost every aspect of your relationship concerning power. Dominion and takeover privileges exact a heavy price on this couple as each of you brings to the partnership the habit of being in control. Surrendering the control prerogative (even as to who gets to feed the dog which brand of glop) will seem impossible. Neither of you is accustomed to negotiating. Talk about struggle!

Without benefit of bickering or even a little friendly couple game-playing, one of you may either up and leave in a huff, or else out of duty, you stay and spend the remainder of your lives together in resigned polite silence, bitching under your collective breaths about how annoyed you are at having to endure the other's dictates. Neither of you ever explodes, whines, or complains much. Oxen just grumble on.

The lovemaking between the pair of you is often remarkably satisfying for both. Again, neither one nor the other, although very sensual, is exactly an outright sex pistol. Foreplay, seduction and romanticism are definitely not part of this picture. But never mind. Sex, for you two, is therapeutically necessary and needs to be efficacious rather than fraught with sentimentality.

Kids? Oh, yes. You two will make terrific (if a tad strict and sanctimonious) parents. Have yourself a Dragon baby to add pizzazz and festivity. Or why not treat yourself to a chatty little Rat child or a clever, fun-loving Monkey? Each of these will fulfill your otherwise slightly stodgy lives with fantasy, mischief, and merriment. You might want to Snake child, too. The Ox is captivated by the Snake's immense beauty and the Snake is urged along to activity by the Ox's grave sense of purpose. If you can help it—need I warn you?—don't have an Ox baby. Enough drudge is, after all, quite enough.

Ox with Tiger

No matter who wears the pants in this relationship, somebody will end up being sat on. Empire-builders that you are, you two make better rivals than allies. Unless one of you is prepared to take a permanent backseat as chief of staff and forego the role of general, you will have trouble staying balanced as a couple.

The main centers of friction belong to what therapists like to call "control issues". In this cumbersome, four-fisted couple, you will be hard put to share power. When the roof wants repair, each will think you know best what color, when it should be done, and how much repair should be sought. And, indeed, you will both be right (for what you want). Ox, of course, prefers sober, neutral tones and classical styles, whereas Tiger will prefer something electrifying, special, or new-fangled. Ox is less likely to keep his or her counsel on the subject, not interject an opinion, or so much as breathe a choice. Tiger will opine. Loud and clear. Not Ox. Ox waits.

You two are forever wallowing in deep decision-making doo-doo. For Tiger, there is always enough money in the till for pet projects. The Tiger who wants flying buttresses on an alpine chalet is prepared to go the extra financial mile to pay for them. Not the Ox. The Ox is a reasonable, careful, well-intentioned planner who only agreed to the cantilevers because the builder promised they would reinforce the house. If Ox considers Tiger's flying buttress decision too zany, Ox will refuse to pay for it. And vice versa. If Tiger thinks Ox's desire for a solid new kitchen counter to replace the worn-out pink Formica from the fifties is not "fun" enough, or prefers to order Italian granite for the guest bathroom and forego Ox's counters, Tiger will claim there is no money for the counters.

The Ox/Tiger power war is permanent, ongoing, and wearing. Usually, not much actual battle gets waged because Ox is so quiet, long-suffering, and patient. In this marriage, in fact, the terribly charming Tiger always thinks he or she is getting away with one spoiled brat scheme after the other. But not to worry. The Ox has a computer for a brain. Ox is toting up all the slights, imputing every single inch of loss, and waiting to get revenge. No sign is more aware than the Ox of the old saw: *Revenge is a meal best eaten cold.* Tigers pounce noisily on victory after victory. Oxen chew their cud silently and wait for just the right moment to get their own back.

Secretly, the dauntless Tiger feels the Ox is dreary and dull. Even more covertly, the Ox feels that the rapacious, high-living Tiger is going to hell in a handbasket and that once in hell, Ox will go it alone with all the family treasury. Usually, the atmosphere in the Tiger/Ox household grows tenser and tenser, until one day the cantilevered buttresses finally cave in and the couple is forced to call the divorce ambulance.

Reconciliation may be possible. Tiger's raw sensuality may eventually thaw the Ox's resolve. In bed with the Tiger, the tight-lipped Ox can let his or her hair down, play at being naughty, and truly enjoy the game. At least a twenty-four-hour truce will result from this couple's successful sexual activities.

If you decide to stay together, you might as well have some kid to distract you from annoying each other. Have yourself a nice sturdy Dragon or a candid no-nonsense Rooster child.

½ Ox with Cat/Rabbit

Cats do well to marry Oxen. They cherish peacefulness, require quiet, and despise conflict. Oxen, likewise, enjoy the placid Cat person's company, take kindly to the Cat's insistence on tradition, and share this creature's taste for silence and seclusion from the madding crowd. As a couple, you will seek the comfort of a rural—if not isolated—home, spend many a long evening occupied with handiwork or fix-it projects involving the care and maintenance of your nest.

Holidays should be festive around your antique-filled home, as you both know how to cooperate to make a good party—complete with punch and presents, carols and smiling children's faces. You, Ox, will provide the nuts and bolts of the party's makings. If there is special lighting to be arranged or streamers to be strung, you are definitely the one chosen for the job. You might not like doing the cooking or being responsible for decorating the tree. But never mind. Cat is capable of all those detailed chores and performs them willingly and with ease.

Of course, Ox must rule the roost. But if the authoritarian Bull doesn't make unreasonable demands, the Cat is content to take a back seat and play with a ball of yarn. Cats feel safe in the presence of a strong and forceful mate. The Cat's sweetness and lavish shows of affection may embarrass the Ox, as he or she finds excessive displays of romance difficult to endure. But in the long run, despite the Ox's stubbornness and the Cat's insistence on a "classy" household atmosphere (somewhat foreign to the Ox's native gaucheness), these two are able to create a harmonious environment in which to ply a very sound marriage.

Cat is prone to fantasizing about a perfect world, castles in Spain, and spacious houses in the glorious south of France surrounded by the "right" people. Ox will be disappointed if he or she discovers that instead of scrubbing the porch railings and scouring out the fridge, the languid Cat has been spending time in a chaise longue, dreamily consuming satin box after satin box of bonbons from Belgium. Oxen sometimes lack tolerance for pursuits of a purely imaginary type and are wont to scold or disapprove when Cats go into their "If only our life were elsewhere ..." number.

Oxen, for their part, sometimes plod though life too churlishly, leaving something to be desired for the refined Cat's well-developed sense of snobbery. But, as you two get on so well in the bedroom (domesticity replaces passion to some degree), Ox won't mind when Cat suggests they try to become more cultivated, more elegant. If the Cat wants a subscription to the symphony, Ox will gladly go out and buy it. Same goes for changing the Ox's mode of dress. If Cat asks Ox gently to stop appearing at the opera in torn T-shirts, Ox will comply, dressing as the Cat instructs. In return, the Ox offers his Cat partner a steady living without stress of hyper-emotional scenes or roller-coaster bank accounts.

Your strongest suit as a couple in love will be your children. The ideal signs for you to try to hatch would be sweet-natured Pig children, agreeable Goats, and love-hungry Snakes. Tigers, Dragons, and Horses will not be easy family members for you two. The Ox doesn't want competition in the domination department.

Ox with Dragon

You two both think you are right *all the time*. Dragons will make their draconian points more noisily, but Oxen will blow them right out of the water after the noise dies down.

Oxen are strong yet modest creatures. They may be proud inside and haughty beyond belief about what they think they ought to be in the world, planning, in fact, to take over and become its Queen or King right after breakfast. But Oxen at least try to appear humble. Dragons, on the other hand, are vain and show it. Dragons preen. They speak up when they don't really know the answer. They talk out of turn in church just to hear themselves. They have ideas about every aspect of everybody's lives, and are 100 percent certain they are 100 percent right. They are to-die-for attractive, as charismatic as Eva Peron or Mickey Mouse; and moreover, Dragons swagger through life as if they have nothing more to learn.

Pretension is a quality much decried by the serious, low-key Ox person. Hence frequent battles arise in the middle of preparations for a business or family dinner party. Ox wants to keep it down to six or eight people—the principals. Ox sees no reason to speak to any but the most important people. Dragon bas already invited the entire office staff—plus the elevator operators from the whole office building, and probably the kid's teachers just to round the crowd out to fifty. The fight is on. Ox, of course, gives in. Does Ox have a choice? Dragon is so convincing and such a party animal that Ox can well believe it may ruin Dragon's life if the show doesn't go on. And show it will be. Dragons love to celebrate and throw shindigs for every occasion. Dragons also love to be seen, to be admired, and to be flirted with. All of the above drive the Ox mad with jealousy. Doesn't this marriage sound restful?

What's worse, the exorbitant Dragon loves to spend money. Dragons are extremely generous and that means they are sometimes wasteful, too. The Ox's reaction to Dragon's profligacy is to become overly budget-conscious, scolding and harping at Dragon about planning for the future. Ox tries to impose a more methodical plan, doling out family's money: investing, saving, socking it away. Dragons have no time for penny-pinching. It's all too plodding and plain. Dragon resists the Ox's influence and goes on spending like a bandit. The stubborn Ox holds fast to the sensible three-year plan. As a result, Dragon may leave in a hurry and only rarely be seen again.

The Dragon's wandering eye unsettles the faithful Ox. Dining with a couple from the office, the Dragon ventures to place his daring hand on the wrong thigh. Incensed, the normally good-tempered Ox seethes with fits of jealousy. What a sight. A galumphing Ox spontaneously combusting without a word.

How can this duo make it work? A mutual respect for home and family might save them from total despair. The Dragon tells wild bedtime stories of variant princes fighting flame-throwing monsters, and Ox helps with the math homework. Through children, marital harmony can be found. Also, the two signs are interested in their community and the environment. Avid recyclers, they volunteer time and teach the populous about ecological issues.

Both enjoy sex. But the Ox's routine approach may bore the drama-loving Dragon, whose romantic nature yearns for theater and enchantment. The Ox expects a regular living schedule, while the Dragon favors a more erratic time code: exorbitant stormy sex followed by quiet time for a week.

If you do marry, please be sure you can live sanely together without outrageous friction for at least two years before embarking on any productive activities. The best kids for you two would be garrulous little Rats, funny-faced Monkeys, and spunky Tiger babies.

🖤🖤🖤🖤 Ox with Snake

Most ultra-attractive Snake people are chronically cold. They shiver and shudder at the slightest breeze and prefer to live in the tropics. But instead, sometimes Snakes live with Oxen who do not live in the torrid zone. The Ox, as we already know, is a slow-moving, hardworking authoritarian soul who always abides where he or she is most needed. The security-conscious Snake feels safe in the clutches of a stronger Ox person and, despite a tendency to philander, will endure in this relationship.

Snakes are known for their heartfelt assistance to others in times of need. They are sought after for advice by friends and family. Snakes give the best of themselves when their nest is well-feathered. An ambiance of penury and emptiness gives the already chilly Snake an even chillier feeling—a feeling of nothingness. Ox always provides cheerfully, works harder than two people, and takes a serious view of all of life's responsibilities. Ox's ponderous, slow rhythm suits the Snake, who never minds pushing harder but who is neither lively nor quick by nature.

Snakes also have trouble getting up in the morning. Again, this trait has a lot to do with being cold all the time. Getting up means being chilly, and Snakes hate chills. But they are ambitions and wish to get on with their day, so they earnestly push themselves to rise up and go. The cozy Ox's hardy influence aids the Snake, sets a fine example, and will often be kindly and sweet about turning up the heat in the bathroom so Snakey doesn't freeze on the way to the shower.

Luckily, neither of you has to worry much about money. The Ox knows better than anyone how to work for food. The Snake attracts money. It's a lucky thing, for the Snake can be rather languid. Your home will undoubtedly bespeak the Snake's impeccable taste for luxurious items of real value and the Ox's ability to pay for them. A wise partner who intends to keep his or her Snake both happy and at home will make certain to serve champagne from crystal glasses and keep lots of the finest caviar in the fridge. Snakes thrive in a comfortable atmosphere of cushioned divans, satin sheets, and elegant bathroom fixtures. They seem to draw strength or derive an improved self-image from living in plush surroundings. Underneath, Oxen don't much mind whether their sheets are made of muslin or gold. But they do like to make their Snake feel good.

But beware: Some Snakes just cannot resist the temptation to flirt— and even to cheat on their mates. The Ox is so true blue that the Snake mate's shenanigans serve only to confuse and sadden. Oddly, if the Snake had to explain this roving-eye policy, he or she would be at a loss—a taste for foreign flesh? A desire to be admired? A need for extra warmth? Never mind. Ox wouldn't understand anyway.

Besides, the Snake is not about to leave hearth and home over a brief affair. Snakes have a clear view of which side their skin is buttered and would not slither out from under a security blanket unless ejected. It is likely that, with time, Ox will learn to tame a bad temper, calm any confusion over the Serpent's wayward ways, and realize that this, too, shall pass. Snakes— no matter how elastic their sexual habits—always cleave to strength and security. Nobody is better equipped to provide a suitable power base than the steady Ox.

Lucky for the Ox, the Snake is the best of bed partners, thinking up all variety of imaginative foreplay and after strokes that Ox never even hoped for in other relationships. A well-advised Ox will never let go of this very special treat of a sexual partner.

Children? Well, why not? Whichever of you stays home with them, it's certain they will benefit from kindly nurturing. The Ox is more of a disciplinarian than the kindly Snake, who may spoil and indulge. But you two agree on so many philosophical aspects of life that the parental control issues will not disturb the harmony. Choose children born in Rooster years. Or why not try a gentle Cat or even a spunky Dragon or a sweet-natured Rat?

Ox with Horse

Horse and Ox living and loving together? Not what I would call connubial bliss. Both want and need to be boss of the stable. I mean, think about it. Horses and Oxen do not even work well together in the fields. Horse's style is prancey and proud. Ox's is stolid and plodding. Yuck!

Oxen notoriously take dominion over their mates. They rule. Or, if they do not rule, they suffer. In the case of a mate-seeking Ox attracted to a terrifically independent, able-bodied, proud-as-punch Horse prospect, I would bet that all the Ox can think of on the first date is how to quiet and calm this driven beast into submission. As for the Horse, Dobbin is examining the dots on the tablecloth and waiting for it to be over so she can get home and turn up the music for some solo dancing in the dark. Horses are not even a teensy bit attracted to someone so obviously bent on folding them in quarters and putting them into a safety deposit box for keeps.

If, by some miracle, you two do find each other palatable enough to actually live together, the home mood will be not unlike that of a large group of high-tension wires at an electricity convention. The Ox will try to mold the haughty Horse into his or her idea of a perfect mate. The Horse will, in turn, ridicule the Ox and make horrible fun of his stodginess, disobey every Ox rule, and make mincemeat out of the Ox's beliefs about how people "should" behave. No matter how burned up the Ox gets, not much will be said about the Horse's rebelliousness. Oxen do not usually confront head-on. They become sad, pout, grow sullen, and stomp the earth, while cooking up some dreadful secret plan to undo the Horse's entire life story. Oh, this match is doomed.

The only way it could work is if one of you had a very compliant Western astrology sign and was willing to give up your desire to run things. Or, for example, if the Ox were to give up the notion of taming the wild Horse, then the Horse might grow more tolerant and loving.

But we all know that the Horse never really belongs to anyone. Horses are wonderful. But they are also selfish creatures who keep their secret selves darkly hidden from view. Oxen are not gifted for tracking buried treasure in other peoples' souls. They like what they can see, touch, and pass judgment on.

You might possibly prosper as business partners. The pair of knows how to work hard. But then you are not great at working in tandem with each other. If you are not obliged to toil at the same station at the same time, you might be able to open a grocery store or hamburger franchise together. One of you could work days and the other nights. That way you would both thrive and you would never have to see each other. Make sure you know who's in charge of finances and who is responsible for scut work—neither of you is gifted for the latter.

Bottom line, the Horse simply will not conform to anything steady, traditional Ox wishes to impose. Even the sex will be of the "Who's on top?" ilk. Horse wants variety, fun, adventure, and jollies in bed. The Ox wants a tried-and-true method of relieving the itch, preferably often, and preferably with someone halfway attractive.

These two just don't agree on anything.

Having children (unless you have proven that you can live together without violence for five years) would be an experiment in cruelty. Abstain.

Ox with Goat

When you two first meet up, the attraction is powerful. But as time passes, there will be less and less room on either side for indulgence of the other's foibles. Nothing makes an Ox more belligerent than caprice. And very few character types are more capricious than Goats. Nothing flummoxes a sensitive Goat more than brute force. And there is no Chinese character type more brutally strong than the Ox. Does Ox/ Goat begin to sound iffy?

You bet it does.

You, sweet-natured Goat, will be swooningly drawn to an apparently solid-as-a-rock Ox mate. You, after all, are forever seeking stability. The Ox embodies your need for structure, for someone to lean on, a cornucopia-type wage earner whose coping capacities far outweighs your own in the financial arena. So, although perhaps you don't see this hefty creature as the most exciting marriage possibility you have ever dreamed of, you know your own limits. Besides, there is something so challenging about your Ox's opacity of spirit. Something you know you can help to fix.

As for you, Ox, a languid, gentle facade makes the Goat person you meet for the first time wildly appealing as well. The Goat, you think, is someone you can handle, please quite easily without a bunch of folderol, and most certainly dominate.

Before taking you too far down the garden path, let me promptly disabuse you of the promise of marital harmony. Just picture yourselves yoked together, working in a field somewhere: the Ox and the Goat? I don't think so. You do not cooperate effectively.

Ox puts up with the Goat's lackadaisical attitude for a while, but will soon come to believe that the Goat is not only lazy, but directionless. A hardworking Ox simply can't understand the Goat's inertia. Happy to be dependent on others, the Goat doesn't feel the need to work, period. "After all," says Goat, "money grows on trees." Especially if the Ox is growing it. The dedicated Ox brings home most of the bacon. And the graceful Goat grazes the bacon-filled trees.

Now the trouble begins. The Goat doesn't want to be forced to be enterprising and will decide to remain close to home rather than brave the big bad workplace every day. The Ox, of course, will do just the opposite, plodding off to the office or shop or business each morning and stockpiling goodies of loot in the bargain.

Now, we already know that the Goat secretly thinks he or she can help the Ox to get over the stodgies. Goats brim with imagination, frivolity, delicacy, and spirituality. Moreover, they long to share these qualities with their partner. But have they ever tried to teach an Ox to fandango? To listen for extrasensory perceptions? To wear a fancy, flowered garment to work? To sleep on satin sheets? Much less to pay for them?

Nope. And trust me when I say that no matter what Goat does to lighten the Ox's load, the Ox will ultimately find a way to flatly refuse aid, piously reminding the poor Goat that, as a serious person, an Ox has no time for New Age silliness, no taste for decadent silken bedclothes, and certainly no eyes to wear any crazy apparel to the office. Ox disapproves of Goat. Being naturally pessimistic, the Goat often suffers from low self-esteem. He or she feels smaller and more helpless with each onslaught of Ox disapprobation. Goat never rebuts the Ox's comments, but is more likely to suddenly complain of a headache or dissolve into tears or fly into a reasonless rage. Ox/Goat is a no-win match wherein each player feels misunderstood—and the wall of incomprehension grows taller by the year.

Also, the inventive Goat finds the Ox's mating call monotonous, and the Ox has trouble keeping up with all the different Goat positions. Even in bed, this is a clumsy couple. I recommend that both these grazers search for greener pastures.

No children, please.

♥♥♥ ½ *Ox with Monkey*

The presence of a jolly Monkey partner is sure to help any old Ox have a cheerier life. Besides, Oxen truly enjoy the company of Monkeys. They see the humor in their every funny line and antic, and get a terrific charge out of watching Monkeys perform. Any reasonable Ox will be thrilled to have found such an agile, nimble-minded mate. As for the Monkey, he or she will greatly benefit from the security and solidity of the Ox partner's work ethic cum well-padded pocketbook.

Oxen can be stodgy creatures who only enjoy life when it's predictable and safe. Oxen fear change unless it's revolution and they are leading. Oxen have clear goals and no-nonsense plans. Monkeys are very different.. They are not heavy-handed at all. Monkeys like fun more than anything else - except perhaps finding solutions to problems (which they also consider to be fun). Whereas Oxen tend to be sticky about their dyed-in-the-wool opinions and shy of exposing their thoughts, Monkeys are anything but timid. They are, in fact, all about making everyone else have a good time. Moreover, they come right out with everything they have on their minds and bare their hearts and souls—almost neurotically.

What I believe keeps this couple together—and Oxen and Monkeys do tend to get married rather a lot—is the mutual admiration they each feel for the other's ability to cope. Oxen handle business and work situations with aplomb and calm. Monkeys are irreverent about social strata and don't put much truck in considering the boss superior to the janitor. This attitude can be suicidal in hierarchic office environments. Ox can show Monkey how better to operate in the social minefield of the workplace, while Monkey keeps serious Ox in stitches cavorting and acting silly in almost every part of their life together.

Oxen are self-involved and suspicious of all newcomers. Monkeys love entertaining and meeting folks they have never before seen and are known for taking up with strangers on the slightest encouragement. The free-spirited Monkey can help the dour Ox to come out of his wormy woodwork, speak up more freely, and even learn to laugh at himself Under the Monkey's humanitarian influence, Oxen have known to become philanthropic and smiley when giving money to the poor.

Monkeys are outside people. They are not much interested in how the house looks or whether it impresses anyone with its decor or cleanliness. Not so the Ox. Oxen love their homes and will work fingers to the bone making the silver shine, the dishes sparkle, and window panes appear invisible. Although Monkeys are pleased by the Ox's endeavors, they claim to have no time for convention and eschew the bourgeois traditions. Fortunately, they do know that we all need a comfy place to sleep at night—which their beloved Ox more than provides.

Monkeys never lose their adoring Ox partners, as they make terrific sex mates. The Monkey is lithe and full of sexual imagination. Monkeys aim to please their lovers and do so in a real spirit of affection, often taking their pleasure from the other's thrills. What could be better for the lumbering Ox, who is anything but imaginative and yet is very sexually active? The energetic Monkey is also able to provide frequent bouts of satisfying sex, which is exactly the sort of thing the hungry Ox needs—quantity and efficiency without too much romantic palaver.

Yes. Do have children. You will certainly want to begin with a Dragon child. You both get on with this volcanic creature and will be able to provide what it takes to set him or her on the right path. You might also consider having a resourceful Rooster. Monkey will admire this character's problem-solving prowess and Ox will adore the cocky kid's resolve. Or have yourselves a Rat baby. You will both have fun listening to this word-conscious genius child whose dynamic energies both entertain and cheer up the whole family.

❤️❤️❤️❤️ *Ox with Rooster*

What good luck that you two should have discovered each other! Chinese astrologers advise Roosters and Oxen to team up for life. Both are steady wage earners. Both have a sense of community and family. Both enjoy the safety and comfort of a settled home life. The show-offy Rooster adds pizzazz. The Ox tells a good story around the fireside. The Rooster's talents inspire the Ox to try new things. The steady-earning Ox fills in the blanks whenever the Rooster's finances fall apart. Moreover, if Ox falls ill or succumbs to depression, resourceful Rooster will find a solution. The match is solid—and not boring.

The pair of you is often accused of being picky. You don't like the fact that your neighbor's pear tree drops its bounty on your groomed lawn. You are not particularly thrilled when your friends let their toddlers loose in your nasturtiums. You would really rather folks didn't bring their dogs into your tidy living room. Both Roosters and Oxen have the reputation of paying an inordinate amount of attention to detail. When you are together—for some unknown reason—you don't get on each other's case about small items. Rooster's cat may shed all over Ox's velvet couch, yet you don't fight about it—at least not for long.

As you both like to get things done and usually proceed in a traditional fashion, your home life is orderly and cozy—without being frilly or hung with silk pelmets. The Ox believes he or she does everything as it should be done. The Rooster doesn't mind and usually follows right along. Roosters don't much want to be in charge, as they prefer to use their time to concoct schemes and do their myriad projects. So the Ox will be welcome to run things at home as well as in the workplace.

As you are equally qualified for wage-earning and Ox makes sound investments, money will be plentiful, but you will never flaunt it. Even the Rooster, who needs to have everything "look right" on the outside, will not overindulge this character trait when living with an Ox. Money is a tool—not a goal. Remember, a rainy day will always arrive when there's a Rooster in the household. Don't squander savings on anything you can't redeem in a millisecond. Rooster will always be on top again. But once in shaky while, you will need to tread some very shallow water.

Ox and Rooster will probably want a traditional wedding with family all around. You will have a good income before you buy your first home. Then you will furnish the house in Rooster's good taste and with Oxie's good sense. When you have made enough money to afford it, you will no doubt purchase a country home. There, you will grow vegetables, tend flowers, and manicure your lawn every weekend.

I don't see you inviting slews of friends out for weekend parties, as you tend to prefer quiet dinners at home with, perhaps, four people from the family or neighborhood whose taste in music is similar to yours or who have some important horticultural info to disclose.

Your sex life will be constant, enjoyable, healthy, and not very outrageous. Even though the Rooster can be flirtatious and seem almost too blatantly sexual at times, he or she is actually quite conservative and usually faithful. Both of you require good sex but neither is unduly romantic. Down-to-earth, plain old sexy sex is your mutual style. And, as you are equally energetic, lots of it!

Children are heartily advised. You will make a Snake child very secure and help him or her perform noble deeds. Or, if you do have that country place, why not birth a sweetie-pie Pig child, whose link to nature is identical to yours. A spiffy Dragon will give you both plenty to think about—as will a headstrong Horse child. Go for it. We need more parents like Ox and Rooster in this crazy world.

½ Ox with Dog

This couple is not perfectly suited to last for the duration. Number one, Dog can be slightly fickle and Ox flirtatious. Oxen are possessive as hell. Dogs pretend not to give a damn but they are woefully hurt by disloyalty. Besides, as a couple, your basic energy vectors are vastly different. Oxen want to rule the world and Dogs want to overturn its rulers from the privacy of their own doghouse. The Ox is out for long and total control over everyone. The Dog longs for nothing more than a safe and simple home where he or she can slam the door in society's face and hole up writing tracts about the shoddy way the garbage gets collected.

If you two have fallen in love and insist on becoming an item, you will discover early on that it's no fun being at leisure together. You are not the sort of duo who spend long winter evenings playing a friendly game of

Scrabble. Each of you will have your own pursuits and may not find those of your mate all that interesting or compelling.

When, finally, the dutiful Dog finds out that the Ox is beating the world the at its own game, plotting coups, and hatching hostile takeovers, Rover will be horrified—criticizing and taking the Ox apart with his incisors. The basic philosophy of each member of this duo is the polar opposite of the other's. Oxen rule, own, pressure, and pillage. Dogs stand by watching and hoping for the Ox's demise. Can we call this a couple?

You see, Dogs are too lucid by half. They can always see the flaws, hunt down the buried bones, and chew the meat off every overweight plan. Dogs will not obey or even bother to respect Oxen who think they know best where to live, how to dress, or which car they should drive. The critical Dog also feels he or she knows what's best and wants no part of the Ox's domination. Dogs cannot obey whom they do not respect. Is there anything you two can safely talk about?

The Ox who truly loves the Dog partner will be baffled by the Dog's rejection of his or her authority, feeling that ones mate should be the first to show fealty. But Dogs, although duty-bound if they see a person in need, cannot be bothered with Ox's bulldozing desire to usurp. Dogs hate power trips. They would much prefer to help an old lady across the street than to stay home licking the boots of an Ox dictator. The Ox, jealous by nature, will sulk and make clumsy attempts at seducing the Dog into "heel and roll over" stay-at-home mode. But Dog is too canny for the dense-minded Ox, whose heavy-handed tactics simply will not work.

As each of your characters is given to righteousness, you will no doubt spend much of your life together lecturing each other. The Ox is always justifying his or her own needs with lavish shows of the kind of medieval generosity, wherein the rich Lord throws food over the wall at the peasants but doesn't want to rub shoulders with them. Conversely, the Dog wants to invite a few homeless people to lunch and a pajama party. Intellectually, your twains just don't meet.

Dog/Ox sex can be extremely playful. In bed, the Dog is amused by the Ox's diligent application of the right pressures in the right place at the right time. In turn, Oxie, you are delighted by the Dog's sprightly flirting and devoted leaps and slurpings. Though it is not your habit, you find that you enjoy Doggy's long-winded foreplay, and make it your business to return the favor. With the proper nudging, out of this union a passion might be created.

If the pair of you can learn to agree to disagree, accept the other's point of view, and settle down together in relative peace, you might actually be able to found a family. The Dog makes an excellent, if fearful and overly protective, parent. The Ox knows better than most how to provide the solidity kids need for a firm foundation in life. I suggest a good prenuptial agreement, a period of adjustment in cohabitation, and a basis in family similarity before having children. If (and when) you have not bitten the heads off each other, try to have yourselves a precocious Tiger cub, a spiffy Monkey, or an anxious (but powerful) Rat child.

❤️❤️❤️ ½ *Ox with Pig*

The Ox and the Pig get on like two cottages thatched together at the roof line. They are equally rural-minded, adore authenticity, and cleave unto all solutions requiring simplicity and purity of purpose. Of course, there may be gross difficulties when attempting to agree on certain types of mutual policy decisions, the handling of money and, worst of all, the acquisition of lots of beautiful stuff—a commodity that Oxen put into a category marked *futilities*. Not to worry. Although Ox frets too much about where the precious money goes, Ox soon notices that Pig naturally attracts wealth.

You see, Oxen are professionally plain-living people. They have no taste for frivolity. They eschew lightheartedness in favor of appearing—and indeed being—serious, solid citizens. The Ox is the bulldozer of the Chinese zodiac. Authority and domination are the Ox's bailiwick. For most Ox couples (unless the Ox's opposite number belongs to another tyrant sign such as Dragon or Tiger), Ox's word is law—without either compunction or embarrassment. Not only must others conform to the Ox's way, but if they do not, they can be cast out forever without warning. Oxen carry grudges—big, lumbering, overweight cargoes of resentment that they may refuse ever to speak of or reconsider so long as they live.

Why, then, is the Pig person such a terrific partner and foil for the heavy-duty Ox character? Because the Pig is so sweet-natured and tolerant as to put the Ox to shame for being such a horrid old stick in the mud. Pigs are kindly and giving, and accepting of the behavior of others. Besides, the Pig is adaptable and generous, convivial and sensual. When confronted with all that gooey-tender Pig niceness, plus all the hot stews and loaves of freshly baked bread, the fine classical music, and the even finer wines and cognacs, the poor old curmudgeonly Ox can easily be made to think that he has succeeded in dominating his congenial mate. Little does Oxie know that Piggy is no fool. Piggy is honest and true as the day is bright, but will still go through Ox's pockets after he or she has drifted heavily off to sleep.

Pigs need to be surrounded by beautiful things. Not in favor of buying anything beyond necessities and comforts, the Ox mate may tempt to curb Piggy's sprees and flagrant buying habits by laying down the law or pulling tighter on the purse strings. But the gentle Pig has little to fear from the Ox's ultimatum. If Pig gets mad enough, Pig pulls one of his or her fits. Ox (and everyone else in the household) is terrified of Pig's ire. A porcine temper tantrum is a rarity indeed. But if you have ever witnessed one, you will not hanker to see another soon. The Ox is anything but self-destructive. So once Pig has pulled a fit, Ox knows enough to butt out and let Piggy wallow in shopping.

At the summit of a beautiful hill in the mountains of some exquisite location, the Ox and the Pig will build their dream house. This home is perfectly well cared for—inside and out. Pigs cook with gusto and imagination. Preparing chutneys and jam, sauces and creams, this devoted Pig mate revels in the use of a splendidly practical as well as beautiful kitchen. Much entertaining goes on in this Pig/Ox household, where Piggy serves only the best of hospitality as well as vittles.

At bedtime, the careful Ox tiptoes about turning off all the lights in the house, and this frequently chubby combo plops into bed. Despite the Ox's native reticence about romance, sex is not ever going to be *ho hum* between these two. Our ultra-sensual Piggy will not have any of Ox's therapeutic, sportsmanlike, get-it-over-with sex. *Au contraire,* the loving Pig prepares the Ox by massaging his or her tired hooves, speaking sweet nothings into his sleepy ears, and initiating the Ox into fancy Piggy foreplay about which you will only learn the delectable ropes if you take up with one of these delightful mud-lovers yourself.

If you two have kids, I suggest you produce them in the years of the gentle, creative Goat, the sensuous and irresistible Snake, the resourceful Rooster, or the refined and elegant Cat. All of these signs will find their lot improved by cohabitation with your solid, nature-loving couple. The Goat will get on the Ox's nerves, but the Pig will protect it. Rooster and the Pig may have differences of opinion, but the Ox will stick up for Rooster's needs. Snakes get along with both of you but will bamboozle the Pig parent. Never mind. Ox will protect Pig. And the Cat will make you both proud and a mite richer.

Tiger

Taken to the extreme, all of our qualities can become frailties. Some of us are generous to a fault, which can be wasteful. Good communicators can also be blabbermouths. Nurturing parents can smother their children. Fortunately, free will allows us to balance the positive and negative sides of our character. The courageous daredevil Tiger was born:

POSITIVE | NEGATIVE

idealistic | fanatical

industrious | workaholic

independent | uncommitted

charismatic | narcissistic

dynamic | coercive

danger-loving | self-destructive

Tiger with Tiger

Burning bright? You bet. Brighter than is possible without burnout. Tiger people make excellent friends and terrific business partners. But as most Tigers think only of victory and want quick results in any and everything they do, it's difficult to imagine them maintaining a long-standing relationship. Tigers deplore tired, commonsense marital concepts such as: *compromise your ideals, mend your ways, and take a backseat.* Tiger One will want it his way, and Tiger Two will want it hers. They may have a vivid discussion or two about who is right or wrong. But it will end there. Each will walk out one door of and be back whenever they feel like it.

Peripatetic by nature, the Tiger never ceases to prowl—looking for love, fun, excitement, and well, maybe just someone else to lay charm on. Charm, seduction and open-faced friendliness are all part of a bag of tricks uniquely native to Tigers, who lavish their goodwill on everybody from the grocer to the garage mechanic to the dry cleaners and the cop who stops them for speeding. Tigers are very *nice* people.

Except when they meet their match. Except when they stop being nice and grow cross and irritable because someone is trying to stand in the way of their parade, scotch their plans, nick their territory, snitch their cookies, or move their computer over a millimeter or two.

Tigers make all their own decisions. Tigers are the people who, when you tell them the name of the highest mountain in North Korea, pipe right up and say, "I knew that." Tigers stalk about the earth doing what comes aturally (to them) and often being right. They thrive on victory, wilt in failure.

Now place two of these nomadic, know-it-all creatures side by side in a non- hierarchic idyllic love relationship. *Kaboom!* They go off like a fireworks display. And then drizzle back to earth all soggy and sorry.

In other words, this couple can work. But it cannot work for long.

If you are in one of these doomed relationships and you want to get it "undoomed", I's say, give it a try. But I don't promise anything. Tiger twins? Mmmmmhhhh.

There is passion. Passion and Tigers go together. So a love affair or a smashing one-night stand will definitely work. (If you can agree on "my place or yours", that is.) Your lovemaking could be glorious. There is pizzazz by the pound in each and every Tiger libido. So a good head start is a distinct possibility.

But wait. How about next morning, when it comes time to share the bathroom? Who makes coffee for the Tiger King or Queen? The Tiger King or Queen? I don't think so.

Trouble is, there is no give in this relationship. All right. If one is a Scorpio and the other a Pisces and twelve years younger, it *might* work—for a while. Or if one Tiger is a rich Leo or a powerful Sag, and the other one is twenty-four years younger and born in Libra or Cancer or even Capricorn ... but I am still not keen. If marriage there will be, it will probably be short and to the point. And it may last the the time it does because you work together, hence a common bond of interest holds you together. Tigers do work well as a team.

Children? If one of you absolutely wants to spawn little children of this union, let him or her ask for a little divorce first. Okay?

Tiger with Cat/Rabbit

I confess never to have heard of a longstanding Tiger/Cat liaison, marriage, or live-in partnership. What's wrong with this pair of cats trying to make it as a couple? Plenty.

Tigers live for change and victory over adversity. Tigers think of money as a necessary evil, and are not particularly concerned with its long-term accumulation as they trust it will always be there. Tigers go after the biggest challenges, are not above committing violence if they if they deem something is in their way, and are often more dangerously confrontational than wisdom would dictate.

Cats live for peace and quiet. They dream of having sufficient capital to survive all nine of their lives without worry clouding the horizon. They deplore change, eschew violence, and shrink in horror from anybody vaguely confrontational.

Moreover, the Tiger's and the Cat's natural styles of living are polar opposites, and create a true clash at every attempt to get together on living space, entertaining, or holiday plans. Cat wants to live in abject splendor, surrounded by antiques and Grandma's inherited Limoges china. Tiger wants to decorate with whatever is expedient and attractive and to hell with the style. Cat longs to invite small groups of very select people to dine in candlelit harmony. Tiger wants to get everyone together to eat, drink, and argue far into the night and giggle until they can't breathe anymore. Cat wants to vacation in Venice and stay at the palace. Tiger prefers to travel in Ireland in the rain out of season, thereby saving enough to throw in a jaunt to the Cotswolds and a weekend in Paris at a neat student hotel in the grubbiest bohemian neighborhood.

Imagine these two feline creatures attempting to live side by side, establish a family, make a home for some unsuspecting offspring, and live happily ever after. As we say in France, *"C'est impossible."*'

But it might also be a case of *"C'est la vie."* Especially if you two are already ensconced in a relationship and strongly desire to hold on to it.

The only way I could see this working at all is if you two had separate private incomes. Cautious Cat could stash his or hers safely in a trust fund so that Tiger won't squander it all. Lucky Tiger could spend the family fortune in one place or lose it in a single poker game, and suddenly gain it all back with interest by investing it in something outrageous like sardine futures in the Korean highlands.

Bed? Sex? Passion? I doubt it. Cats are squeamishly slow and languorous about their sensuality. Tigers are brash, enthusiastic to a fault, and go at sex in the same frantic, eclectic fashion they do everything else. I conjure an image of two very dissatisfied pussycats sleeping on very opposing sides of a lumpy marital couch.

You might possibly be able to patch this match together with tons of therapy, a lucky harmonious Western astrological configuration, and truckloads of good old-fashioned luck. Until you have accomplished this patching process, however, I advise against procreation. In case you ever managed to build yourselves a sound basis for a family, you could try for a sweet-natured puppy Dog baby. You will each gain greatly from what this adorable pet of a child has to teach you.

Tiger with Dragon

Despite a tendency to overdramatize your individual issues, you two can make excellent lifetime partners. It's true that an undercurrent of "Who's the boss around here anyway?" will be ever present and may interfere with harmony between Tiger and Dragon. Yet you two have an implicit understanding about many of life's problems—and neither of you are afraid to go ahead and implement radical solutions.

You are both ego-centered. Dragons need flattery, spotlights, and praise. Tigers need to be appreciated and seen to be sensible, righteous, and efficient. It may take some time to iron out the kinks, but Tiger and Dragon both benefit from mutual respect and reciprocal admiration. Oh yes, the Tiger is less tolerant of sentimentality than the weepy Dragon, who cries at the sight of a broken rubber band. And the Dragon is far, far too noisy for the Tiger's sensitive ears to tolerate. Too, Dragons are name-droppers and snobs. Tigers are pushy and independent to a fault. But these flaws become details in the bigger picture between all-seeing Dragon and Tiger lovers.

Doling out departments may, at first, get in the way. You both want to rule every area of your relationship. For example, you have a real estate opportunity: Tiger wants to talk. Dragon wants to yell. Tiger wants to shout.

Dragon will bellow. This dead-end methodology could become tedious. Because you are both intelligent, results-oriented people, you will soon see the folly (and perhaps even the humor) in your shriekings and decide in a twinkling to buy that house in Idaho, even though it's too expensive and interest rates are too high.

Not to worry about money. You will have enough and then some. Both of you like to work and be paid handsomely for your efforts. Neither is a sissy about asking for just desserts. Don't argue about who gets to handle the finances. You will do it best if you do it together. If accounting bores you both, when finally you have the means, hire yourselves a budget-conscious accountant.

People love to come to your home. You are a generous pair who know how to share both your spoils and your toys. You gracefully take turns ruling the roost, choosing the party themes, and coming to a solid agreement on how to decorate the house or educate the kids.

Tiger/Dragon sex is fabulous. Strong, steamy, and delicious. You own a pair of equally matched, determined libidos. You adore making love together—and will be capable (if you watch your steps) of maintaining loyalty and sexual fidelity for many, many years. Your energies match, too. Unless one of you is ill or out of sorts, the pattern of your sexual experience together should pan out as regular and intense.

This relationship is a promising one for marriage. Battles will be waged, power lines will sizzle and sometimes burst. But at the end of the day, the ravishing Dragon sets the tawny Tiger on fire and the electrical storms revert to the bedroom, where they belong.

Kids? Have oodles. Dragons love to live with noise. Tiger puts up with the din because Dragon is such a darling. Your best choices for offspring are dutiful Dogs, merry little Monkeys, and relentless Rats. You might enjoy having yourselves a sweet-natured Pig child or a headstrong Horse for good measure. Dragon and Tiger kids will be happy additions to your household as well—the more the merrier.

💘💘 *Tiger with Snake*

This is an exciting but difficult match to keep balanced. You are compatible without being alike. In fact, your compatibilities are grounded in your differences. If you can work things out, you'll have some fascinating times together.

You are both ferociously strong—in two entirely different ways. The Tiger bombs around, leaping and pouncing on every new idea, thrashing through the underbrush of life, and hoping against hope never to have to slow down, give up any territory, tell so much as one lie, or lose a single battle. Snakes move quietly and liquidly, slithering in and out here and there, listening and assessing, spying and deducing, attracting and prevaricating their way among life's most powerful influences. Tigers rule and control. So do Snakes. Tigers want star billing. So do Snakes. Tigers are charismatic. So are Snakes—big time!

Snakes take it slow. Tigers are in a big hurry. Snakes ponder. Tigers leave the pondering to hindsight. Snakes philosophize. Tigers psyche people out. Snakes are wont to lie abed mornings. Tigers leap from the covers to attack a new day. Snakes covet silken sheets and dream of being permanently wrapped in thick, warm bath towels at tropical spas. Tigers will sleep anywhere as long as it's reasonably flea-free, and bath wraps make them feel hot under the collar—as do spas.

If you work at it, you two can exert a positive influence on one another. A deliberate Snake can slow a tempestuous Tiger down. This may irk the Tiger. But it also may make the Tiger think twice before he jumps off that next cliff. A Tiger can spur the low-energy Snake to action with words and some good old Tiger enthusiasm. The Snake may resist Tiger's attempts to spark him off. But not much discourages an eager Tiger in dynamo mode—except perhaps the sting of an unwilling Snake mate.

Money will constitute a hurdle for you two. Snakes seem to be extremely careful about money, yet they spend lavishly on luxuries. Snakes hate to pay utility bills, so they may secretly put a summer down payment on a $5,000 fur coat they hope to wear in winter when the house cools down. Tigers make money and spend it. Then they make more. But Tigers are not much for lavishness, and take pleasure in driving around in a battered pickup truck wearing last year's leather jacket. Clashes about values inevitably crop up between you two. Tiger must learn to be more compassionate. Snakes may wish they could cut back, but they probably cannot.

When things do go wrong between the two of you, they go exceedingly awry. Snakes are quite easily tempted by infidelity. They are too attractive for their own good. So, when the Cat's away—which the Tiger so frequently is—well, the Snake may play. Tigers can be fairly annoying in many areas of cohabitation, but they are usually not unfaithful. Tiger's reaction to Snake's strayings may emerge as impressive fits of temper. Snakes feel sorely guilty for their sins, and by reaction may actually up and leave with their new lover. Tiger will of course be outraged and inconsolable. What principled Tigers see as rank betrayal of a sacred covenant, the luxury-loving Snake may see as expedient.

Also, the sex is not perfect at first. Tigers are too heated, hasty, and impetuous for the slow-moving Snake. Snakes are so languid and sensual in a dark, cool way that the Tiger gets confused before things have a chance to heat up. You can hope for better sex to come along with a deeper knowledge of your mutual characters. I advise entering therapy for a few years until you can better comprehend where the other person is coming from emotionally. In this way, you will build a sound, more mutual love life together.

If one day (after you have resolved your differences) you do have children, you might choose to bear yourselves a brave Rooster or a Horse child. It might be tempting to have yourselves a Monkey or an Ox, since Snakes get on so well with Oxen and Tigers go well with Monkeys. But for the children's sakes, I would abstain. If you want true excitement, have yourselves a dashing Dragon baby.

❤️❤️❤️½ *Tiger with Horse*

You two get along handsomely. You both have an independent spirit, and find it easy to adore and respect each other. Tiger may be working on the Grand Dam of Mongolia while Horse is performing at the Santa Fe Opera. But neither of you will be singing the blues because it is understood-- a pact between Horses and Tigers—that you don't get in each other's way.

Mostly, I advice people never to try to pack two stars into one household. With the Horse and Tiger, however, I can lift that caveat. Both are strong. Usually, if a depression comes along, the Horse is up and the Tiger's down—or vice versa. No boredom here either. These two are active, lusty life-grabbers. Both of you know how to be creative in your work and world activities, and yet at home you leave your inflated ego in the closet. Tiger and Horse agree on a lot too. You both love the same styles of furniture and trust each other's taste in everything from politics to holiday venues. On the other hand, when you disagree, neither of you is afraid to argue with the other. Mutual respect, of course, is the basis of this peaceable method of dealing with trouble.

Although many aspects of your life together jibe, there is one essential difference between you. The Tiger is a hothead who goes for new-ness, pounces heedlessly on change, and takes gigantic risks for the thrill of it. Not so the Horse. The Horse may boil over, say outrageous things, give the impression of abandoning his or her senses. But Horses are pragmatic first and emotional second. They will not make heedless decisions about changing jobs or mates or couches unless there is a sound basis for them. They won't pull up roots and move somewhere for a healthy change of scenery either. When there's money in the bank and all the insurances and credit cards are paid up, then will Horses accompany their Tiger mate on one of those pounce-first, think-later adventures.

Horses respect money much more than Tigers do. Tigers tolerate money, but don't have much affection for the stuff. Both of you are supremely employable people. You will undoubtedly make it your business to do well in business or in creative endeavors. But let the sensible Horse person handle the funds. Tigers may find the most brilliant ways of investing or even of getting more money—but Horses know how to stash it in that bank and keep it there.

A Tiger/Horse household will be a neatly arranged place where friends are welcome when planned for. Neither of you is particularly gifted for spontaneous parties where neighbors stop in with their cousins from Cleveland. No. Your parties will be well attended by a select few and may turn into long nights of political discussion and tumult-- improvisational you are not.

The initial sexual attraction is volcanic. And both Tigers and Horse are imaginative enough and faithful enough to keep sex exciting over the long haul.

If you are thinking of being married or are already together in a live-in way, I advise you to establish a safe, secure household before starting a family. In family matters, the Horse's conservatism curbs the Tiger's hotheadedness. You work hard together to raise a fine family in a very "proper" way. Yet, thanks to the Tiger's rebelliousness, the kids will get some relief from the severity of Horsey's approach. Still, neither one of you is particularly stay-at-home, so you will need to provide a house large enough to accommodate live-in help and include some family space for kids and adults to enjoy for joint activities. As for which signs you should aim for when you have children, I would advise three really basic compatible ones: Goat, Dog, and Pig. But do not have either a Goat or a Dog as an only child. The Goat needs to feel safe and surrounded, and the Dog longs for companionship. One Pig child could be happy with neat parents like you. The Pig has in fact, much to teach a Tiger/Horse couple as—unlike either Tigers or Horses—Pigs are tolerant and pliable. They know how to be spontaneous and are guaranteed to help you find your own gooey center without a map.

Tiger with Goat

You may not want to base your future on this match. Sex, yes. Passion, yes. Getting along as friends, yes. But long-term, long-winded, long-suffering, for better or for worse—not by the hair of your chinny chin chins.

Tigers like change, derring-do, adventure, and risk. Goats like all of those things and many, many more—providing they have the one thing they love more than anything else in the universe—security. Now, you can lead Tigers to security, but you cannot make them stay there. Tiger hates routine. If a Tiger buys a house, he or she wants to tear all the walls down, rebuild the house from the bottom up and inside out. Then, maybe the Tiger will live in it for a few minutes or even years. But ultimately, even after having done mucho repairs and plenty renovations, Tiger sells out, moves on to another house project, and tears that one apart... and you know the rest.

So consider the poor shivering, sensitive, gentle Goat, whose sole life concern is finding and keeping a secure place where there's enough (if not more than enough) food and drink and means to thrive and accomplish some sort of creative endeavor in an atmosphere free from want. Imagine this clinging-vine Goat person married to an on-the-go nomadic spouse. It's positively laughable. Except the Goat does not find it amusing. Goats do not take live-in relationships lightly. If Goats marry and settle down, that is precisely what they had in mind—settling They do not find it too humorous when their beloved mate suddenly ups and sells the house because the shutters need painting.

Faced with Tiger's tenuous arrangements, Goats freak. They lose it. They have no way of maintaining peace of mind in the absence of their object of affection/security blanket. Tigers one day grow impatient with Goat's neediness and *"C'est fini!"* Roger. Over and out.

If you are an established Goat/Tiger couple, you have already seen what I mean. Yet, if you are not yet espoused and merely living in the first flush of love paralysis, you may think I am insane to advise against such a smoothly-running engagement.

Trust me. As soon as the children and responsibilities begin to pile up and Tiger is off to work in Africa, the cracks will begin to show in the walls and ceiling of your marital life. Goats hate to be left on their own to assume the load of house holding and bill-paying, and so on. Tiger regrets, but he or she cannot come home just yet. Goat does not cry and scream and beg and plead. Oh no. The Goat hangs up in a huff, grows sullen and more pessimistic than usual, and forgets to feed the bambinos. The Goat may even slip into a depression and forget to feed the Goat. Or worse. The Goat may begin feeding that nice-looking person he or she met at the movies last week. Now we approach the emotional blackmail portion of the story. Tiger calls back. Goat is a mess. Tiger feels guilty and comes home. Then comes the next call from Africa. Tiger explains, "I must leave again for a while, darling." Goat re-freaks. After a few harrowing days, Goat calls Tiger home in emergency mode. Tiger comes home. Goat goes all blissful and Tiger grows more and more miserable. Get the picture?

My suggestion to the pair of you, Goat and Tiger, is to have yourselves a rip-roaring affair. Your sexual attraction is intensely passionate. You agree on many, many issues. Tiger appreciates the Goat's laidback attitudes. Goat admires the Tiger's ability to deal with the world. Go for the long-standing sexual heyday. Remain lifelong loving friends if you want. But do not tie your little red wagons together for the purposes of cohabitation or marriage. No. *No.* A thousand times no.

Children? Never.

💘💘💘 *Tiger with Monkey*

Monkeys and Tigers make fabulous companions. They share an upbeat tone, and both tend to attack life each day as though it were a large slice of Grandma's best chocolate cake. This complicity of energy often causes these two to fall in love. On top of the love, excitement is a second treat in this relationship. Tigers and Monkeys think alike. They both adore strategy and are intrigued by complex human interactions. Chinese scholars don't always agree with me, but I feel that Tiger/Monkey is a happy match. Luckily, the issues of money and power are naturally set aside between these two people. The Monkey's spurts should not cloud the otherwise sunny atmosphere that informs this couple's mutual admiration.

Tigers sometimes find the prying nature of the Monkey rather irritating. Monkeys; by nature, are inquisitive and need to know what is inside every package, who is responsible for every bill in the household, and sometimes insist heavily on whom to blame when the cat isn't put out at night. The loner Tiger often feels imposed on by Monkey's questions. In these situations, Tiger wishes only to disappear and not continue this conversation. Deep down, the painted beast considers the Monkey annoyingly picky and judgmental. The Tiger wants to avoid silly issues, to remain rigorously independent, and to not have to respond at all. If snoopy Monkey pushes too hard, curiosity might just kill the Monkey instead of the cat.

Tigers can be moralizers, forever sermonizing and handing out free tips on everything from indigestion to Indians. If there is one thing Monkey cannot do, it's taking advice gracefully. Monkeys are the solvers. They always want to think they know best what to do in any given situation—and they are frequently right. When the meddlesome Tiger hands out freebie hints and the Monkey goes blithely ahead with plan A, having turned a totally deaf car to Tiger's counsel, Tiger gets mighty bent out of shape. Monkey laughs. Tiger seethes. A disagreement ensues.

Even though these two occasionally spat and fall out, they invariably patch things up and move ahead with their relationship. Neither the Monkey nor the Tiger is a born grudge holder. The living of a good life, to them, is all too important to allow it to be burdened by a heavy unpaid emotional debt. Once their differences blow over, the Tiger and the Monkey usually fall back into each other's arms and commence their characteristic giggling at the world all over again.

The sounder elements in this cheery couple belong to their reciprocal and complementary talents. Monkeys know instinctively how to solve sinuous, complicated problems. Tigers are forever involving themselves in sinuous, complicated scrapes. Monkey steps right in and lifts Tiger out of the deepest poop. And what's more, Tiger really appreciates Monkey's clever strategies. Tigers enjoy the spotlight. Monkeys hate to be targeted for top billing. This way, Tiger gets to shine and preen and be adored by the public, while Monkey remains willingly in the background, steering Tiger by the tail like a master puppeteer.

Money is rarely an issue between the Tiger and the Monkey. Monkey is probably the more careful spender, but these two have an equally devil-may-care attitude toward cash; they enjoy throwing it around and reveling in their own mutual generosity. This couple lavishes presents on each other. Of the two of you, I'd venture the Monkey is a bit more serious about keeping some money for a rainy day, so do put the investment responsibilities in Monkey's capable hands. Tiger makes money. But Tiger also spends it like a bandit.

As a couple, you are eminently talented at great, hearty fun-filled sex. Have as many children as you want. Monkeys never grow up, so they usually enjoy being surrounded by kids. Tigers like to preach and give orders, so they can care for the whole lot and get a kick out of being the family hotshot. I advise Dog babies, Horse kids, Dragon cubs, and of course, gentle, sweet Pigs. To keep the happy family train for a long, long time, you might want to add on a Rooster caboose. Those canny little Rooster guys always do their older parents proud.

Tiger with Rooster

Marriage? I used to think this relationship would be overly turbulent. Then I changed my mind. Finally, in these times, when life is so hectic anyway, I can see a terrible Tiger hitched to a cocky Rooster for a veritable tilt-a-whirl lifestyle wherein perhaps kids won't have a place—but never mind. Couples do survive without children.

Roosters are adventurous folks who have absolutely no hesitation about ending one relationship and moving on to another. No that Roosters break their word or throw dust in the face of promises—on the contrary. But when a relationship goes sour, a partner races off with someone else or somehow loses interest in the Rooster, he or she never stays around long. Roosters are not snivelers or torch-bearers. They do not allow their ex to see them weeping and wailing or even try to make that same ex feel bad about what happened. It's *ciao* and *au revoir,* see ya round sometime. Tigers are fairly similar in their attitudes toward breakups. When its over, Tigers move on.

The reason I go into this aspect of Rooster and Tiger love behavior is to indicate that neither Tigers nor Roosters dwell on emotional masters. Tiger needs someone steady who enjoys life and knows how to have a good time even when Tiger isn't around—someone independent. Roosters need the same thing. They do not think of their love affairs or marriages as two people melting together into one dreamlike entity. Rather, Rooster-Tiger marriages contain two very distinct people who stay together because of a special synergy they feel they create as a pair. The Rooster who gets this zany notion to paint gold stars on the dining room ceiling wants a partner who begins cutting out stencils and mixing gold paint. Same for Tiger. The Tiger who decides to wear a papier-mâché headdress to a masquerade hall wants a mate who will begin collecting newspapers and glue. Rooster and Tiger form an excellent team. But they are not the sort of people who say, "*We* think the president is full of dreary platitudes." Tiger says, "I think the president thus and and such," and Rooster then expresses his or her own opinion quite separately.

The major difficulty you will encounter in getting along turns around who gets to be the boss. Each of you is very competent and likes to live your own life your own way. There is little compliance or flexibility here. My advice about this serious hitch in the eventual harmony of your couple is to delegate departments in your life as either all Rooster's or all Tiger's. Tiger cooks and Rooster cleans. Or Rooster plays handyperson and Tiger pays all the bills. If you don't tread on each other's flower beds, life will run more smoothly around that Rooster/Tiger homestead.

The issue of money will be a problem in this relationship. Tigers make money but usually not before the age of forty, when they settle down to accomplishing one career at a time. Roosters make money in spurts. They are very capable and quite careful about saving and investing. But the Chinese claim that the fate of all Roosters is to have gobs of money one year and none at all the next. So, where finances concerned, you would be well advised to make arrangements for rainy-day cash to be stashed by someone more economical than either you. Get an honest business counselor to manage your affairs-and—and do as you are told: Do not take off for a romantic trip to Hawaii even though there's no money in the savings account.

You will undoubtedly enjoy the comforts of more than one home. You both like building and gardening. You are probably both good cooks. You have excellent mutual taste in furniture and are manual and creative when it comes to decorating. I advise you to invest in ruined houses and fix them up for resale. As a second business or hobby, you two could not do something more suited to your talent.

Sex is fantastic. The Rooster is energetic and imaginative in bed. Moreover, Roosters are exciting people who adore the joys of all aspects of living. What could be more adventurous than sex? Tiger is impulsive and loves thinking up new sexual games and positions. Your love life will be full of intensity, grand gestures, and words of undying passion.

No children, please. Too much moving around.

💘💘💘💘 Tiger with Dog

You two really do get along. Not that your styles or characters are remotely alike. Nor are you opposites. You complete each other. You understand each other. You get excited about the same things in life. You also care enormously about each other's welfare.

The Dog, of course, is a born pessimist. Dogs suspect the world of being mismanaged by a wall-to-wall conspiracy—right down to the guy behind the counter at the deli who forgets to give Doggy mayo on his turkey sandwich. Tigers are mostly optimistic. If they don't get any mayo on their turkey sandwich, they decide that they're better off without—mayonnaise is bad for people anyway.

Why then do Dog and Tiger harmonize so successfully? Because there is an absolutely synergistic sense of cooperation between you. Whether Doggy carries the heart and Tiger brings the muscle or vice versa, your party is a huge success. Whatever the issue—politics, business, human relationships, holiday plans, or how kids should be raised, the Tiger and the Dog can and will come to a compromise. You do not always agree... far from it. There will be plenty of growling and gnashing in this couple. But between you lives a special compassionate place where, when you both manage to quiet down and look at the other person's point of view, the only solution is a peaceful one.

Dogs are *cause* people. They are forever coming up with new ways to solve the problems of humanity, remedies for social ills, and discovering the rotted, wiggly board in the new deck you just had built off of your master suite. The Dog sniffs out injustice. But he or she is not satisfied to merely trot into the kitchen and tell Tiger, "Hey, honey, the baby is about to drop through the floor because Bill-the-Carpenter built it all wrong. Oh no. The Dog wants to see that justice is done. So here comes the Tiger's role. Dog will rarely want to ring up Bill to complain about the dry rot in the floor. Dog is timid and antisocial. Here, Tiger springs into action—"Goddamn that fool

Bill!" Tiger races to the phone and takes care of Bill: "You jerk! How dare you? Whatever possessed you to buy us cheap wood?" Case closed. Dog snuffs out the grievance and Tiger dares to bring it to light. Dog cooks up schemes. Tiger voices them.

Where money is concerned, you ought not to have much to fight about. The Dog is a far more careful spender than the Tiger. But as you usually fall into step about what to buy when and for which reasons, you find a common ground before impulse-purchasing the latest luxury model car or deciding to go with a more modest four-wheel-drive vehicle to get you over rough country roads. It's odd, but in this couple, the Tiger will often concede power to the less pushy, less vocal Dog. Bottom line—the Tiger (who trusts nobody) trusts the Dog. Dog ought to handle finances.

Your home will be a more peaceful haven if both of you work and you hire someone to look after the place while you're gone. Neither you is a particularly gifted stay-at-home, as you are both sincerely involved in your work lives and need to feel occupied in the world to be happy. Dogs engage in all variety of employment demanding precision, criticism, and poring over detailed documents. Tigers prefer being leaders: captains of industry, builders, movers, and shakers. You could even work together. The Dog might be an architect. The Tiger a contractor. You might have words over certain aesthetic elements of your work. But you would always find a way to compromise for the sake of the project.

Sexually, you are super compatible. More aggressive, the Tiger will often initiate lovemaking. Dogs need to be calmed. Tiger knows how to foresee this need and handle it without allowing their own ego problems to get in the way. For Dog and Tiger, I predict a long and healthy sex life of which ought to emerge several of the most interesting little pests ever born.

You will both get along with Horse children. You admire their energy and can help them deal with their upstart nature. I also like the idea of a Dragon child living in your home. Dragons will pep up the celebratory side of your lives. Little Pig or Cat children might also flourish with you two as parents. But be certain neither of them has Western astrology signs that conflict with yours, as they are soft people and might, otherwise drown in your sometimes fractious home environment.

❤️❤️❤️ *Tiger with Pig*

Initially, you two are hardly attracted to each other at all. Tigers are muscular, short-of-haunch, and move stealthily. The Pig, conversely, tends to lollygag along and have a roundish body—not always plump, but well-cushioned. The physical magnetism of your couple is not obvious when you first meet.

Your mode of living is also different from the outset, as Piggy enjoys a countrified, if luxurious, convivial lifestyle complete with lots of company in the form of family, pets, and even errant neighbors dropping in. Tiger at home is a private sort of person who likes to keep things in order and rarely invites people to come visit unless all is pre-arranged. Tiger is more of a control freak than the Pig, who prefers to leave control up to the gods and even his guests. Pigs trust Life. Tiger does not.

Both of you also appreciate the finer things in life. Tiger has a fondness for education, reading, and learning about all manner of exotica. Pig is a culture vulture, knows every gallery and museum within a hundred miles by heart, has traveled to every land of castle, king, temple, and pyramid, and brings home treasures of real value. Stories (told by Piggy at those big dinner parties you love to throw) of your travels and intellectual pursuits will delight more than one guest in your entertaining lifetime.

There will be some problems. The flip side of Piggy's good nature is a frighteningly ferocious temper. And the underside of Tiger's charmed broad-based life approach is chronic procrastination and constant absences. Pigs like to do things "right." Pigs are scrupulous and rather let themselves be bamboozled. Tiger (probably not home at the time of the incident) is outraged when he discovers that Pig has let wool be pulled once again over those squinty little eyes. Tiger scolds. Pig throws a tantrum. The roof blows off the house. You will have to learn to tolerate each other's faults. But, for the sake company, don't fight it out. Get professional help instead.

Whatever way it goes down, the fact is that our Pig/Tiger combo grows slowly into a mutual admiration society. Pig is wowed by Tiger's ability to win others over and get things done. Tiger is comforted by Piggy's ability to kick back and watch as projects develop. Pig, with a gentle tolerance of all and nothing, finds Tiger's hands-on approach intriguing—kind of disarmingly cute, really. As for you, Tiger, you may at first perceive the Pig's acquiescence and general openhearted approach as weakness. But as time passes, the Tiger comes to realize that Piggy is amazingly strong—but in a different way from Tiger. Tigers attack. Pigs lie back and wait. Tigers say no. Pigs say maybe. Finally, when the Tiger takes a look at results, he or she is amazed to discover how often Pig's objectives have been met just as effectively as Tiger's—that it was all a question of style.

When they team up, Pig and Tiger are unbeatable. It's good cop, bad cop time—and they are equally terrific at playing mind games. Much commerce can be accomplished by these two in cleverly designer business schemes where nobody gets hurt and the Tiggy/Pig duo make lots of money—which they will share without argument, as neither Pig Tiger is one to worry much about where the next penny is coming from. They both attract lucre, but Pigs should manage finances. Tigers are squanderers.

Your physical relationship will grow slowly, being at first only mutually comforting and later growing into a passionate, fervent lifelong attachment. Pig is sensual but sometimes timid at first, afraid of Tiger's direct approach. Tiger is a fabulous sex partner but, unless informed, not always sensitive to the needs of his mate. It will take some time for you two to engage. But once you do, it can be forever. My prescription? Hundreds of cuddles.

Do have kids. Pig will give into them. Tiger will try to run the show. On balance, they won't have a disappointing life. Hatch yourselves a baby Goat (Pigs adore Goats and vice versa) for Tiger to boss around. Or why not have a Dragon baby whom you can both admire? Or an Ox for ballast? Rat children would be happy in this household, too.

Cat/Rabbit

Taken to the extreme, all of our qualities can become frailties. Some of us are generous to a fault, which can be wasteful. Good communicators can also be blabbermouths. Nurturing parents can smother their children. Fortunately, free will allows us to balance the positive and negative sides of our character. The Cat/Rabbit, an evasive diplomat, was born:

POSITIVE | NEGATIVE

sensitive | squeamish

pennywise | miserly

tactful | untruthful

well-mannered | snooty

discreet | evasive

ambitious | ruthless

💘💘💘 Cat/Rabbit with Cat/Rabbit

Cats/Rabbits like peace and quiet. They need lots of security, too. They are not content to take risks or change venues often. So, to survive as a double-Cat couple, you will need to make certain of your reserves: a portfolio of stocks, a real estate empire, and savings and retirement accounts galore.

You also need great gobs of comfort in order to cohabit successfully. You will both want to live in a posh neighborhood. A château would be ideal. But barring that, you will settle for a sprawling, splendid mansion or ten-room apartment. Every gadget in the big country kitchen will need to be polished and in excellent working order. No missing bolts or errant screws to cloud the perfection and efficacy of your purrfect cuisine. Same goes for the living areas. Deep velvet couches. Elegant hardwoods. Armoires from France. Chests and gateleg tables from jolly old England. Tradition and Cozy might, in fact, be your pet names for each other. You both like it warm and toasty, so you will require at least one fireplace and plenty of thermostatic control.

You also enjoy puttering in the garden and around the house, dressed in the latest L. L. Bean upscale booties, and wielding spades and trowels bought in the chicest nursery stores. If all of the above-mentioned decor can be achieved by a Cat couple (and there is no character-related reason why it cannot) you can indeed share a very calm, peaceful existence together.

You also have similar ideas about where to take your vacations. I can see it now. Brochures piled neatly on the mahogany end table, waiting to be pored over during an evening's *tête à tête*. Your choice of travel destinations will be safe, too. You'll take the family to New England and rent a large house on the beach. Or you will decide to spend a cultural summer at an art colony. Most adventurous holidays will happen when you venture as far as wild and woolly England. There, you will visit castles and gardens, stroll through cathedrals, and learn university towns' street names by heart.

If problems arise between you, they are likely to emanate from outside influences. A noisy neighbor or a begging relative could become a thorn in your collective paw. Here, as one of you may be more sentimental than the other, you may disagree. Discord displeases Cats. You may flee the very thought of a spat. Tensions over unspoken differences of opinion may cause the usually fluffy ambiance in the household to seize up. Hissing sounds may be heard through closed doors. But you may have to actually start therapy to get yourselves to talk openly about what's really troubling one or the other.

It would be good (but unlikely, as you are both squeamish about blood) if one of you were a doctor or some sort of health practitioner. Cats tend to be hypochondriacs. Yours will be a household fraught with headache, pains in various joints, bad backs, and mysterious complaints that have no explanation. Chronic complaints commonly plague Cats.

Money? Not really an issue. You are equally industrious and, in your quiet, efficient way, know how to, earn a solid good living.

What about the sex between two Cats? Well, as you have guessed, Cat's idea of bliss is holing up together in their four-poster bed and reading books about money, long ago things, home decorating, and rock gardens. Occasionally it might seem amusing to have a little romp together in this cushioned hay. But passion—fiery, wild, fall-on-your-face, steam-out-the-ears passion-will be absent.

Which, oddly enough, doesn't discourage this relationship from working quite well.

Its enemy? Boredom. If someone more tangy appears from outside this couple's usual ken, plunges headfirst into an affair with one or the other of these Cats, and drags him or her off to Katmandu ... don't be surprised. The trick to maintaining a good relationship for a long, long time is to never forget to let the Cat back in before going to bed.

The wholesome, intelligent, and caring aura in which you two will undoubtedly want to live will be particularly salutary for creative little Goat kids, clingy, loving Snakelets, and dutiful Dogs. Pigs will be happiest born into this household, as they require the selfsame variety of refinements as do Cats and will rarely feel offended by anything in their environment.

Cat/Rabbit with Dragon

Imagine a Dragon/Cat couple. To me, it sounds absurd. I have trouble conceiving of such a lopsided duo. But okay. Let's have a go. The Cat is quiet, reserved, diplomatic, and seeks safety. The Dragon is noisy, outgoing, brash, and confronts every risk and challenge with an eager, toothy smile. Now, if the Dragon had a strong desire to care for the Cat, to protect and nurture the Cat mate, perhaps their life together could be pleasant. Dragons are lovers first and protectors second. Dragons plan their entourage with strength in mind. Dragons want obeisance from their allies in order to advance their own causes. In this environment, Cats don't have a chance—unless they decide, for some weird reason, to become self-sacrificing and efface their own personality in favor of the Dragons. Except for Cancer/Cats and perhaps Pisces/Cats, I don't think self-sacrifice is in the Cat's nature.

Cats can and do live in many different households and survive. But in certain, quiet, cushioned homes, Cats seem to thrive, are rarely nervous, and tend to gravitate toward any unsuspecting guest whose lap is sufficiently ample to hold them. In other, more raucous, feisty homes, we often find house Cats grow skittish, jumpy, and timid. They skulk about like criminals, hiding under furniture or climbing heavy draperies to escape contact with strangers. In other words, Cats deplore conflict, noise, and chaos.

No matter what they do, Dragons steal the show. Whither they perch, Dragons take up a lot of room. Their intensive behavior is never ill meant. It's simply in the Dragon nature to think *I am first* everywhere I go. Dragons are loud, demanding, openhearted, and generous. People notice Dragons.

Cats do their utmost to avoid being seen or heard, while Dragons are forever driving through your living room to *inform* you that children should be routinely spanked because Dragons think it's right. Dragons tender unsolicited outspoken opinions on everything and rarely leave anyone the last word. Cats hate to be criticized. Dragons criticize anything they didn't invent, discover, or give birth to. Cats abhor pyrotechnic displays of wealth and rollicking bash-type parties. Dragons throw only such parties. Cars give refined, elegant dinners for a few well-informed friends who sit around after dinner talking of Michelangelo. Divergence takes precedence over similarity in this combination of characters. I cannot see it as much more than a passing flirtation—over in a week at most.

Where money is concerned, the Cat/Dragon alliance will be disastrous. Cats invest, sit on their capital, and spend cautiously, solely on high-quality merchandise. They only love luxury if it represents true value—Cats surround themselves with silks, gold leaf, finest finishes, and hand-rubbed antique buffets. Nothing is ever garish or showy. Dragons? They spend money like sailors on leave, buying up everything from hair-cutting gadgets to outrageous items of clothing (the better to be *seen* in, my dear) to flashy sports cars. You two will rarely agree on how to manage money.

There is one case where this relationship might work. If the crusty old Dragon is getting on in years and desires to acquire what one friend's mom calls "a nurse and a purse," he or she would be well-advised to grab a Cat for a mate. Cats lend a conservative tone to the Dragon's life, add class to his or her act, and usually have managed to set aside lots of retirement cash with which to hire Dragon's caregivers.

The Cat is not enormously passionate or sex-hungry. The Dragon is a veritable steam bath of ecstasy in sexual behavior. Ordinarily, I wouldn't give either of you a nickel for your joint sexual experience. However, if the Dragon is waning and growing less demanding, a younger, more supple Cat partner might be just what the doctor would prescribe. A May-December marriage might work.

Children? Not a good idea. A younger Dragon/Cat couple may not last long enough the raise kids. The older couple? Well, Dragons do live a long time. Perhaps you could adopt a beautiful little Snake child to spoil.

💘💘💘 ½ Cat/Rabbit with Snake

Twin sensibilities can mean a great deal when attempting to maintain a long-term relationship slated for marriage and family-raising. You will definitely get along first as friends, then later as lovers. Much about your characters is alike, many of your opinions match, and (a definite plus) you like the same sorts of people. So the Cat/Snake mix is a solid one based on mutual respect and admiration.

What I see as very positive about this relationship is that you usually do not come together in some sort of *love at first sight* frenzy of sexual attraction. The Cat is seduced by the Snake's ravishing beauty, but laid back enough not to instantly let the Snake know it. The Snake is intrigued by the Cat's singular reserve and quietude, impressed by his or her vast intelligence and gift of witty speech and then gently attracted to the Cat's subtle sensuality. Each is challenged by the other's aura. Neither is obliged to perform some baroque act of heroism to entice the other into a joint venture.

Moreover, Cats like to stay home. Snakes don't mind roaming but they love to return home after a while to find a loving person waiting patiently. Snakes are intuitive. They figure things out before they happen. They go to the heart of a matter before the matter matters. Cats, too, have great intuition. They have a sixth sense about who is evil and who isn't, who will behave decorously at an elegant dinner party, and who will cause dissension. Conversation is never dull around the Cat/ Snake home fire.

Although Snakes are too extravagant by half for the conservative Cat's taste, Cat usually learns to tolerate lavish shopping sprees as, in the bargain, Snake usually fills the house with glorious art treasures and accessories—which helps the slightly snobbish Cat keep up appearances. Snake will want to own too many clothes and slinky fast cars for Cat's sedate four-door sedan taste. But compromise will soon arrive as Cat cunningly chooses to drive a Rolls-Royce and sexy Snake a spiffy Lamborghini. Joking aside, you are both born money masters, so, at whatever level your lifestyle begins, you can be certain that your joint efforts will increase your incomes and raise your social stratum a notch or two before your life is through.

The sexual side of your relationship will sometimes be strained by the wages of infidelity. Neither of you is particularly well-known for your constancy in sexual matters. One day or another, peccadilloes will begin to show up. Trouble is, the passion between you is not all that enormous. Cat is slow to warm to sexual activity. Conversely, Snakes need little prodding to be ready for sex at almost any moment, anywhere. In other signs, this difference might not prove problematical. But in a Cat/Snake marriage, neither of you is about to cajole the other into suitable sexual play. You are, however, both very reasonable folk and may simply decide to maintain the marriage for the sake of family and appearances and agree to find your passions elsewhere. In other words, please don't break up your happy household because of a partner's single sexual slip-up.

You will definitely want to have children. Your couple (aside from the sometimes lukewarm sex) is extremely well-balanced. Your philosophies are not too divergent and your tastes and goals are similar. A sound basis for a family is present. Please try to have Pig babies or little Goat kids. These sweet-natured children will benefit from your refined home environment and take easily to the cultural nature of your dynamic. Roosters, Dogs, and Rats are not advised, as the Cat has difficulty getting on with critical sorts. Snakes and Cats don't get along too well with arrogant Horses, but both of you would be good as parents of an Ox child who works hard and brings honor to the family. Tigers are too brash and Dragons too noisy to fit in at your house.

Cat/Rabbit with Horse

A dim future lies in store for these two. If you have already embarked on a Cat/Horse relationship, you know what I mean. It will be difficult to reconcile your differences, as your goals and methods of achieving them are extremely different. You have little common ground in style or dynamic on which you might base a long-lasting love or family life.

Both Cats and Horses are pragmatic. They enjoy dreaming of success and want to get somewhere in life before they die. Neither Horses nor Cats are particularly dependent, either. You are two distinctly sovereign characters who do not rush about seeking security in the eyes or the pocketbooks of others. Neither of you hankers to be cared for or nurtured. Yet something intangible about your separate modes of operation will hinder long-term felicity as a couple.

The Cat seeks a sedate, quiet lifestyle replete with symbols of tradition and custom: antique furniture, plush carpets, fine art, delicate foodstuffs, and not too much adventurous change to ruffle the surface. Cats who can afford to usually choose to live in retreat mode, spending masses of time and energy in the early part of their lives building bastions around their personal property in an effort to keep away probing or rambunctious intruders. Cats are secretive and snobbish. They are choosy about the people they cultivate as friends. No self-respecting Cat person would willingly go off on a bear hunt, join the army during a war, or seek out wild and woolly sports challenges that might put their skins in jeopardy.

Horses are born independent. More than almost anything (except perhaps money), Horses go after social and personal success. They are haughty in their manner, high stepping, and outspoken in their style. Horses need attention but are not willing to admit it. They often behave as though they require nothing from family or friends, but secretly they long for approbation on every front. Horses plan for a busy, adventurous lifestyle wherein they can travel and meet new people whom they are constantly persuading of their talents and convincing of their integrity. Horses make excellent public figures, often specializing in politics or entertainment. They know how to perform for an audience and are delighted when their ideas and positions are voted on or accepted by their admiring public. Horses want nothing much to do with old-fashioned appurtenances, preferring the design of a clean, modern interior to a heavily curtained home furnished in antiques. Horses can also live well out of a suitcase and are not much bothered by what others think of their social class or manners. Horses are originals who may wear a garish or rakish hat to top off a super-conservative dress or suit.

The intensely different choices characteristically made by these two determined, individual creatures would render a lifelong relationship impossible to manage. I can foresee endless arguments about why Horse is never at home politely attending to snooty guests at Cat's posh cocktail gatherings. Where Horse flaunts, Cat conserves. Where Cat name-drops, Horse blurts social blunders apace. Where Horse travels afar, Cat sits nervously by the fireside musing over a migraine and wishing for a more cooperative mate.

Nasty spats will arise over why money that Cat has been amassing under the mattress is being spent foolishly by Horse on all variety of fantasy and folly. Sex? If you must. Cat likes lovemaking to be romantic and to happen in four-poster beds from the Elizabethan period hung with silken draped *baladaquins* and dressed in purest linens. Horse prefers a hearty gallop in the hay and is not at all fussy about where it happens—as long as it happens efficiently and with gusto. Oh no, Cats and, Horses—much as I love you both—I cannot advise a union between you.

Forget about children until after the divorce, when you have found a new partner more suitable to your way of living.

💘💘💘💘 Cat/Rabbit with Goat

Goats need safe, secure environments in which to live while plying their creativity. Cats are willing to provide just that-and then some! So you two have a sound personal basis for long-term cohabitation. You are equally sensitive to things natural, adore animals, seek out bucolic countrysides, and steer clear of politics and other worldly or mudslinging occupations. You are probably best suited to holing up somewhere in the boondocks in a lavish, traditional-style manor with wall-to-wall pets and a river running by.

Cats like to think of themselves as refined. Their tastes are old-fashioned, conventional, non-eccentric. Cats save old string and rubber bands, care immensely about decorum, and insist on manners. Cats admire delicacy of behavior in others, and attempt to create an entourage they deem worthy of their (real or imagined) elevated social stratum. Cats are squeamish about dirt, discord, and health matters. They are forever coming down with a new ailment. Cars are diplomatic and intelligent. They love culture, classical music, and aspire to wealth—and when they get it, they know very well how to keep it.

Not only is the Goat the very sort of person that Cats are attracted to, but Goats are often seen to go after Cats as well. Love aside, Goat's main reason for tethering themselves is rarely mere physical magnetism. Goats seek freedom from want. They look for somebody *possible* and even tough, whose bank account can finance their life of creativity. Goats do not wish to be heaped with responsibility, nor do they care to flaunt the mantle of wealth. They just want to be cared for, fed, and nurtured so they, in turn, can play with and care for pets and children, paint or write, or make music or sculpture or theater or films, or simply do an elegant sufficiency of nothing at all. Goats are not afraid to tender strong opinions on everything from philosophy to poetic license, and they become extremely arrogant in the bargain. But while opining and posturing, Goats like to be supported.

You are both pessimistic. Sometimes, you believe that the world is a terrible, dangerous place, and that you cannot possibly succeed in it. These combined fears may cause tension. Two frightened souls are decidedly worse than only one. If the workplace is such a fearsome and dangerous spot to be in, which of you will venture out to earn the family fortune? You, Goat, will find excuses based on your excessive sensitivity. You, Cat, may find excuses based on your fear of contracting a contagions illness or having to deal with conflict, for which you have no gift at all.

If the Cat can be persuaded to go after money, stash it and keep it safe for both of you, then you may look forward to a felicitous home life for a long, long time. Or ... if one or both of you has inherited funds, then the only real challenge will be to invest well and watch your spending. In this regard, Goats should not be encouraged to manage the money. Cats are best at that.

Your sex life could be a real treat. Goats are gentle, but randy, creatures who need plenty of sexual activity. Cats know best how to make love when embedded in designer sheets, silk pajamas, and slathered in redolent creams and lotions. Goats don't really care to do much about luxury but are well-adapted to enjoying it when it's there for the taking. Also, Cats need lots of romantic blandishment and low lighting to become aroused. Goats are manually clever and will make it their business to provide the proper setting. Sex (when Cat is not otherwise engaged in a migraine or a hang-nail crisis) between you promises to be thrilling, slow, and satisfying. Fidelity is not an issue here. While neither of you is particularly good at undying devotion, you are unlikely to break up your happy home for the sake of a passing fancy. Discretion is something you both understand implicitly.

Have children? Why not? But perhaps only one or at most two kids should be brought into your peaceful, sedate world. Otherwise, the tone will become overly rambunctious and the Persian carpets might also suffer. Try giving birth to a Piglet. Pigs are your natural partners. They delight in your elegance, learn to love your cultural bent, and appreciate your *objets d'art* from an early age. A Dog might also be a welcome addition. But his or her sharp remarks might shock or upset you. What you will adore about puppy dog children is their sweet devotion and royalty to your family image. Dogs rarely fail their loved ones.

🖤🖤🖤 ½ *Cat/Rabbit with Monkey*

My fellow Chinese astrologers think this a sound match. I have never felt positive about its long-term success. Cats are so ... reserved. Monkeys lurch laughingly about, swinging from one project to another, speculating on this or that new person or plan, gabbling on about unheard-of sillinesses, or rushing out to help a lady whose grass edger got stuck in her disposal—I just don't know. Yet I have to confess that I know two very good marriages where one partner is Monkey and the other Cat. So who am I to argue with science?

Cats usually have scads of education, so their trade may be law or investing or textiles or decorating or newspapers. Whatever their *métier*, it is sure to be backed up by method and transacted in the fairest possible manner. Cats also like to entertain their clients in the best restaurants. They adore appearing to be discreetly rich. But they do not flaunt wealth. Cats keep up appearances and are often hugely successful because of this trait.

The Monkey is the problem-solver. Moreover, Monkeys do not like to be in the limelight. They will not be happy dealing with clients or small talking customers out of their shekels. Monkeys are happiest when they are lending a hand, helping out, giving someone a leg up, and especially staying out of the line of fire.

Problems may arise out of the difficulty Cat has in understanding why the Monkey needs so many friends around all the time. Cat wants a calm life, devoid of conflict and free of shouting. Monkey is not like that. Monkey adores company and will invite and feed all manner of noisy, funky friends who frolic until all hours, while Cat sits there chewing his claws, worrying about how Monkey will get up in the morning to do the accounts. Oddly, even though Monkeys are problem-solvers .by nature, this impending dissonance doesn't even graze their psyche. Monkey thinks Cat is having a whale of a time discussing Rilke with his or her ex, the hippie from Alaska.

Spats may ensue. But as Monkeys don't usually see their own problems nearly so clearly as they see the issues of others, they may simply go on doing what the Cat disapproves of. Neither of you is gifted for processing your differences, as you both fear conflict. Cat will leave the house rather than have to encounter the hippie from Alaska. Monkey will try to pretend Alaska never existed and make a joke about it, relating it in rollicking detail to all the friends who call you for the next, few days.

Luckily, you will not have disagreements over money. The Cat earns a living by treading safely in areas of commerce where tradition has proven money can be made. Yet, in this couple, it is the Monkey who cares for the money. The Cat turns it over to the wily Monkey, who collects it, keeps track of it, and counts it. Monkey pays the employees, the dentist and the school bills. When it works, there is something about this couple's common interest in what the Cat does to make a living that keeps them so happily bonded. The Cat never minds providing when he or she can depend on a mate's true ability to assist from behind the scenes. Cats are, in fact, very content to allow the cunning Monkey full run of their elegant household. They will work ever harder and longer bouts to be sure Monkey can upgrade the furniture, buy some real art treasures, marbleize the kitchen counters, have a lovely new automobile to drive to the bank—in short, to stay happy and clever as long as they both shall live.

The sex between you is good but not great. Neither of you minds that aspect of your life together too much, as your real reason to be a couple is the perpetuating of an intelligent relationship wherein you both implicitly understand certain unspoken things and not too much has to be rehashed day after stultifying day.

You will have children. And I think that's great. Monkeys make super parents. They play games and indulge their kids with all manner of zany devices. Cat plays the heavy in this instance, but is secretly amused by the fun everyone has at his or her expense. Have a Monkey or Goat or Pig child—or why not have all three?

Cat/Rabbit with Rooster

If you two came into my office asking for advice about your engagement, your lifelong plans, or your chances for succeeding at the above, I would shake my head from side to side and wonder how in the world you ever dreamed up such a weirdo scheme.

Cats aspire to an elegant, quiet, flatline F-KG readout sort of life where finally, after years of work and accumulation, they can hope to enjoy peace and quiet, no intrusions from without, and a chance to sit in their brocade wing chair, boning up on Aegean artifacts. Roosters are flamboyant creatures whose lives are never one-dimensional or without major upheaval. Roosters get bored with a stay-at-home life and are forever seeking to infuse their existence with excitement and adventure. They never stop. Roosters travel and take tap-dancing lessons and redesign their gardens and take down all the curtains and put up new ones and paint garden vegetables on the kitchen ceiling just for fun.

This is not a marriage. If it is anything at all, this is more like a weeklong fantasy relationship wherein you two earnest, good-hearted people were trying to do each other a sweet favor by agreeing to marry each other. It probably won't work. Stay together if you can. Try all you want to work things out. I wish you the best of good luck. But prepare for the fur and feathers to fly at least once per twenty-four-hour period as you attempt to find a common ground through civilized discussion and compromise.

Roosters make pronouncements. *I will not!* is a common Rooster comment. *That is not so!* is another. Negotiation is not really the Rooster's strong suit. Rooster would rather not be there at all than to be required to have dinner with your bourgeois family one more time. And Cat? Well, Cat is not against compromise. In fact, Cat is a diplomat born. But Cat also respects tradition and esteems family. Here (as in many other areas of discussion), Cat is torn. But Cat can't say that to Rooster because Rooster has already gone too far and created a conflict. You, Cat, despise conflict. So you simply take to your boudoir or retire to your mahogany-paneled study and pour it out.

Result? Nothing gets done. Rooster has dinner in Hong Kong alone and will be home in August, when it's warmer. Cat puts on a pale face, has dinner alone with the family, and complains a lot about a bad back and getting by without Rooster around to lift things.

Money? Oh, boy! Roosters make money. But they also spend it. They love gadgets and want to own at least one horse and a couple of houses in Europe and some really cool Italian-designer duds and a set of expansive shocking pink dinnerware to go with those turquoise plastic spoons brought back from that fifties' store in Chicago. With what Roosters spend in one year on such useful items as fake metal ivies that creep down your bathroom wall and serve as towel racks too, Cat could have bought the Mona Lisa. Tastes and priorities between the two of you make the management of mutual monies an absolute bust.

About the sex ... mediocre. Or should I say listless? The Cat has romantic needs, which Roosters, by their very nature, deem ridiculous. Roosters are, after all, roosters. They set about having some good, raunchy scratch-and-bite sex, while Cat's lying amid the scrambled lacy bedclothes counting flies on the ceiling. Oh, please, Cat and Rooster, don't do this to each other. Have an affair if you want to. Take a vacation together. But do not marry up. (If I was wrong, drop me a line. Any input is good input.)

I will mention the children because it's that time now. But do the kids a favor and leave them out of this. One day, you will each find a more favorable mate with whom to raise a family. With a lopsided Cat/Rooster marriage, you won't even be able to raise a petunia without fighting about it.

½ Cat/Rabbit with Dog

In our culture, we think of Dogs and Cats as natural enemies. But that is not so everywhere. In Chinese astrology, the Cat gets on swimmingly with the dutiful Dog. They share an understanding of how life ought to be lived, a mutual respect for the other's choices and tastes, and a belief in charity first and self-interest later. You make excellent lifetime companions.

A shared belief in humanity's basic goodness will draw and keep you two together as a couple. You will no doubt seek to live in a town where culture and museums exist side by side with theatrical and musical productions and viewing exhibitions. One day, when you have enough money, you will probably also build or buy a country place. Dogs make excellent builders and designers of homes, and Cats make fabulous choices in decorating and accessorizing them. As a couple, you will never lack for joint activities and, as we all know, doing projects together can help a pair of earnest people over many a rough spot.

Yours will be a cerebral couple, bound by ideas and ideals. You will often be discouraged by world events or political setbacks over which you have no control. Dogs are pessimistic and moody. They worry and fret over sometimes real and sometimes imagined happenings. Cats worry, too. Especially about health and confrontation. As a couple, then, you will have to master a tendency to discouragement and hermitlike retreat. As each of you is caring and loving, your occasional bouts with gloom shouldn't last very long. As one of you is down the other can help him or her back up the slippery slope to hopefulness.

As you have probably guessed, Cat people are conservative about public displays of affection. Cats, in fact, do very little public displaying of anything, feel safer in private, and wouldn't tell a soul if one of the children got lice or an F on a report card. Surprisingly, the good old wagging Dog doesn't fancy public display or and is not usually fond of excessive socializing either. The Dog, in fact tends to be secretive and even suspicious.

I expect your married life will be lived in a secluded manner, without the intrusion of many strangers or newcomers who haven't been carefully vetted by the Dog's most accurate fraud sniffer-outer, passed the Cat's draconian manners test, and shown their pedigrees at the door.

The Cat will need to have a pleasant home in which to live and raise a family in peaceful harmony. Cats are not afraid of working for a living, and with luck will be able to earn enough to provide the necessary funds for their share of this domain. The Dog is also a diligent worker. Dogs like to be of service and often choose careers where looking out for others is involved. Dogs usually make a good living but are not particularly concerned about amassing fortunes. In fact, they disapprove of fortunes, believing that money is there to be spent and should never be inherited, as inheritance kills ambition in the heir. Dogs tend to think we all should help one another, shoulder equal responsibility, and mutually see to the needs of our fellows. Cats don't disagree. Cats approve of charitable acts and are forever lending a helping hand. Cats, however, do not mix with the needy. They pass yesterday's brioche over the castle wall, then race back to the library to check on the butler's progress with dinner arrangements. If you do marry, give the Cat the purse strings.

In things sexual, there will be a period of adjustment to weather. Eager Dogs do have a habit of jumping up on people and licking their faces all over. At first, the Dog may be a tad too solicitous and slurpy for the Cat's reserved self to bear. But in time, as you are both such reasonable and truly caring souls, the Cat's shell of decorum will melt away and you two will grow more and more tender and affectionate. Your lovemaking, like your life together, will blossom as it grows more caring, satisfying, and reciprocally intense. No great imaginative fantasy or masquerade sex scenarios are on the docket for Cat and Dog sex. But when you share sweet love, who needs theatrics?

Having kids? I suggest you try for a Pig child first. Pigs, especially eldest-child Pigs, are happy and kindly in the same the way you parents are together. He or she will adore the cultural and intellectual pursuits you both enjoy. A Tiger baby would be happy in your home too, except watch out for the turbulence. Or why not try for another Cat or Dog? You would all get on famously in that pretty big old house you designed together.

💘💘💘💘 *Cat/Rabbit with Pig*

Cat/Rabbit and Pig want the same things in life. But you do have two very different methods of getting them. Cat is a laid-back, delicate-natured person devoted to nonviolence and nonintervention. The Pig is a scrupulously good, slightly naive, and determinedly ambitions liver of life as it comes. The Pig is far more tolerant than the Cat. The Cat is far more refined than the Pig. Still, as both of you want the same things: gold, jewels, paintings, antiques, palatial homes, luxury hotels, marble floors, vast bathtubs, culture and tradition—plus plenty of money to spend to maintain what you have and to buy up the remainder of what you do not yet own—you two have plenty to do to spend a lifetime together.

There is a major difference between you—Pigs need to add gourmet cuisine and lots of it to their list of luxury desires. Cats enjoy fine eating but they are not always willing to spend large amounts of time and money—and then hours at table—for the sake of the *meal*. Pigs do. Pigs are food people. Watch a Pig eat sometime and you will see what I mean. Sharing a meal with most Pig folks might be called *dining with wolves*. It will be up to the sophisticated Cat mate to help Piggy clean up his or her manners and cut down on fat and carbohydrate intake. Otherwise, Cat will end up using Piggy as a couch cushion instead of a spouse.

As for finances, in all likelihood you will both be gainfully employed. In the city, Cat will run an art gallery whilst Pig trots the globe selling authentic nineteenth-century etchings. Or Cat will be a decorator and Piggy will build elegant apartment buildings. In the country or the provinces, Cat will run a country-style bed and breakfast and Pig will raise organic vegetables. Careers will never be a problem for you two so long as you stay clear of too much turbulence. Pollution is the allergic Cat's enemy, and evil characters who misuse others are the Pig's. The countryside will be a safer venue in which to ply your contented life.

You should keep joint accounts, pore over the bills and expenditures together, make your big purchase decisions together. Cat is likely to be slightly more conservative about investing in a new car or fridge when the old one is still working fine. But Piggy can be persuasive and is, in any case, often the member of this pair who attracts the most money. Pigs (bless 'em) are endowed with an eerie faculty for earning money. Whenever Cat is laid up with one of his or her chronic complaints, Piggy will always be able to provide for both of them.

The sex between you will be delicious. Cat likes romance, frills, satiny bed sheets, and ruffled canopy curtains. Cat likes to be seduced and cajoled and foreplayed. Pig finds such sexual manners both challenging and essential. Pig loves to cajole others, indulge their idiosyncrasies, and please their palates. You two are in for a lot of years of very sweet, highly sensual, and sometimes even down and dirty (thanks to Piggy) passion. Enjoy!

Kids? Yes. By all means. Have slews. You both get along with creative Goats, dutiful Dogs, and irresistible Snakes. If you want a fiercer household atmosphere (and I doubt that you do), you can try adding on a tawny little Tiger, a feisty Dragon, or even (especially if you live in the country) a serious little Ox person.

DRAGON

Taken to the extreme, all of our qualities can become frailties. Some of us are generous to a fault, which can be wasteful. Good communicators can also be blabbermouths. Nurturing parents can smother their children. Fortunately, free will allows us to balance the positive and negative sides of our character. The magnificent dauntless Dragon was born:

POSITIVE | NEGATIVE

vibrant | overbearing

magnanimous | grandiose

principled | intractable

compelling | overpowering

noble | high-handed

sentimental | maudlin

🏹 *Dragon with Dragon*

All the *noblesse* in the world—without a smattering of *oblige*. At best, this incendiary relationship promises to explode almost daily into sparring matches of a grandeur hitherto untested by human people In the beginning, there is gigantic passion. In the end, there may be hellfire and messy divorce.

If you are involved in a Dragon/Dragon love affair you will already know whereof I speak. Dragons consider themselves the worthy of the worthiest, greater than the greatest, bigger than life, and more deserving of time and attention from a mate (and everybody else) than is conceivable for us mere mortals.

Perhaps it's the mythical aspect of this sign that makes Dragons imagine they have no obligation to adhere to the mundane, boring rules of ordinary life. You Dragons are born special. You are well aware of that fact and make no bones about sending yourself flowers and blowing your own horn. In short, you are anything but shy about making your uniqueness known to the test of humanity by means of your loud, imposing, and self-propelled manner.

Dragons are charismatic and irresistibly charming. But it is not common for them to be utterly perfect for each other. There might, of course, be mitigating factors such as thoroughly compatible Western signs that, because of their talent for harmonizing, might drown out the din of the Dragons' fire-breathing power squabbles. A Scorpio/Dragon with Pisces/Dragon, for example, might do well as a dynamic Dragon duo. The Pisces knows how to surrender ego to the cause of progress. The imperious Scorpio/Dragon appreciates both the Pisces' flexibility and the Dragon strength rolled into one person. So, even though I don't recommend Dragons take up with each other for life, that match could work.

Trouble is, most days at Dragon Manor are not very festive. The name of the day-to-day game is Ego. The game itself consists of a permanent joust over who gets to be supreme ruler of the roost. One Dragon will surely want to hold full sway at the workplace, in the household, the bedroom, the nursery, the garden, and possibly even the garage.

Likewise, the other Dragon wants to make all of the decisions. Both want to manage the money and dictate who gets to spend it on what, and why. Both will attempt to take over the children's upbringing, and are likely to wrestle each other to the floor at regular intervals over who gets to read which section of the newspaper first.

Despite an intense sexual attraction between two Dragons, the problems involved in keeping this weighty boat on an even keel are truly more trouble than they are worth.

For an unsuspecting kid, having two Dragon parents is definitely not better than having one. But if this duo of Dragons wants to have children, they should try for a Snake or Pig child. Both are simple of spirit and able to handle the Dragon's ego-driven personality without crumbling and losing sight of their own needs. Or try a Goat, whose gentle presence might even invite some peace and quiet into the Dragon family's digs.

Dragon with Snake

Dragons adore entering a chic restaurant with an irresistibly beautiful person on their arm. Snakes enhance, beautify, and lend a touch of class to everyone and every place they frequent. In fact, in order to thoroughly appreciate a Snake's allure, you almost have to be dauntless like a Dragon. How this couple fares over the long run will greatly depend on how well they learn to share the spotlight.

Dragons like to have top billing. They love being the king or queen of the castle and have great aspirations about staying right up there on top of the mountain controlling the volcano's eruptions. But Dragons have to work at keeping their top positions. Snakes are also ambitious—more quietly driven—but greedily ambitious all the same. Snakes not only want to star in the show, they want all the money and fame that goes with the role. Yet, staying on top of the mountain is rarely an issue for Snakes because their adoring public won't let them come down.

The combative Dragon is without an adversary in this relationship, but he or she is not without a wily and useful ally. If a truce can be struck between Dragon and Snake over who will own both spotlight and throne, much gain is promised. The team of slithery Snake and dashing Dragon is fairly invincible—both socially and in business or professional work.

Your money affairs are favorably aspected. Snakes spend a lot of cash on accessories, massage, skin care, hairdressers, and beautiful goods. Dragons tend not to care so much for "stuff" unless it's useful gadgetry or can be consumed on the spot. However, despite a basic difference of opinion about what to spend money on, you will always have so much that each of you will be able to satisfy his or her needs and still have funds to put away for your old age.

Your relationship will experience peaks and valleys—sometimes it's because Dragons are so egomaniacal and never mince their words. And other times, it's because Snakes can be both coldhearted and manipulative. If Dragon wants Snake to stop being so damned flirtatious at parties, Snake will probably smile coyly and do exactly as he or she pleases. Snakes do not give in to emotional blackmail or take orders well. Snakes pretend not to hear Dragons yelling and shrieking about how insanely jealous they get when ... "Cool it, Draggy," whispers the levelheaded Snake to a steaming partner. "You'll explode if you keep that up." Dragons, poor things, despite their ferociousness, are syrupy sentimentalists. They suffer easily—not only from jealousy—but also from broken hearts. Loss of a loved one's affections can prove unbearable to the tenderhearted Dragon. Hence, fickle Snakes are advised to keep their peccadilloes out of the Dragon's face.

The sex between Dragon and Snake is fantastic. It's no surprise to find them attracted to each other in the first place. Dragons are flamboyant and loud, generous and emotive. Snakes are beautiful, but they are rarely noisy.

The Dragon approaches the Snake with flattery. "You are absolutely the most delectable creature I have ever laid eyes on," gushes the Dragon. What vain Snake could resist? Moreover, as time goes by, the sexual rapport warms and deepens. Snake (a caring and very humanitarian person underneath the cool) begins to sense the Dragon's growing sentimental attachment; which touches the Snake's dearest side. You will develop a serious, and passionate, liaison.

You ought to try living together for a while before you get pregnant. Depending on how you get along in close quarters, you will judge for yourselves if the liaison can turn into a real family-rearing Mom and Pop show. There is a lot of ego to unload before you're ready to give yourselves over to the needs of children. Wait two years. If your household is peaceful and you have the means, go ahead and have a child. Choose from among Roosters, Monkeys, Horses, and Oxen, as these signs have strong senses of self and can handle self-centered people like you two.

💘💘💘💘 *Dragon with Horse*

Madly in Love these two can be. The very idea of spending the night together keeps them both chugging along during daytime hours. They are as physically compatible as chewing and gum. Rather than beat about the hydrangeas, I might as well admit that these two initially get together because of sex. And, if they stay together, the sex grows more and more fabulous.

Something about their mutual magnetism makes it impossible for Horse and Dragon to resist each other's physical charms. They will certainly be the kind of couple who flirt and caress unabashedly in any and every circumstance. Both of these creatures are born performers. Dragons crave outside attention so fervently that they practically invite people to watch them take showers. Horses, innately more discreet than their Dragon partners, may downplay their natural urge to be exhibitionists. But just you wait. At the very first opportunity, Horses gallop right up onstage and prance eagerly about, wishing only to be applauded and paid public homage.

Dragons consider themselves superior to normal mortals of any sign. While this Dragon pretension doesn't get in the way in relationships with compliant Pig partners or dependent Goat lovers, Horses are not known for humility or acquiescence. Horses are monsters of independence. Dragons need an exaggerated amount of attention from their partners. Horses want attention too. But if they cannot concurrently run everything in the precise manner to which they have become accustomed, the Horse will forego all contact, withdraw their own affection from the love-hungry Dragon, and split the corral. Horses will not pay the heavy price of obedience for peacekeeping's sake. Nope. Horse does it Horse's way or Horse doesn't do it. Period.

Each of these characters is also proud, headstrong, and irritable by nature. The sexual attraction is indeed wondrous between them. But what of the getting along in between times? Not so easy. Dragons hate authority unless they are doing the bossing. Horses likewise refuse to be dominated.

Dragons are overly generous with parties and friends and are sometimes altogether wanton with money. Horses love money and often spend it to impress others (and themselves) with how much they earn, which, because they work so hard, is a lot. Horses thrill at spending large sums on outrageous gorgeousness that lend prestige to their image. Where a Dragon might throw a huge ball for his or her own (or a loved one's) birthday, laying out fortunes on food, drink, and music, the Horse, a slave to appearances, will spontaneously rush out and buy a BMW and a ranch mink bedspread—in the same day!

Because the two of you are so heavily endowed with excess, I am tempted to say that you can definitely look forward to a glorious affair—even a lifelong love affair. But I hesitate to advise you to marry up for the long haul. I foresee a stormy household atmosphere complete with slamming doors, divorce threats, frequent abandonings and reconciliations, and far too much empty-headed spending of monies in an effort to make things better each time one of you walks out on the other.

Marriage might work better if the Horse were the male in love with the Dragon female. While Dragon women are not all ravishingly beautiful the way Snake women are, they attract men as honey draws ants. Horses, despite their well-deserved reputation for maintaining independence, have a fatal flaw. They can watch every gram of self-assuredness be drained from their souls by a great love—especially a difficult great love. Horses, as practical and down-to-earth as they are, have been known to give up everything for the sake of the one huge love of their life. If that love happened to be a Dragon, and the Dragon accepted the marriage contract, then this relationship might work. Obviously, the Horse who is paralyzed with love will relinquish authority, give up bad habits, and even become putty in the claws of the fascinating Dragon, who will bask in the adoration of the sexy, worshipful Horse.

No children. Too much ego on both sides for the children to get a wish in edgewise. Besides, being the child of this horny couple be downright embarrassing. All that heavy petting in the kitchen!

💘💘💘 Dragon with Goat

Frankly, I have never seen a Dragon married to a Goat. Because of that, although Chinese astrologers often tell me that this can be a sound marriage, I wonder. Is that opinion culturally biased? My occidental self has this sneaky feeling that the daring Dragon would eat the gentle Goat in one gulp at teatime and then go out looking for his brother or sister.

Dragon is able to provide a strong center post around which the Goat can gambol to hearts' content in utter security. Goats dream only of being tethered in a fertile field so that they can get on with the business of being both creative and dreamy. Dragons like to be in control. So far so good.

However…if the very creative Goat ever wants to get anything personal accomplished, an ego conflict may arise. Dragons occupy center stage. Their house is a "Dragon house," where their family lives with the head Dragon in a Dragonesque style doing Dragonish things together with the Dragon. Dragons are charmingly tyrannical. Goats do not mind playing second fiddle to their mates. But they do mind being told what to do and when to do it. Goats are rebellious and have no respect for deadlines, time schedules, dates, or the too-rigorous plans of others. Goats do everything in their own time—sometimes brilliantly, but always in their own time. Goat might stay up for three days running to edit out all the commas from a 3,000-page manuscript. Then that same Goat may fall from his or her chair sound asleep on the floor of the office for three more days. No matter that nobody can get in or out, use the facilities, or turn the lights on during Goat's sleeping period. Goat is the absentminded genius and wishes to be treated as such.

Dragons are genius rulers. Goats are genius dependents who can be flexible when it serves their purpose. If Dragon yells and screams because Goat's inert form has been cluttering the office floor for three days, Goats will get up sleepily, apologize, and fall asleep somewhere else. But next time Goat has one of those endless jobs to do, he or she will once again fall down dead in place asleep. Not to get Dragon's goat … just because Goat forgets to do stuff that people—especially bossy people—deem indispensable. The Goat's languid mind flaps about open-endedly, which is part of his charm. But the Dragon doesn't have much patience with flakiness and may spend much of this time in a towering rage, trying to get Goatsy to shape up.

As for the day-to-day, I find it hard to envision. Yet, if Dragon is away a lot and doesn't worry about Goat letting the house burn down because he or she forgot something major was cooking on the stove, this match could prove to be lots of fun. Dragons are not always handy with tools or pleased to engage in manual labor. Goats don't mind digging their hands into the dirt or building a shed all by themselves (as long as no one dictates when the project must be finished).

The Dragon should definitely manage the couple's money. Goats cannot be given funds in great gobs, as they find exotic ways of spending it all up before nightfall. But since Dragons can also be squanderers, perhaps you should hire a good accountant to protect you both from each other's lack of economy.

The sex between you two might indeed be splendid fun. Both of you have enormous sexual drive. Dragon loves to be the king of the bed. Goat adores the feeling of being thrust about and loved and bustled in all directions. Because you both have colorful imaginations and delightful fantasies, I see a long and durable sex life for your couple.

If you want to have kids, I advise you first to get yourselves an able nanny. She can take care of all three of you. Dragon is not one to be home nurturing all day and night. Goat is. But Goat needs company and extra security. Have a Pig baby. Oh yes, do have a Piglet. You will be the happiest trio ever.

Dragon with Monkey

Because of their ability to amuse and beguile us, we sometimes imagine that Monkeys hog the spotlight. As for Dragons, they are, after all, the celestial celebrators, and the head honchos. You might think that two characters would clash. But it doesn't work quite that way. Indeed, the Monkey and the Dragon are a fairly hand-in-hand, even a down-the-aisle pair, whose driving vector can be entertainment—of themselves and of loved ones—and even sometimes of perfect strangers.

Dragon is born at center stage. The most loving parents may complain that they cannot take their attention from little Draggy for a millisecond. Not that the Dragon child will be naughty when not stared at—oh no—the Dragon child is simply that magnetic, that dazzling figure in a household. People come to visit a home where a Dragon kid lives. They walk in, smile politely at other family members, and go looking in all the rooms until they find the Dragon: the center, the hub of life around that ranch. Dragon is the Force.

Monkey kids, conversely, like to play the clown from within the safety of their own peer groups. Monkey's aim may not be to actually join in the fun, but rather to make the fun happen by punching in a hilarious line or pointing up an action just at the perfect moment. Monkeys are the Greek chorus. Through their sage observations, they make us more acutely aware of our own behavior. Monkeys talk a lot and sometimes yammer on and on about unrelated subjects. But Monkeys are always there—scrutinizing, signifying, and reminding us all just how silly (or interesting) a life can be.

So, when a star-quality Dragon meets a magical Monkey person, they usually click. Monkey admires the Dragon's haughty carriage and ease of communication. Monkeys are somewhat neurotic and (surprisingly) may even be shy. Watching the great Dragon lover stalk out, hop on his motorcycle, and zoom off into the night makes little Monkey's heart go pitter-pat.

Dragon, too, feels satisfied to hook up with a clever Monkey mate. Dragons are often too sure of themselves by half. Because they often allow their egos to supercede their brains, Dragons sometimes make giant goofs and suddenly find themselves drowning in their own follies. A thoughtful strategist like the Monkey will never allow Dragon to get as far as the goof precipice. Instead, Monkey will reason with the reluctant Dragon, logically point out the microscopic termite holes in the plank Dragon wants to walk on, and—yes—Monkey will save the day before it has a chance to dawn. Dragon will, of course, rush out and tell everybody that the decision not to tread that wormy plank was uniquely his or her own. But never mind. Monkey never wanted first place. Monkey is blissful as .the power behind the throne.

Money? Not really a problem here. You both have the will to succeed at what you do. As Dragons have a way of spending to impress others, Monkey should hold the purse strings in this couple and dole out funds to Dragon where needed—and proven to be needed. Dragon respects Monkey's wishes—because Dragon respects Monkey's fertile brain.

Your sex life will be passion-filled. Dragons are very interesting love partners. But they can be dauntingly self-propelled when thrashing under those covers. Dragon lovers want everything their way. The quilt can't be tucked under because it makes them feel hemmed in. The windows have to be open for air to flow through. Dragon prefers the saddle position to the missionary position. And on and on. In these matters, Monkeys are rather compliant. They love sex and truly adore their dashing Dragon partner—so they might go along for the ride. But watch out, Dragon! When your pet Monkey gets tired of being tossed around like a plush animal, you may find Monkey living in Prague doing a course on ecological crop spraying while trying to forget his or her great Dragon love.

Kids? Yes. If you have lived together for at least two years in harmony, have a suitable home, and enough Monkey money, have children. Try having little Rats, Oxen, and even a tiny Tiger cub. Although you won't be surprised, you will see: After the kids arrive, your relationship will be cemented for life.

💘💘💘 *Dragon with Rooster*

Here is a sometimes thorny (but workable) relationship based initially on intellectual attraction. You are both strong-minded folks who spend time and energy polishing your appearance before coming on stage to show off for the world. In this way, providing you can afford twin bathrooms and dressing areas and acres of closets, you may indeed have a fine, live-in love affair on which to build a sound future.

On first meeting, everybody loves a Rooster. The Rooster is always impeccably turned out, has a pleasant word to say to everyone and about many things, and is always willing and enthusiastic to participate. Roosters are also very generous, never showing up without presents and foodstuffs galore to shower on friends and hosts. Roosters are not sentimental, keeping up a screen of defense against syrupy emotion and mawkish behavior. But don't be fooled by this flinty façade. Underneath they harbor some of the most tender of souls. They tend to blurt out home truths rather often, but we only love them more for their candor.

Dragons are also very tenderhearted beneath their sharp, flamboyant exterior. They are also quite dandified and certainly like to be seen as attractive. But unlike the sedate, well-mannered Rooster, Dragons are ostentations. They clamor for attention. And they get it.

Together, this pair has a very fine chance of success because they share many of the same goals and desires. Roosters want a professional life, prosperous and healthy family, and chance for lots of adventure in travel, social life, and leisure activities. Roosters are not slouches or slackers. They know how to work hard. But they don't always like to make a lifestyle of working. They need time out for pleasure, reading, writing, movie-watching and party-going. Roosters seek a good, happy life among their peers. But they don't necessarily have to rule the roost or grab the spotlight. Roosters are content to work side by side in teams or with their partners to achieve the goal of goals—which, in their estimation, is time to enjoy peace of mind and harmony in love.

Dragons must occupy the driver's seat. Either Dragons get to rule the roost, or they just up and take their dolly dishes and sashay on back up that mountain from whence they descended to deign play with you in the first place. Dragons can be boringly self-satisfied, and rapaciously grabby. But they are cute as the dickens and charismatic as hell.

Moreover, you will both make money. Tons of it. But Rooster's fortunes will tend to fluctuate wildly, so Dragon should be the keeper of the keys to the safe in this household. But not to worry. Dragons can be pests but they are very generous to those they love.

Clever Dragons assert their position by insinuating their magnetic aura into the Rooster's life, penetrating his or her most secret heart center.

Roosters, with their spiffy good manners and careful conservatism, cannot resist these incursions. They find Dragons delectably irreverent. In a twinkle, Dragon sweeps Rooster off his or her nervous little claws and onto the nearest mattress or squishy divan in hopes of taking outrageous advantage of the delighted Rooster's virtue.

In bed, Roosters and Dragons may find things a tad uneven. Roosters love sex, but they tend not to be very romantic or theatrical about it. Dragons prefer their sex complete with marching bands and harlequins playing tambourines. The Rooster is rather put off by these displays and yearns to be back in the barnyard with all those willing partners. "Life," thinks the Rooster partner of a dashing Dragon while lying there hoping the marching band will soon depart, "used to be so simple." True enough, dear Rooster. But was it as much fun? I doubt it.

Yes, go ahead and have a couple of kids. The responsibilities of family life will exercise cruise control on the breakneck pace of the Dragon/Rooster home. Once the kids arrive, you can throw away the tranquilizers. You would both be happy as parents of a beautiful little Snake baby, a hardworking Ox, or even a frolicsome Monkey.

½ *Dragon with Dog*

The grouch quotient is astronomically high between you two characters. Although the initial attraction may seem irresistible, it usually doesn't work out in the long run. Dogs and Dragons are both swooningly seductive. But you haven't got the same ideals, do not share a lifestyle program, and have nothing in common when it comes to sharing your toys.

Dragons shine, dashing about impressing others with their pizzazz, their earnest intention to be seen and heard. Dragons are festive people. They will throw a bash for a hundred people, give a masquerade ball for casts of thousands, or cook a sit-down dinner for thirty at the slightest provocation. Dragons need to be surrounded, to play lords or ladyships. They need to be looked up to as not only the bosses of the world, but also as the royal benefactors who lavish fortune (both good and bad) on their lowly beloved subjects. They play the benevolent despot to the hilt. In common parlance, the Dragon character type is better known as a control freak.

Despotism is what Dogs despise the most. And so-called well-intentioned despotism really makes them want to puke. Dogs don't believe in rulers at all and ally themselves most closely with liberal, glad-handed, socially conscious types. Dogs go to great lengths to avoid being seen as even vaguely snooty or regal, and wish, in fact, that all hierarchies could be stamped out posthaste. In common parlance, the Dog character type is, at best, anarchistic.

Moreover, Dogs stay in a lot. They do not mingle gladly—especially with fools. Nor do Dogs particularly enjoy attending a fête just because it's Patricia's first day of menopause or Jim's Mom's sister needs a bridal shower on the occasion of her third marriage. Doggy will sulk in his doghouse and Dragon will play lord of the manor, oblivious to his or her emotional state.

It's quite simple, really. The pair of you will never be on the same wavelength. Dogs are quite naturally pessimistic. Dragons are always up. Dogs are skeptical and suspicions. Dragons draw everybody into their confidence for nothing else than the joy of having company. Dog spend their lives poring over the details of various causes for the betterment of humankind. Dogs are honorable first, ambitious last. In their haste to succeed, Dragons have been known to step over dead bodies—sometimes it looks as though it's raining corpses. Dragons believe in politics. Dogs do not. Chinese sages say that you two are born enemies.

I tend to agree.

Will you have a life together? Is it worth even talking about who should handle the money and who has more or less? Obviously, Dragons take more money out of life than Dogs do. You may reply that Dragons need more money because they dress up for parties all the time, and Dogs never go anywhere and so can be satisfied with one or two hair shirts. This is true. Dogs hate to bother with clothes and basically think that owning more stuff is merely owning more clutter. Dragons favor mansions decorated with gilded sconces and high-ceilinged ballrooms in which to throw their lavish parties. They often dress garishly and own mucho closets full of all-occasion duds. So yes, money is also an issue—perhaps even *the* issue-- between you. Dragons squander. Dogs conserve.

About the sex ... Mmmmmhhh. Dragons are hungry buggers in the sensuality department. They always want more, bigger, and better scenarios and routines with which to spice up their busy sex life. They can be faithful, but only if their love life contains enough drama to keep them entertained. For the plainspoken, good-hearted, care-giving Dog, the Dragon's bedtime theatrics are a giant bore. Doggy would rather make it with a pretty fire hydrant than deal with Dragon's exorbitant thespian needs.

Needless to add, if you decide (against my advice, of course) to have children, you should do so with eventual single-parenthood in mind. And frankly, I would not wish to be there for the custody battle. O la la! All those chomps and snarls and showers of volcanic Dragon ash.

❤ ❤ ❤ ❤ *Dragon with Pig*

Oh happy day! Oh lucky you! Compliant, reliable Pigs are just exactly what the Chinese astrologers ordered for the dashingly sentimental Dragon. There is something reassuringly special about how you two relate to each other—something intangible akin to a mixture of understanding and pure compassion one for the other's plight in life. It's as though you were meant to be together all of your born days.

Dragons are bossy, uppity creatures. They take themselves and their needs and their lives seriously. Some people think that because Dragons are so festive and noisy, colorful, and a tad snooty, that they are shallow. This assessment is unfair. Dragons are outrageously self-possessed. But if you can burrow under the scaly exterior, you will be surprised to find a sweetie-pie person who loves with boundless generosity of spirit.

Pigs are more obviously giving, tolerant, and accepting of the needs of others. If you tell a Pig person that you just had a nervous breakdown, the Pig will rush right out and buy you a bottle of tranquilizers. Pigs are lovely, benevolent, scrupulous, good-hearted folks who do not simply tolerate Dragons. They adore them. And it is reciprocal.

Pigs are born to be of service and Dragons need to be served. On one level, we might think that the feisty Dragon is taking advantage of the poor, naïve Pig. But that is not so. Certainly, Pig people are too generous with their kindness and will stoop to ridiculous depths to please their Dragon lovers. But we have to remember that Pigs are content nurturing those they love. Besides, they truly admire and revere their adorable Dragon partners. Ditto for Dragons. When they hitch up with a Pig partner, they do so because they are in love with the purity of spirit and true candor and honesty of the Pig character. Yes. Dragons like the fact that Pigs are so malleable. But malleable does not mean stupid. Pigs know when they are being exploited. And trust me, Pigs have their ways of controlling Dragons—right back!

It's usually Piggy who holds the purse in the family. Dragon hates to do accounts, and must ask Pig for an allowance. Second, as Dragons are sexually energetic beyond the norm and the apple of their eye is Piggy, Piggy has weaponry untold with which to keep old Draggy in line. Third, the Pig always organizes and runs the home for our couple. If things don't go Piggy's way—and this does happen—Piggy might just pack up all of Dragon's swashbuckler costumes, set them on the doorstep, and change the locks.

Yet most Dragon/Pig marriages endure. But Pigs who marry Dragons are not always starry-eyed gaga happy, anymore than Dragons who marry Pigs live in the lap of La La Land forever and ever amen either. The Dragon/Pig marriage is interesting and mobile, waxing and waning all the time to suit the circumstances, and evolving with the needs of each member of the tribe.

The relationship endures for good reason. Dragons adore Pigs and Pigs adore them back. Each takes care of the other in ways the other one cannot. Dragon is out there exteriorizing all over creation, while Piggy stays closer to home (also raking in shekels for sure as Pigs simply *get* money), polishing the infrastructure so that Dragon can continue to hold up that heavy self-image.

Happily, the sex is fabulous between you two. Pig is the very essence of sensuality born. Dragon, as we know, has sexual energy to burn. The combination of the two is fairly unbeatable and will benefit from a long life of truly exciting passion. Pig's lusty rustic sensuality keeps Dragon on his or her scaly toes, while Dragon's sheer magnificence keeps the admiring Pig hooked for life.

Oh, yes. Do have yourselves some children. I recommend a Goat baby, whose creative spirit will delight Piggy and who will feel protected by Dragon's fiery persona. Or, why not hatch a Cat child? Cat's gentle nature will fit in nicely, seducing the exuberant Dragon and pleasing the doting Pig parent with an inborn cultural sense and good taste to match.

SNAKE

Taken to the extreme, all of our qualities can become frailties. Some of us are generous to a fault, which can be wasteful. Good communicators can also be blabbermouths. Nurturing parents can smother their children. Fortunately, free will allows us to balance the positive and negative sides of our character. The tantalizingly attractive Snake was born:

POSITIVE | NEGATIVE

intuitive | paranormal

compromising | manipulative

helpful | invasive

sophisticated | condescending

discreet | covert

sensual | fickle

Snake with Snake

This twin Snake match occurs often, as both Snake people instantly recognize in each other a joint need for beaucoup sex, kilometers of luxurious surroundings, and a deep interest in things philosophical. But does it last? Think about Jacqueline Kennedy Onassis—a Snake *par excellence*. She got married twice, and both men were rich and famous Snakes! For well-known reasons, these marriages did not last. Fact is, twin Snake marriages usually do not.

Snakes are wise people whose advice is often sought by friends and family. The Snake's uncanny intuition can gauge things psychic quicker than you can say cobra. They are always heartbreakingly attractive and keep their bodies in excellent shape.

Not only do they always look wonderful, but Snakes enjoy a privileged spiritual relationship with each other because they can see around corners. This talent affords two Snakes living together many hours of conversations about such intriguing matters as politics, psychology, history and philosophy. They can also predict when events will happen and sometimes even know how to control them. Because of this intellectual or psychic connection, any Snake couple's life promises to be—if nothing else—provocative.

Money issues will abound between two Snakes. Snakes are weird about finance. They spend big sums on luxuries, as though a highly-priced item had more intrinsic value than a high-quality, low-priced one. If Tiffany, Cartier, Van Cleef and Bulgari have mailing lists, I would bet they contain a preponderance of Snake customers. If both of you are out spending, who will watch the store? Who is going to be responsible for making and keeping the money? Fact is, both of you are capable of pinching your last pennies because you hate to spend your own money on basics. If the rent isn't paid, you can be sure Van Cleef's latest bill is.

Snakes are obsessively possessive, yet are not known for their constancy in marriage. Don't ask me why, but Snakes have a reputation for straying. Some claim that Snakes are out-and-out philanderers who cheat on husbands and wives for the thrill of it. Despite their wisdom and philosophy, their common sense and capacity for deep-thinking, there is a part of all Snakes that lives for sexual contact, for the heat of intimacy between two writhing bodies, and ... for the attention they get from many different admirers. I have never known or encountered a Snake person who has not experienced this need and, in some way, acted out its ramifications.

For a Snake couple, when one (or both) begin to take sexual detours, fights and shouting matches ensue. Accusations and apparitions of the green-eyed monster begin to explode all over the place and the relationship becomes seriously endangered. No mate can truly comprehend why their beloved (and sexually active within the relationship) Snake partner has betrayed them. And should that same uncomprehending mate decide to give Snake a taste of his or her own medicine—the Snake might indeed then feel this to be the ultimate betrayal. And ask for a divorce.

But, although the facts are there, this assumption is not entirely fair. There is a real reason for Snake infidelity: this magnetically beautiful person's need to be physically admired, appreciated, and—believe it or not—helpful. Ms. Snake may be cheating on her Snake hubby with Ted, but in her mind she isn't really hurting hubby because he doesn't know and besides, Ted doesn't mean anything to her, *that* way. Ted, you have to understand, needs Ms. Snake to help him through his nasty divorce. She's only giving him a boost through his own muck. Snakes tend to believe their own lies. No amount of finger-shaking and scolding and trying to make her listen to reason will change things. When hubby freaks out because of Ted, she will stop seeing Ted. Or she won't. Then hubby may take revenge and begin seeing ex-Mrs. Ted. Tumult reigns.

Don't have any kids unless you have lived happily together in your plush home for at least five years in preparation for the responsibility of staying the course to raise the children. Remember, marriage means fidelity, which is difficult enough for you two to master. But children mean twenty years of constancy, of putting the other person first, and of getting up in the middle of the night for any piddling reason at all. If you feel you are up to it, go ahead and have a Rooster or Ox baby. They will give you two very strong reasons to tough it through.

½ *Snake with Horse*

At the outset, these two are drawn together by physical attraction. Even though they are usually strapping and tall, carry themselves proudly, and lend much grace to their movements, Horse people think of themselves as bland-looking. Snakes are gorgeous—whether or not they're strictly beautiful according to the book, Snakes are born with the kind of features we think of as seductive. Snakes are tantalizingly irresistible. And Horses are only human. Plus, Horses feel that the presence of a snazzy Snake by their side enhances their own appearance. Unfortunately, this will not last. Their differences will eventually do them in.

Horses and Snakes are not at all alike. The Snake relies on magnetism, seeks security, and dispenses wisdom and charity. The Horse relies on hard work, seeks independence, and dispenses persuasive opinions and inappropriate outbursts. One attracts the other by virtue of these great differences. The Snake finds the practical, nose-to-the-grindstone Horse charming and reassuring. The Snake senses that an industrious Horse lover or mate may indeed bring along the security that Snake so believes necessary to his or her own survival and that of an eventual family. On his or her side, the Horse will admire the Snake's wisdom and philosophical approach to problem-solving. Also, the self-serving Horse respects the Snake's considerate, generous nature and natural bent for being kindly.

Theoretically, this team should work out nicely. However, the long run has a way of wearing out the tempestuous Horse's welcome in the life of the quiet, slow-moving Snake. Horses don't listen very well, nor are they particularly interested in the plight of the poor and downtrodden. This disappoints the Snake, who always feels sorry for those less fortunate and sincerely wants to assist them. For the Horse's part, the Snake is a tad more than disappointing. To the Horse, the Snake is a possessive, smothering mate who won't let him or her have his head, run the show, or tell off the world. Moreover, the true-blue Horse is a paragon of sexual fidelity. Not so the inconsistent Snake, who sometimes feels the urge to make love with someone a bit different from his or her mate—if only to boost the new sex partner's self-esteem during a particularly bad patch.

As for money, you two could not choose a more piquant subject of dispute. Horses adore money. First, last, and always, the Horse is pragmatic and will always lean in the direction whence the money is flowing. If Snake has a lot of money, Horse will be glad to help him save it and spend it and invest it and so on. Horse will even work very, very hard to help preserve the Snake's capital. Snakes love money too. Snake, however, will be happy to take Horse's capital and spend it on sports cars, racehorses, and other expensive material things that the Snake needs in order to feel ever more and more secure. This spendthrift side of Snakes (who can also be mighty stingy when it comes to coughing up half the utility bill) will not only cause riots in the Snake/Horse relationship, but it will ultimately create a rift that could lead to a divorce.

The sex will be excellent, at first. The Horse is fatally attracted to the Snake's body and becomes glued to the Snake's mystical soul. Besides, when Horses fall madly in love, they can't extricate themselves. They are very concrete, earthy lovers who take their own feelings so seriously that when they actually do feel love they imagine it will have no end. They don't even question passion. If it's there at all it is there for the first (and maybe only) time ever, and they do not wish for it to depart. Snakes are more circumspect. They may be intellectually in love with Horsey and want to own his or her body and possess his or her spirit and even raise a family with Horse. But

Snakes are anything but naive. They do not really believe that passion lasts forever. Snakes are in close touch with their own feelings and intuitions. On the Snake side, the sexual passion may wane. Never on the Horse's. Somebody's gonna get hurt here, and I think his or her name is Dobbin.

If, by some miracle, you two underwent sufficient therapy or managed to overcome your differences and stayed together forever, you could have one child—either a gentle Goat or a dashing Dragon would be terrific.

Snake with Goat

If beauty really were truth and truth beauty, this relationship would be among the world's finest. You two are positively beautiful together. But although you two characters are inexorably drawn to each other's auras of loveliness, artistry, and creativity, life's harsh realities eventually stare you both down. Truth has a funny way of spilling the cracks of beauty and, in the case of the Snake/Goat relationship, the name of this bitter truth is money.

Snakes, of course, know how to provide. They are soft-spoken, slow-moving creatures whose attractiveness is legendary and whose natural languor belies a real knack for working hard to make their way in the world. Snakes may act lazy. But they are not.

Goats are ephemeral, dreamy, gentle people whose attractiveness is also epic. But where Snakes are sizzlingly tantalizing, Goats are swoony, gossamer folks whose four feet never quite touch the ground. Goats are gorgeously creative, but they are not ambitious. Oh, they may social climb a bit, but actual Goat ambition is very often vicarious. Goat loves Snake, whom he sincerely hopes and dreams will one day become rich. As for Goat, becoming personally rich isn't even a temptation. Too much like work.

Goat will gladly assist and advise and adjust and applaud and even home-make so that their beloved Snake can go out every day and face the workplace. But Goat would rather be take care of by Snake (or anyone else) than actually do the providing.

Both of you are big spenders. Those elegant cars and quadruple digit-priced pets you both like to own do not come cheap. Yet, even though you realize that perhaps there is not enough in the family budget to buy six pedigreed Persian cats, neither of you knows how to deprive the other of their adorable furry company. Same goes for clothing, hotel suites and jewelry, secondary residences and a pony for the little ones. You two will need to hire a meanie business manager/accountant if you ever hope to be able to get through life without experiencing at least one bankruptcy.

Aside from the money issue, you two ought to make a very artistic, cultured couple. You both enjoy attending expositions, going to the theater, sitting front row center at the opera and the ballet, wearing the latest designer costumes to the masquerade charity ball, and just generally gearing up for whatever sports and holidays require special purchases. At your house, decorating the Christmas tree, sprucing the house for Thanksgiving, or inventing theme parties will be a treat that both of you will delight in sharing.

Between two so luxuriously sensual people as Goat and Snake, sexual activity around your house promises to be positively opulent. Nothing will be too outrageously kinky or imaginative to get up to in bed. You both have a rich fantasy life and are able to actualize some of your wildest dreams while engaged in the act of love. Your bedroom will no doubt be hung with heavy silken fabrics and designed for privacy and pleasure. When you are not making love, you two will usually be found petting, cuddling, reading erotic literature or even watching soft porn on video. You are a passionate duo indeed.

By the way, fidelity is not in the cards for either of you. Dealing with occasional flirting and extramarital sexcapades is bound to cause you both some pain from time to time. But neither of you is famous for your undying devotion in the passion department. Chances are, you will work our reciprocal ways out of these hanky-panky crises better than most. In any case, Snake is possessive and Goat is dependent, so your mutual infidelities are not likely to be reason enough for either of you to want to split up.

If your finances are in order, you might want to have a number of kids. Goats (even males) are extremely motherly and know well how to nurture and cajole little ones into happy adults. The Snake will see that the children are cultured and steeped in art and reading. You family additions will be little Roosters, tiny Oxen, baby Pigs, and Cats.

½ *Snake with Monkey*

I confess I envy you your lifelong passion. You two seem eminently suited to be married to each other. Monkey will remain passionately attached to Snake, turning a blind eye to Snake's occasional roamings, and provide a fun-filled environment in which the Snake can feel both secure and fulfilled.

This unlikely combination begins when the peppy, spirited Monkey is insanely attracted to the slow, handsome, and alluring Snake. Snake's magical magnetism can cause the Monkey to fall, derrière over teakettle, in Love. Monkey seems to have found a partner who not only fulfills every dreamy physical specification, but also offers an intellectual equal with whom to hold long-winded court for hours and hours, talking of every subject on earth and never tiring of each other's company.

The Snake has many of the same feelings about a Monkey lover. Monkeys are sprightly, witty, and full of the sort of boundless energy Snake simply doesn't have. Also, Monkey is amusing and able to solve problems, give advice about money, and carry out many schemes that Snake, because of the Snake's native languor, would otherwise leave aside for lack of dynamism. In short, the Monkey provides a motor for the Snake's myriad plans and ideas, generally agrees with the Snake's charitable causes, and helps the retiring Snake come into society.

Don't forget that for Monkeys, the most pleasing jobs are always those wherein they assist someone who enjoys being in the limelight. The Monkey is at his or her best as the brains behind the throne. Monkeys want to stay in the background thinking up newer and cleverer ways to solve all the problems of their employees, friends, and loved ones. Luckily, Snakes adore being in the spotlight and are not likely to discard the king or queen of the world role in a hurry either. So what could be better? Monkeys run the show from the wings, and Snakes sit in the seat of reverence and authority.

One thing will definitely cause trouble here. The Monkey has about one millisecond's patience for laggards, and the Snake hates to be hustled or hurried along. While Snake is still adding and subtracting cuff links and wafting hair spray onto the preparation for his or her public appearance, Monkey has gotten dressed, started the car, devoured *Time* magazine, and has started on *War and Peace*, while foot-tapping the accelerator in exasperation.

Also, as Monkeys enjoy following their heart's desires, they are not always easy to pin down emotionally. They seem to fly off in many different directions at once pretty much all the time they are alive. Snakes are possessive—obsessively so. Monkey's insistence on owning freedom of movement and even pulling the occasional disappearing act will no doubt flummox and even frighten the Snake, who fears and despairs over even a momentary loss of security. Yet, it is a fact. Monkeys must roam free. If the, Snake cannot learn to deal with this Monkey exigency, the relationship will be doomed from the jump.

Money should not be an issue between you two. Snake spends a lot on frivolities and pretties and luxuries. But as long as there is disposable cash (and Monkey is competent both at investing and earning great sums), Monkey doesn't really mind. In fact, one of Monkey's best traits in this regard is the desire to give presents to loved ones as tokens of passion and esteem. In fact, where Snakes might tend to be a little tightfisted about personal money matters, clever Monkeys will jolly them out of this bad habit.

Need I say that the sex is pure heaven? Both of you love to be entwined, attached, and, in love. Monkey may not always be able to produce that torrid, seamy tone in lovemaking that so seduces the sensuality-addicted Snake. But never mind, you are both intelligent and agile of spirit. Whatever difficulties you have in the bedroom will get worked out more easily than with many, many other couples because you (thank Zeus!) know how to talk everything through together.

Children? Yes. When you calculate the birth dates of your kids, try to aim for a Rooster or a baby Ox, a powerful little Rat-born charmer, or even a blustery powerhouse Dragon.

Snake with Rooster

A sterling match if there ever was one! Snakes and Roosters get along beautifully. Rooster admires the loveliness of Snake's physical attributes. Snake can't get enough of the feisty Rooster's special attentions. You are equally attracted to each other's intellect, agreeing on many points, and always receiving sound advice when you consult each other about life's multifarious issues.

It's fortunate that both of you are quite conservative and luxury-loving. You adore culture, sponsor the arts, and believe very strongly in continuing education. It may, at first, seem as though the Snake is a mite too glittery and sophisticated for the rough and ready Rooster to handle. But Roosters are deceiving. They can muster almost any sort of persona needed to adapt to the situation. If anyone can handle the slippery Snake, it's the feisty, flinty Rooster.

If one were to rely solely on appearances, you two might well be thought of as superficial or at least highly materialistic. Chic wardrobes, napery, fine china, and top-quality foodstuffs characterize your lifestyle. This glow of refinement might possibly dupe outsiders into imagining you two as social climbers or snobs. But they would be very wrong. Rooster and Snake are more akin to a pair of old, bearded philosophers who sit around the hearth, jabbering day and night about how to improve the world. No matter that their home has just been photographed for *Architectural Digest,* or that they have hired the most famous landscape architect alive to design them a perennial garden, Mr. and Mrs. Snaky-Rooster are much more thought-oriented than all that. These folks are busy planners and doers of serious good deeds in the community as well as among friends and family. They both benefit from a sharp intelligence and delight in the intensity of their shared ideals.

Roosters move about at a zany, hectic pace, hurrying and scurrying everywhere at once, getting all their professional work done early—so they can go shopping, work out, and hurry home to start dinner while watching a video on how to speak perfect Catalan. After a fine meal, they might finish a sculpture or start another watercolor. Roosters never stop learning, growing, and applying their myriad talents to as many projects as the day will hold.

Snakes, of course, sometimes have trouble getting started. The Rooster's frenzied motion might at first actually repel the languid Snake. But as this couple gets to know each other better, the Snake is inspired to undertake more activities, to get more involved in social life, and to respond to challenge without fear of failure. Rooster is not only a good role model but a good teacher for the hesitant, security-conscious Snake to follow.

Snakes are voraciously luxury-loving and cannot keep their hands off the "best" of everything life has to offer. Roosters also like handsome home furnishings and finely accessorized housing. But they are more likely to buy a solid, one-of-a-kind designer couch built to last a lifetime than to decide every other month to change decorating schemes or plead for a whole new living room suite because of a family wedding or other celebration. Snakes have an odd view of money. They are penny-pinching about necessities and lavish spenders when it comes to jewels and furs, sports cars, and clothing. Of the two of you, Rooster is by far the most stable about money.

You are very well-matched sexually. The Rooster is drop-dead seduced by the Snake's slinky charisma, and the Snake deems the Rooster's well-tended physique a passion party treat. Snakes do tend to be possessive to the extreme. But the Rooster doesn't mind, as he or she is naturally faithful and devoted—having little time to dally with outsiders as there is so much else to do in life besides engage in hanky-panky. The Snake will, of course, indulge in some sidelining. But as long as Snaky remains discreet, Rooster will not be outraged. Certainly, if he or she finds out, Rooster may be hurt. Rooster prefers, however, not to be confronted by them.

In short, your couple promises to become an ironclad contract and even a long-term marriage wherein a family can be both nurtured (by the Snake parent) and taught lots of amazing skills (by the Rooster). You might want to try to have a hardworking little Ox baby, a clever Monkey, or a gentle Goat, whose creative gifts will enhance your family's very culturally receptive household.

Snake with Dog

Providing you both desire it strongly enough, a marriage might just happen here. A solid union will, however, require major efforts on both sides. Your goal is compromise. For that, you will need to cultivate acres of mutual understanding.

Snakes are desultory yet intelligent creatures whose motives and methods are often cryptic and secretive. They plot and plan strategies far in advance of carrying out projects, and may ruthlessly slither over a goodly number of dead bodies to achieve those objectives. Paradoxically, Snakes are also extremely charitable people who frequently reach out to lend a hand or cheer up a sorrowful or victimized friend or acquaintance. The Snake advances at his or her own deliberate cadence to speed up or make adjustments in either style or manner to suit a mate. Snakes are also fully aware of their rapacious sexuality and their remarkable ability to tug at the hearts of those who feel drawn to their charms.

These traits in themselves are really quite delectable. Most of us are enchanted by Snakes and bewitched by their outstanding beauty. But Dogs are different. Yes. The famous reptilian attraction is still very much present, and the urge to get to know the Snake at close range pulls the Dog's short hairs. But Dogs are suspicious, wary creatures and do not take easily to folks whom they fear may be capable of cruelty or ruse. Dogs have a built-in BS detector that sets off an alarm in their brain—even when the rest of their body is melting with passionate desire for the Snake's special brand of sensuality. Despite themselves, Dogs are constantly on their guard against dishonesty and injustice. For them, the enigmatic Snake is just on the borderline between good and evil—and it takes a while before the Dog trusts the Snake to enter his or her intimate personal circle. The image I get here is one of a testy pooch walking around and around a superbly beautiful coiled-up serpent—not quite knowing what to make of the gorgeous thing, yet not being able to leave it alone.

When they do get together, Snakes and Dogs begin as good friends and discover that, although they come at their ideals from two very different positions, they enjoy similar notions about justice and believe fervently in righting social wrongs. As your friendship deepens, your mutual attraction will grow. As you learn to love each other, Snake will deign to descend from his or her vaulted pedestal of sophistication, and Doggy will drop some of his sarcasm and harsh critical commentary. In a very old-fashioned way, you will probably not become lovers until well after you have been chums for a time.

Wealth issues may cast a shadow between you two. Snakes concentrate a lot of energy on the getting and spending of large sums. They are not always squanderers, but love to lay out large amounts of money on luxury items. Basically, the Dog disapproves of overt shows of luxe and wishes he or she was not obliged to own much of anything at all. If Dog cares for the family finances, Snake will be miserably deprived. If Snake handles the money, the Dog will growl and snap all the time about waste. In my opinion, you should each handle money and only pool your funds for basic household matters

The sex will be marvelous. In the beginning, because Dog is so straight-arrow and direct, Snake may feel a mite underwhelmed. But in time, with Snake's gentle insistence and clever methods of persuasion and teaching, Doggy will slow down and start to enjoy the Snake's slippery sexuality. If the Dog does not adapt to the Snake's voracity, Snake may be tempted to sniff about elsewhere for some action. The Snake's flirty nature is exactly what worries the Dog about this character in the first place. Discovering Snake's outside interests would destroy the loyal Dog's tender ego and could even cause a nervous breakdown.

If you do manage to stay together for a long while, you will be quite content with each other's good company. After a few years, you probably should have a couple of kids. Both of you have the capacity for becoming fine humanitarian nurturers. Your best bets for children would be a bold Tiger or resourceful Rooster child. Failing either of those you will also be happy with a loving Pig baby or even a talented little Goat kid.

❤❤❤ Snake with Pig

This relationship is a cautionary tale: A very innocent, tolerant, understanding Pig person sooner or later gets smothered by the possessive stranglehold of a splendiferously gorgeous lover named Snake. Piggy falls plumb in love with Snake's quiet beauty, and schemes to seduce and eventually even to own the Snake. Snake, experiencing the willingness, and generosity of the Pig, who loves and cherishes without reserve, is also smitten. In the first chapter, you two spend much time staring into each other's eyes, wondering how you could be so lucky. But by the final page of this saga, the pudgy Pig has grown very thin and morose, and the Snake wriggles away to find a more challenging lover in a faraway fairyland called Oz. Snake/Pig love is not for the fainthearted.

If the two of you manage to weave yourselves a life together, you undoubtedly attend expositions, concerts, theatrical productions, and other cultural events. You create a lavishly decorated household and invite many relatives and friends for champagne brunches and candlelight dinners with *foie gras* and caviar. You both fancy gilt frames around your masterpieces of fine art, which are hung on walls covered in silk or damask fabrics. Heavily lined drapes and bronze-sculpted sconces characterize your home's décor. You will always enjoy inviting guests to your table, too, as the Pig is often both an accomplished cook and an excellent host or hostess. Moreover, the Snake won't mind appearing in glamorous finery, enthroned at table's end, receiving kudos and comments about the elegance of the table settings and the glories of the flower arrangements.

Piggy should manage the finances. Pigs are good with money and somehow attract it without half trying. Snakes usually work hard for money, as they are extremely ambitions and clever. But they do spend it all at one time in huge bunches on everything from electronic gadgets to accessories for the bedroom, of which they already own twenty-seven models. Let Pig run the money show. Pigs are generous and will happily provide Snake huge allowances for buying all the finery they need.

Your sex life will be a joy for both of you. Piggy is the wallowy sensual type who loves to roll around a lot during sex and twist the sheets to pieces in passionate revelries. Food along with sex stimulates Pig's most excitable parts. Snake is turned on by the Pig's delight in things sensual and will cooperate fully with any and all fantasy erotica the Pig can think up.

At about three-quarters through the cautionary tale of which I spoke earlier, you will witness the first signs of the decline of the Pig/Snake harmony. This usually comes about because of Snake's eternally flirtatious nature. Whilst ensconced at the head of the table, Snake secretly playing footsie with a guest. Piggy, in sweet naiveté, continues to revel in the belief that Snake is unswervingly faithful. Then Pig finds out. Now the formerly peaceful, harmonious, and convivial home environment becomes a tense battlefield in a cold war masterminded by a hideously jealous but still tolerant and indulgent Pig who, rather than blame the Snake, decides to keep

Snaky bound and gagged. Snake, who does not take kindly to this inhibiting, confining treatment, complains and withholds sexual favors in retaliation. Pig decides then to move the family to the remotest countryside—removing temptation from Snake's surroundings. Snake ends up bedding the barmaid or the gardener, and the house of Piggy/Snake falls into ruin. Scandal ensues. Pig is shamed and martyred. Pig ends up alone, mourning the loss forevermore of a time when everything seemed so perfect.

If you do manage to keep this act together—if Pig can learn to handle Snake's flirty nature and Snake can allow Pig to be free to move about at will without punching a love time clock every second, the idea of marriage is not out of the question.

Should you marry and stay together, you might want to try your children during Rooster and Goat years. The Rooster boosts the family energy level, and the creative Goat pleases such cultured parents as you with his or her talents and abilities in artistic fields. You might also get on well with a Cat child or even a baby Ox.

HORSE

Taken to the extreme, all of our qualities can become frailties. Some of us are generous to a fault, which can be wasteful. Good communicators can also be blabbermouths. Nurturing parents can smother their children. Fortunately, free will allows us to balance the positive and negative sides of our character .The proud, headstrong Horse was born:

POSITIVE | NEGATIVE

enthusiastic | zealous

amusing | intrusive

industrious | driven

logical | ruthless

talented | self-satisfied

generous | prodigal

½ Horse with Horse

A team of Horses traditionally works hard and gets the job done. It's the old-fashioned way, but it is still an efficient method of working the fields. Human Horse people are no exception. They work well together, and each pulls his or her own weight and runs a tight ship, bringing home money and enjoying a shared grand passion—their own! Horses, who are independent souls, interested in anything and everything they deem fun and intriguing to do, make good partners for each other—and, parallel to their physical attraction, manage to maintain a good friendship. Projects get undertaken willingly in assisting the other in getting things accomplished. With these two running the show, nothing seems impossible—moving house, traveling around the world, building a boat, trekking the Himalayas, retracing the steps of Buddha, or running a successful political campaign—all seem like child's play for a pair of enterprising work-oriented Horses.

Horses are, above all, practical. Your home will be handsomely traditional, well-designed, and efficient. You both need to live in an environment that allows for your hobbies and talents to coexist with family life. Art studios, music-mixing rooms, well-equipped home offices, and even cinema production facilities are not rare in two-Horse houses.

An idle Horse is an unhappy Horse. As a Horse couple, you will probably both work outside the home, command good salaries, and get the most of your money in purchases and (providing you resist the temptation to gamble) investments. Although the Horse works well alone, you might also go into business together. Two Horses running a shop or service business is common.

I do see one problem: Horses have vile tempers. They do not handle their anger with grace or reserve, but usually flare up, shout, and scream their fury at being mistreated or misunderstood. Of course, a good team, working cooperatively, can handle these outbursts. But supposing you happen to find fault with your Horse partner? Now, the soup thickens. Rows, big fights of gigantic proportion—complete with accusations, condemnations, lawsuits, and perhaps even rifts of some duration—will occur. The Horse does eventually cool down and become reasonable again after one of these emotional tornadoes. But in the meanwhile ... it's hell.

It's clear to me that the perpetuation of your relation as a pair of Horses in love will depend on how much genuine compassion and understanding you can develop together by discussing your differences of opinion and by meshing your various ideals. When one of you wants to move to Europe to pursue a career as a bandleader and the other wants to go to Hawaii and invest in commercial real estate, there will be some gigantic geographical gaps to overcome. Whether you can tolerate and indulge the other's need for independent action and advancement in fields other than those you might choose will be the key to finding harmony here. Some couples therapy certainly could not hurt, as it might school you in how to fight productively instead of staging so many unfruitful wars.

Your sex life will be a perpetual hoot! You are both passionate about physical love and cherish the idea of a lifelong involvement with the person you choose. Horses are somewhat conservative, but they are the type of romantics who dream of staging lovemaking marathons on desert islands or in other exotic venues. Fantasy will undoubtedly play a large role in your very solidly grounded sexual future. Disloyalty on either side may break you up forever. Beware of the temptation for getting revenge through extracurricular sexcapades. For the essentially faithful Horse character, the infidelity of a beloved mate is intolerable. Can divorce be far behind?

If you want children, please wait until you have worked out your personal couple issues (at least two years of cohabitation) before having them. Plan carefully, and you will lighten your load by giving birth to a sweet-natured creative Goat kid, a tolerant and understanding Piglet, or a justice-seeking Doggie baby. Your Horse couple will benefit greatly from the introduction of softer elements into your home.

❤️❤️❤️❤️ Horse with Goat

This combination will survive the worst rigors of cohabitation and age because of a natural harmony between their characters. This concordant combining of two very different, yet not really polarized, types makes for a relationship based on individual needs and mutual fulfillment of those same needs. You make a fine pair.

Horses are independent. They make no bones of the fact that life ought to be run the way they see fit. Horses make pronouncements and blurt platitudes that sometimes leave much to be desired in the logic department. Horses are, as my mother used to say, "full of themselves." Even when they have no basis for self-confidence or esteem in a certain field, they always act as though they invented the world. Horses have opinions on everything, claim to know how to solve all the problems of humankind, and haven't got much time to listen to yours. A natural sense of self-importance and a little healthy arrogance can be useful in many areas. Thanks to these traits, the Horse is very impressive, capable, and usually successful at what he or she undertakes professionally.

The Horse's personal life is another pair of socks altogether. Horses wear natural blinders. They really cannot see or think laterally unless taken by the reins and led in that direction. Work, thinks the headstrong Horse, is the saving grace of the world. If he or she works and is productive and self-supporting—the rest will fall into place. This haughty attitude doesn't always make the Horse the most delicious love partner in the zodiac. Not everybody can get on with a Horse.

This, my friends, is where the gossamer Goat comes gamboling into the Horse's sumptuously supplied breakfast nook, pulls up the most comfortable chair in the house, and sets about talking the straight-dealing Horse into the ethereal, lateral realm, where Goats come from in the first place. Goats are damned attractive to steadfast, squared-off people like Horses. Goats drift instead of walk, dream instead of think, and only fly into rages when their security is threatened. *Such poetry,* thinks the flatfooted Horse. *Such insight and flair for the artistic.* As for the Goat, he or-she is grazing happily in Goat nirvana, safe in the knowledge that there is one thing Horses love above all else, and that is the steady accumulation of wealth. Knowing this, Goat determines posthaste to plight Horse his or her instantaneous troth and get on with the rest of life.

And the match is not a mistake. Not in the least. The Goat's flaky, wafty nature dovetails neatly into the Horse's, ultraconservative one. When finally you two get together and fall in love, the Horse is fascinated and the Goat is (at last) secure. Horse will take care. Horse will work and make enough money and even distribute evenhandedly (maybe) so that Goat can feel totally free either to pursue some eccentric artistic bent or to stay blissfully at home, in organized (thanks to Horse's demands) surroundings, taking excellent care of the family's dreams. Horse spurs Goat to be a tad more practical and confident. Goat calms the knotted spirit of the overworked, excitable, overly anxious Horse. Goats depend. Horses provide.

This calming effect the Goat has on the Horse's high tension level is, of course, manifest first in their daily life. But later on—when the lights are at their lowest and Horse's psyche is still alive with anxieties racing amok, causing insomnia and worse—a gentle Goat mate will be there to hold and comfort, to listen and cajole, to flatter and sing lullabies to the poor stressed-out Horse. And finally, Goat will be there to make glorious love to that Horse lover—Goatly love designed to quiet a sturdy but strung-out spirit and empty out the cares of all of Horsey's hectic days at one go. You are remarkably well-matched. Enjoy.

As for children, providing the Goat (male or female) is willing to take on the nurturing role, you should have many. I suggest Pig babies for their sweet jolly presence, or Tiger babies to liven up the nursery. Or why not little Cat and Dog children, whose harmonious characters add refinement and caring respectively to your already refined and caring household.

½ *Horse with Monkey*

Here we find two very spirited, willful people. They are first attracted to each other because of a mutual desire to be social together, to go forth as a couple at parties and gatherings, charming people with their interminable talking and chatter, entertaining the troops, as it were. Both Monkey and Horse are interested and intrigued by current events, wishing to stay abreast of everything new that comes down the pike, and they are busy ,busy, busy helping others to keep up as well. Monkey sends out news clippings of everything he or she reads in every single publication known to humankind. Horse calls up the world all day and night to let them in on developments as they happen. Now that I think of it, these two would make a great anchor team. Monkey with the witty, perky talkativeness. Horse with the serious know-it-all attitude. Unbeatable before the cameras and (although Monkey often shies from fame) very articulate indeed.

But cameras aside, the Horse/Monkey combination runs the risk of being one of the most difficult relationships to husband properly. The social attraction is there for sure. You form a good "couple" in the strictest traditional sense. You are capable of creating a household together that grows out of your mutual hard work and shared taste for the unusual in decoration. You are able to pick out paintings you both like, buy valuable antiques, and agree on how money gets spent.

Yet, on a deeper level, when it comes to communicating feelings and sharing emotional information, you two have a very difficult time expressing your problems to each other. Monkeys are highly neurotic. They live close to their feelings without really ever being able to identify them or want to alter them by much. Monkeys live by their wits and are easily pushed to hysteria, but they are just as quick to defuse. The Horse is more like a pan of milk—chugging along nicely, simmering on the stove, then suddenly boiling over. But despite these quick outbursts and sometimes most unpleasant rages,

Horse people are almost never able to understand their motivations sufficiently to know how to make the necessary behavioral changes.

We end up with a functioning couple unable to read each other's needs and thus handicapped when they seek to deepen understanding in their relationship. Why? Because they don't have the natural tools for comprehending the real reasons for emotional slipups in the first place. I recommend therapy for each, and, if you wish to keep your couple intact and afloat in its initial harmonious state, couples' counseling as well.

You will be largely in agreement about finances, except when the Monkey goes overboard, giving presents to every relative and friend alive at holidays and birthdays. Monkeys are generous to a fault because deep down they are really very shallow about money and don't care a whit for the first or the last penny they ever earned. Horse is far and away the more conservative of the two, but Horse still likes to spend money—big time! You are hereby advised to hire yourselves a good business manager.

Your initially shy sex life will grow and become brilliant. Horses are so vigorous and energetic in bed that the more cerebral Monkey may first be somewhat overwhelmed. Moreover, the Monkey should be aware in advance that Horses need rather more sex than the Monkey is used to. In time, because the two of you are both realistic and instinctively know how to work out your practical problems, you will find yourselves delightfully compatible and hypersexually active.

Choose to have children after you have gotten to know each other well first. Give it a few years of cohabitation and financial stability before going all out for family life. When you do have kids, try to plan them in the years of the pleasant cultured Pig, the dramatic homebody Ox, or—*l'enfant terrible*—the ballistic Tiger.

❤️❤️❤️ Horse with Rooster

In the past few years, I have altered my opinion of this union. I have found that the Horse and Rooster can indeed form a successful couple. You enjoy not only sexual attraction, common conservatism, shared ideals, and a well-developed sense of adventure; but you truly like being together in the world, creating your own circle of common friends as well as cooperating on projects such as gardening, cooking, and traveling to exotic places.

The Rooster is almost as dandified as the Horse. You both love clothes and feel that appearances are all-important. Although you favor different styles in decoration and wardrobe, you enjoy shopping for furniture and buying top-of-the-line products in everything from foodstuffs to automobiles. Roosters never undertake any project or responsibility that they are not certain to be fully prepared to carry out. Horses are more likely to leap before they look, jumping into opportunities and waiting for the fallout to see if there will be a profitable outcome.

Despite a sometimes superficially rebellious and devil-may-care attitude, you are nevertheless both ultraconservative vis-à-vis the world and society. Neither of you can ever be accused of true eccentricity, as you both tend to prefer to color within the lines in life, clinging to tenets and beliefs that came down to you from your family.

Horses often behave in an outrageous or irreverent fashion, sticking out their necks before weighing their words. They are capable of insulting, teasing or criticizing their testy Rooster mate into an exacerbated state of nerves without half trying, and will sometimes do this just for the fun of it. Rooster does not take kindly to such taunting, and is in fact deeply wounded by the Horse's teasing. In turn, Rooster can exasperate the headstrong Horse by refusing to participate in spontaneous or improvisational events that Horsey cooks up. Rooster likes to plan ahead. So when called on to perform on the spot, Rooster balks, pouts, and goes into rapid reverse, escaping into a private realm and ignoring Horse for days. When finally the Rooster does come right out and complain, you can be sure not a word is minced. The Rooster is known for excessive candor and will say exactly what he or she is thinking—which can cut the proud Horse to the quick.

One way of keeping this very strong friendship alive for a very long time is to avoid spending all of your time together. The Rooster is a solitary sort of person who needs time alone, time to read and study, see different friends, make long-term plans, pay bills, and maybe just hang on the phone. Horse is not exactly a solitary type, but rather is described as "independent." Horses do not so much isolate as they move about their world alone, visiting this one and that, inviting family and friends to their home for meals, traveling by themselves to places where they have a particular interest, such as a ski area or geological dig. Each of you likes to maintain freedom of movement. Hence the confinement of a home and family will put pressure on your relationship, as somebody some of the time will need to be there for the kids, the dogs, the garden, and so on. Spacing out your intimacy will make this marriage last.

Finances will not be a particular problem between you so long as each of you retains control of his or her financial life. You should share certain expenses but never pool all your resources as, again, you want to feel free to move about at will. Rooster's financial picture will have more highs and lows than a loop-the-loop at a carnival. Horses are steadier and far more basely materialistic than Roosters—which gives the Horse one more thing to lord over the diligent Rooster and tease him or her about.

As your relationship will always be shifting and evolving—sometimes rather more stormily than you would like—having children is a dicey prospect. But if you are married and have managed to solve some of the spikier problems, have established a satisfactory household, live in some degree of harmony, then go ahead and have two-- Tiger cubs will be a delightful addition as will little Dog children. A Snake or Ox baby will also love living in your interesting home.

💘💘💘💘 *Horse with Dog*

The Horse and the Dog are good friends—through all tribulation as well as in joy, they are slated to live side by side, trotting along paw in hoof down the Yellow brick road toward the Emerald City of marriage and family.

The Dog is just plain good people. He or she is fair, concerned with justice, loyalty, and the determination to do what is right always and in all ways. Dog is often sorely disappointed with and by others who do not exhibit the same general feelings of goodwill and doing the right thing. As a result, Dogs evolve slowly but surely toward an anxious state bordering at its worst on paranoia, always fearing the worst and finally suspecting everybody of trying to do in everybody else.

The Horse is more self-centered and self-serving, it's true. But Horses are also more positive and upbeat. They have the unique gift of being able to quiet the panicky Dog, who respects the Horse's opinion. Even more, the Dog respects the Horse's diligence and willingness to put shoulder to the wheel at all times and in all circumstances. Horses, of course, are not very careful about what they say and can get themselves into hot water with their inappropriate outbursts and sometimes outrageous comments and fits of anger. This trait of the Horse's exasperates the careful Dog, as Dogs do not believe it wise to attract attention. But in another way, the Horse's flights of fanciful behavior serve to show that being in the spotlight for a second or two won't really hurt.

So each of you learns from the other by example. Dog teaches Horse to be less vocal and blunderbuss. Horse teaches Dog to be less fearful and judgmental. What more could a couple want? Well, you might want to enjoy some common activities. And lucky for you both, that is precisely what you will do. Horses and Dogs are both interested in being involved in life. Both are active, effective, and project-oriented. Each of you will enjoy sports. Each of you will believe in causes and take up cudgels to help those less fortunate than yourselves. Neither of you tends to be dependent or needy in the emotional department, as you both manage to stand or fall on your own four feet. When you have decided to come together and stay together, your pact is one made by two thinking people who feel not only a sexual tug to each other, but who know instinctively what is best for them.

Neither of you is threatened by the other's need for quiet time and personal space. As we know, this can be a killer issue. If Dog wants to stay home and work on the computer and Horse feels like going to visit Great Aunt Matilda in Poughkeepsie, nobody gets crazy or whines, "You never go anyplace with me ... You're always working on your damned computer." In your couple, there is room for an individual to breathe and have space.

Dogs are discerning. They have a habit of being ultra critical of all matters concerning society such as government, cliques, clubs, hierarchies, and even religion. Horses may willingly plow themselves into groups and club membership and even political campaigns, arrogantly believing that they might be chosen as head honcho. Here is the fodder you both need for late-night discussions over policy. It is unlikely either of you will ever sway the other. But at least you will never be bored.

Money won't be an issue. The Dog may become discouraged over losses or gross misunderstandings in business dealings, but the Horse will raise Doggy's spirits. The Horse might want to manage the family budget, but I suggest you do it together, as the Dog's cautious approach can be useful in reining in Horsey's tendency to overspend on appearances.

Your sex life promises to be vigorous and satisfactory. Both of you adore the act of love and find it especially fun with each other. You, Horse, may tend to take a mite more pleasure than you are first willing to give. But in time, under the tender influence of the noble-hearted Dog, the Horse will learn that in matters of sex, giving is just as pleasurable as receiving.

Have kids. Lots of kids. But first, be sure that at least one of you chooses to want to be home all the time or else hire yourselves an excellent nanny to assist you in raising those wild little Tigers, docile Cat/Rabbits, compliant Pigs, and feisty Dragons that you are so eager to teach how to be healthy men and women like yourselves.

💘💘💘💘 Horse with Pig

Here is a dandy, long-lasting match. Horses know how to go out into the world and seek their fortune. Pigs know instinctively how to provide comfort and security, culture and opulence, in a happy home atmosphere. Both parties are honest and faithful. Both make excellent parents and are not only mutually supportive, but able to create a solid basis for children and family members who might call on them for refuge and understanding.

Horses and Pigs are both hardy types and are prepared to muck in to get through the rough spots. Horses need to be applauded for their labors. They crave respect and at the same time wish to be cradled and coddled. The Pig is wise and knows how to do both without making the Horse feel either hemmed in or smothered. The Horse, in turn, builds up the Pig's confidence and boosts his or her self-esteem.

As money clings to Pigs and Horses are practical and unafraid of hard work and business, material security ought never to be a problem for them. Still, they must beware. Pigs gamble. In business, Pigs go the whole hog for the biggest prize and often lose the farm in the process. Pigs are enormously naïve. They trust fate. They are optimistic and they are lucky. Whatever happens, money always comes back to the Pig. But Horses don't know this. They are nervous and anxious about losing financial control. In their stubborn, pragmatic approach to life, they cannot believe that Fate ever does anything other than dash their dreams and send unworthy Horses to glue factories in Poland. In short, Horses don't like taking chances. They believe in making their own luck. So if conflict ever there is, in this otherwise happy marriage, it will arise over money—the use of it, the abuse of it.

Making a prosperous, solid-citizen family is the logical extension of Horse and Pig's union. So green light on children. You should have children in the signs of Capricorn or Leo in the Dog, Goat, Cat, or Ox years. As parents, you will be too cloying for Tigers and too conservative for Dragons, and a Horse parent might destroy a child's creativity through constant harping about doing things "right." There is almost no child sign that the Pig cannot get along with—except Snakes, whose neediness will coil itself around Pig's good nature until Pig is smothered to death.

It doesn't take much knowledge of Chinese astrology to understand the modus vivendi of this disciplined, self-sufficient, hardworking, cozy, home-loving couple. Even if the Horse makes all the money, the Pig person is still the coziness provider. Pigs prefer their homes to restaurants. They don't have much in the way of table manners and feel that if they want to slurp their soup and rub their greasy hands in their hair, they will be more comfortable slurping and rubbing in their own dining rooms. Besides, Pigs love inviting guests to share their bounty and test taste all the delicious cuisine they cook up. Conviviality is a Pig's favorite toy.

As for Horses, they don't really mind eating out but are often embarrassed in quiet company because their laugh is too loud, their exuberance too exuberant, their gestures too abrupt and sudden. People are forever surprised by their outrageous social ejaculations. Horses feel naturally insecure in intimate surroundings. Large gatherings however don't faze the Horse. He feels camouflaged and protected by the crowd. But, lucky for them both, Horses who live with Pigs are delighted to bring home the lobster—and even to pay for it. This way, Horse and Pig get to relax in their own home and create all the noisy outbursts and slurpy noodle noises they want.

GOAT

Taken to the extreme, all of our qualities can become frailties. Some of us are generous to a fault, which can be wasteful. Good communicators can also be blabbermouths. Nurturing parents can smother their children. Fortunately, free will allows us to balance the positive and negative sides of our character. The gentle, creative Goat was born:

POSITIVE | NEGATIVE

appealing | flirtatious

generous | wasteful

gentle | weak

sensitive | hyperemotional

observant | pessimistic

caring | flaky

💘💘 Goat with Goat

I view this couple as being in a long torrid love affair. As a marriage, however, I fear it's a difficult one to manage. The pressure on two gentle Goats to create order is often more than the relationship can bear. Nonetheless, with outside help, it can work.

Goats are exorbitantly attracted to each other and perform admirably in bed together. There is not much they don't have in common and plenty that they share in the way of tastes and opinions. Of course, if one of these Goats is, say, a Capricorn and the other a Leo, they are likely to get along better longer than if they have incompatible Western astrological signs.

Goats are attractive, artistic, and even perhaps a bit funky or bohemian. They are sensitive people with a strong bent for the creative. One of you may be a musician or a painter and the other a philosopher or poet. And even if both of you have chosen careers in commerce, law, medicine, or science, there will still be an enormous amount of culture in your home. I see you owning a huge collection of classical and jazz records or a library of early Renaissance chant or of great masterworks. Your house will be decorated with skill and every detail of repair seen to by your clever hands. You will take pleasure in hanging delicate fabrics ay your windows, arranging the furniture in unusual patterns and planning the lighting so it enhances a lovely flower arrangement one of you has accomplished to please the other.

You are also probably the proud owners of several gorgeous pedigreed longhair cats or show dogs. Both of you adore animals and prefer to live in the country than to hang about in the polluted city. Nature and its glories suit you better than urban life, which plays havoc with your allergies and chronic ailments such as arthritis and liver problems. Moreover, you both adore gourmet foods and enjoy the fun of inviting a score or more people to your place for meals, wine, and lively conversation. If you cannot actually live in the countryside, you will no doubt make it a point to own a secondary residence where you can take long walks and enjoy the clean air together.

Not much dissension should arise between you two—except over money. Goats enjoy living with someone who has more funds than they do or who will, at least, be able to provide a large share of the family's income. They are notoriously dependent folks, which means that the Goat is an excellent helpmate for a control-freak type who wants to organize the world and doesn't mind taking sweet-natured Goat in the bargain. But two gentle Goats undoubtedly view their combined lack of structure with some trepidation—"Who," they may wonder, "is going to be responsible for watching the store?" Goats are profoundly pessimistic and will worry themselves into an early grave if something is not done to relieve the pressure of creating a personal infrastructure.

Worst of all, neither of you seems to particularly treasure the job of house administrator. Arguments and rifts can arise over such matters as who paid what bills and how the pair of you can ever hope to survive without some outside order. My advice? Get yourself a business manager who can do the accounting and investing for you, warn you against overspending, and give you a real idea of what resources you have at your disposal. Ideally, one Goat in this couple should have a private income. A steady flow of money from a source other than one of your brow's sweat would solve many a problem between you.

As for the sex ... it's fabulous. You are both romantic and interested in enjoying the act of lovemaking. When you put your minds to creating a perfect setting for cuddling, billing, and cooing, you will certainly not scrimp on effort or atmosphere. You share a strong interest in sexuality and may build yourselves a wondrously imaginative sex life where your most evocative erotic dreams can actually come true. Watch each other for signs of infidelity ... a Goat pastime if ever there was one.

If you can manage to put together a structured home life and wish to have children to keep your pets company, you should try to keep your family small. A single Pig child would be the perfect choice. Otherwise you might have a Cat baby or a beautiful little Snake. Limiting responsibilities will make it easier for you to husband your combined strengths for the necessary nurturing to take place.

❤️❤️ *Goat with Monkey*

On the face of it, this couple appears to be slated for a long, balanced marriage of their strengths and weaknesses, which complement each other. Monkeys and Goats do have a lot of fun together. But, for this couple, what starts out with one member of the couple helping the other to live more fully and successfully may just end up with one leaning heavily on the other and the other being bored silly.

Monkeys are funny people. They like to amuse others and solve their problems and they tend not to take life all that seriously. Goats are flaky and pessimistic. They have lots of problems with self-esteem and they need buoying up all the time. Unlike Monkeys, Goats take life very seriously.

Also, Goat usually needs to depend on Monkey to go out and earn money to provide for them both. Monkey doesn't mind. The Goat is so lighthearted (and headed) that the Monkey finds pleasure in having a cheerful partner at the end of long day of work. Besides, Monkeys are ever so generous. They want to give presents and see that others are comfortable-- Monkeys are born crowd-pleasers, and Goats really appreciate their humor and fun-loving approach.

If the Goat is fearful of setting forth into the world to make his or her fortune alone, the very energy that Monkey diffuses will give the Goat courage and boost a sluggish ego. No excuse the Goat finds for not participating in the rat race will be sufficient. The Monkey will always find a way to encourage the reluctant Goat and teach him or her how to better face the possibility of failure or betrayal. The benevolent Monkey has a secret plan. (Monkeys are not always perfectly open about their feelings.) Monkey thinks that if Goaty can prove himself professionally, he or she will gain self-confidence, squelch his pessimism, and brave it alone. Although the Monkey is no fool, this is a fool's errand. The Goat may seem to be making progress toward standing alone, but is really being propped up by the Monkey's encouraging belief that the Goat can do it. If Monkey pulls the applause meter plug, Goat will go into instant decline.

As time goes along, the Monkey realizes that as the Goat's life partner, he or she is in charge of the Goat's general morale—for the rest of their days! Monkey finds this prospect not only worrisome, but boring beyond words. And Monkey hates to be confined. Yes. Monkey loves Goat. But Goat's growing dependence on Monkey may become an addiction that the Monkey cannot abide maintaining. A good therapist would help define things here.

Despite a strong physical attraction, your sexual life will be a bit slow getting started. Monkeys aren't exactly the most romantic creatures alive, and Goats are. Goats are sensitive, gentle, and receptive in bed. They love sentimental music, all-night cuddling, and petting. Monkeys love sex, too. But they do tend to be less moon in June and more getting down to business in the act of love. There is a healthy gymnastic tone to the Monkey's lovemaking and there is always lots of it. Goats might be very sensual. But they are more interested in protracted bouts of languorous lovemaking than in flinging garments about the room three times a day and getting the show on the road quickie style. Over time, you will work these things out between you and the sex will improve immeasurably. Goats know how to soften up even the most agile and nervous of Monkeys.

Should you get over some of your hurdles and decide to stay together for a lifetime, you ought to have children. In your case, it will cement you as a couple. Goats are natural nurturers and they feel very confident raising kids. Monkeys are not always terrific at nurturing, so here we see a balance between your strengths emerging. It would be wise to hatch yourselves an Ox or Pig child first. Then you might want to have yourselves a feisty little

Dragon or Tiger, or even a Rooster kid. These last three will liven up your household for sure.

Goat with Rooster

Goats and Roosters do not find eternal happiness together. They are very, very different, both in attitude and ideals. Their relationship could be improved considerably if their occidental astrological signs were particularly harmonious—such as Scorpio/Rooster and Pisces/Goat, or Virgo/Goat and Sagittarius/Rooster. The problems would also diminish if Rooster's career involved travel, leaving the Goat at home to a slower pace more suited to the Goatly nature. In general, this is not a good match.

Goats like to be home in a safe place alone with family or pets—or both—free within secure boundaries to find ways to be creative and to produce artistic works, working outside the rigid Rooster's routine structures and guidelines. Roosters are extremely industrious people who cannot tolerate laziness or lack of industry on the part of members of their entourage. Roosters work hard for their money, scratching a living out of nothing and feeling strongly (even crankily) that they are always working too hard for what little profit they reap. Roosters never feel they have enough time off, enough leisure to read or travel or do "what Rooster wants." Hence the Rooster's view of the languorous Goat, who tends to loll about quite a lot at odd hours seeming to do nothing at all except dream and moon and "be creative, " is not always flattering. "Why," thinks the industrious Rooster person, "am I the only one who works around here?" Moreover, being known for candor, the Rooster person might simply ask the Goat partner, "When, pray tell, do you think you will be getting a job?"

The brusque remark is certain to break the Goat's tender little heart. To rebut the Rooster's sharp comment, Goat may ask Rooster to sit down and discuss these heady matters more in depth, trying to help the Rooster understand that a Goat's way of approaching life and work are not necessarily like the Rooster's, that Goats need to take their time to muster strength and courage. Goats don't just go out and get a *job*, for heaven's sake! Roosters hate discussing their emotions, have very firm and clear ideas about how life works or doesn't, and really feel such probings are a lot of dilatory flimflam.

You two are stylistically different. Goat wants a quiet house in the country safely tucked away in the hills. Rooster wants up-to-the-wattle involvement in the world's activities, travel exotic places, knowledge of oddball cultures, and experimentation. Goats float. Rooster wants to fly. Two very different ways of moving over the earth are at work here. How can such polarized differences be reconciled? I am not sure they can.

Money becomes an issue almost immediately. Goats can only produce when the field is fertile under their hooves. It's not that Roosters mind providing for Goats if they are in love; Roosters are really very generous. But although the Rooster works very hard and long hours, money doesn't come easily. Peaks and valleys in cash flow are the story of the Rooster's life. This fact alone turns the Goat into a nervous wreck, as not knowing where the next nickel is coming from is enough to give a Goat apoplexy. So you will never be in accord about money. If Rooster's having a hard time earning more, the Goat will be paralytically undone as to really be unable to get a job—out of fear of failure or success or some such pessimistic mindset.

You may end up being able to live together and have a regular sex life, but I am not sure how. The Rooster will no doubt do the falling in love here. Goats are gigantically attractive and loving people. The sex will be great so long as the Rooster is head over claws in love. Goats are wonderful in bed. But when things mature a bit and they begin to chat about their pasts and their future, Rooster will discover that Goat is very self-centered, set in his or her ways, and totally unable to keep his or her word. This last is totally against everything the Rooster believes in, as is the Goat's exceptionally relative fidelity. Sex will soon wilt as disagreements abound.

No amount of ideally suited children could undo the tension in this couple's household.

Goat with Dog

On the face of it, these two have trouble getting along. Dog is snappish, direct, cynical, and sarcastic. Goat is ultra-sensitive and easily wounded and angered. How these two can reconcile personalities is more important than how they will reconcile character. Underneath the superficial behavior that both exhibit are two very sensitive, sensual and sweet-natured folks. Goat has much to offer Dog in the strategy and householding department, while Dog can indeed serve Goat well as an example of lofty ideals and what to do about them. But first, they have to pierce the wall of superficial misunderstanding between them.

In the beginning, Dog will be attracted to the Goat's beauty and soft nature. As Dogs are often harsh, dry, and slightly cranky at the world, when a beautiful, serene, easygoing Goat comes loping along, Dog feels that he or she can either save Goat from harm or else (if the Dog is enlightened) learn from him or her.

Here again, because we are dealing with two ultra-sensitive people, their Western astrological signs will matter greatly. Suppose, for example, that the Dog is a laid-back Libra who meets up with a seemingly naive and easily hurt Sagittarius/Goat. Here we have a foundation on which to build a very solid relationship. Under the steady influence of the truly strong but soft Sag/Goat person, Libra/Dog will soon be swayed to lower his or her guard, melt together with the sexy sweetness of the Sag/Goat, and slowly but surely relinquish what was only a stance of suspicion and misanthropy in the first place. Dog learns to trust Goat in this scenario—but only after many moons of watching Goat operate his or her special magic on the world.

Dogs don't usually confront much. When they do, it's because they have been piqued into action by something very irritating indeed. Goat doesn't confront much either—except when protected by Dog and in the name of Dog's welfare. Then Goat can be a genius at confrontation—more subtly—manipulation. Goats must feel safe and well fed in order to be happy. Dogs must protect and provide to feel happy. If you get the drift here, these two are (underneath the surface personalities) meant for each other.

Interestingly, the slightly hermitlike Dog existence is very much threatened by the swoony, dreamlike Goat's presence. The Goat insinuates him or herself into the Dog's inner sanctum by subtle means such as moving in clothing in paper bags and forgetting to go back home some evenings. In time, Goat will be the Dog's live-in houseguest and eventually the Dog's spouse. It's inevitable. Goats are so loving and clever, and Dogs are sitting puppies for the Goat's nonviolent strategy.

Money? Well, it's the Dog who will provide the money, but the Goat (especially in the frugal Dog's presence) will be a more economical character, thanks to the beloved Dog. You watch. These two will end up having a very happy life. It doesn't take therapy, either. It just takes time and lots and lots of compassionate love.

Speaking of love, there is a deep, enduring passion to be developed here as well. The Dog may need some encouragement to get started, as Dogs fear intimacy and long to find just the right person before they will entrust their real sexuality to an outsider. Goats are easy about sex. They like to be giving and open in matters sexual and will seduce the Dog inch by inch toward a long-lasting passion for which the Dog will be eternally grateful and content.

Children? Oh, yes. You should have kids. If you marry and settle into your private niche home, where all is lovely and glows with Goatly good taste in objects and fabrics, furnishings, and carpets, you may want to wait a year or so until Doggy gets ready for parenthood. Then hatch a couple of little ones, such as a terrible Tiger or a merry Monkey baby. You would also get along beautifully—perhaps best—with a roly-poly Piglet.

Goat with Pig

This little Piggy, you will recall, goes to market. Moreover, at market, this little Piggy makes gobs of money. Then this little Piggy usually sets this little Piggy up in some glorious penthouse or country palace (or both), and from there begins to look for someone to share all this market value with. And who better than with the alluring Goat? Piggy is a sensual sort who loves to bask in the arms of Love and often cavorts amidst bevies of handsome gents or breathtakingly beautiful ladies. With a Goat partner, Pig will gallantly offer every goody from candy to money to dinners in Hong Kong and houses on the moon. It's Piggy's generous way. Piggy loves to be loved, and hates to say no to someone he or she cares for.

Piggy is also extraordinarily tolerant, good-natured (except when particularly badly misused), open-minded, and intelligent. Piggy admires culture, animal husbandry, ecological crusades, and the arts in every form. Piggies surround themselves with symbols of simple authenticity, gold and silver jewelry, real gemstones, and the best-quality leathers and silks. Despite its occasional jovial departures into bold-faced ribaldry, Piggies have natural class.

Now Pigs cannot bear junk in their lives. But they do (almost more than is good for them) suffer fools gladly. Pig is always the one in the family who ends up taking in old Uncle Joe or Aunt Gladys, who could never make a real living out in the world. Pigs are the kids who stay with their aging parents until the bitter end, no matter what. They are good, loyal, kind, and sharp as tacks. They are also hugely jealous and possessive.

Where does Goat come into the Pig's picture? Well, Goats are born lovers, creators, and artists. Goats shouldn't really be forced to go out and work in hierarchies or struggle uphill against tough odds. Goats should, however, be forced to play the piano, take drawing lessons, or learn to sculpt or write poetry. Once they have acquired their craft (and it might be the craft of selling insurance), Goats should try to be settled and tethered in a fertile field or home environment where they can ply their creative pursuit in the utmost of security and safety. Lucky Goats will be sponsored by their mates, adopted and cosseted and cared for. In return for this care, Goats give lots of love, bushels of sweetness, brilliant ideas, creative projects, excellent householding skills, and an uncommon sense of strategy in moments of crux.

Who is best equipped to fill the bill for Goat? Why, Piggy of course! Piggy is the lover, live-in supporter, and appreciator of the mannered Goat's admirable talents. Piggy supplies the security. Goat supplies an ample lap into which Piggy can throw buckets of golden trinkets and silken fabrics, then lie down and wallow in them till the cows come home. It's a perfectly lovely relationship. Pig and Goat make up a couple guaranteed to survive the rigors and vicissitudes of marriage, children, and family squabbles, and truly can vow to stay together until death splits them up.

Problems? Maybe one or two. If Goat is true to form, he or she will undoubtedly be tempted to stray from the path of perfect fidelity. It's the nature of the beast. A second, more serious, issue might arise if Piggy suddenly loses the family fortune: Goat would fall apart. And trust me, a freaked-out poverty-stricken Goat is not somebody a bankrupt Piggy wants to spend any time with. So Piggy, if you love a Goat, stay rich.

Finances? You have the picture already. Pig takes care of Goat. Goat gets a generous allowance and no exaggerated overdraft privileges.

The sex between Goats and Pigs is transcendent. Heaven. Your sensitivities are so completely allied that each motion and gesture of the act of love between you moves, without prompting or discomfort, toward the ultimate goal of melting together as one. Better still, the more you two do it, the, better it gets. Your love is a gift from Mother Nature.

Allow some time at the beginning of your marriage to establish your gorgeously appointed household. Spend some years enjoying the glow of harmony that surrounds you. Travel together. Then settle into your bucolic abode and have slews of kids. Your best bets for maintaining the desired level of peacefulness of your home will be Cat children, Dog kids, Baby Oxen and ... why not? Other Pigs and Goats, too.

MONKEY

Taken to the extreme, all of our qualities can become frailties. Some of us are generous to a fault, which can be wasteful. Good communicators can also be blabbermouths. Nurturing parents can smother their children. Fortunately, free will allows us to balance the positive and negative sides of our character .The Merry Monkey was born:

POSITIVE | NEGATIVE

inventive | tricky

loving | smothering

intelligent | smarty-pants

zany | neurotic

autonomous | isolated

faithful | possessive

💘💘💘 Monkey with Monkey

This couple will enjoy each other's company, make each other laugh, and generally form a duo whose plans and projects distinguish them as people of real quality who do not waste their time.

Monkeys are ever so sociable. And they love action. They are busily engaged in being busily engaged. They live to attend fascinating theater productions, see all the new films as they come out, read the news every single morning, involve themselves in charitable pursuits, travel to visit friends and relatives, take courses in exotic subjects, and delve into studies of everything from Creole cooking to Victorian violins. How, we wonder, does a Monkey couple ever manage to stay home to spend time together?

Fact is, they don't. The above-mentioned Monkey activities are frequently accomplished solo or with friends outside the Monkey couple's. There is nothing of the clinging vine in the true Monkey personality. As much as Monkeys adore having a mate who serves as an anchor and guarantees procreation, they do not need a mate with whom to sit home by the fireside or to accompany them to events or to do chores with. Monkeys are basically independent creatures who—luckily—for the survival of this couple—do not really require the full-time presence of their mate to be happy.

Monkeys, moreover, do not care a whit about social protocol, useless rules of status, snobbery, or class distinction. Naturally, this laissez-faire point of view contributes to the harmony in a Monkey/Monkey couple. Nobody in this relationship loses sleep over keeping up with the Joneses or down with the Smiths. One can even say that Monkeys revel in their eccentricities. They live very much according to their own philosophy, and to hell with the way some people may feel things might be done differently or better. Monkeys raise their kids to care only about basic important things like love and loyalty and morality, hard work and being clever, as the keys to a solid future. They will rarely teach them about adhering to strict regulations, as they would much rather encourage free-thinking than imprison their offspring in society's straitjacket.

This lack of concern for tradition and custom is obvious in the Monkey couple's home decor too. You might be surprised to find that they have an antique white-porcelain bidet with golden swan faucetry plunked smack in the middle of their living room. Why? just because Monkeys like it that way. Monkeys are professionally weird and amusing folks. A pair of them is double the fun.

Financially, you two simians might encounter some difficulty. Neither of you has the least regard for organizing accounts and keeping records. The very idea of doing paperwork when you could be attending a forum on rock music or studying trapeze artistry seems an imposition of the worst order. Most of your disputes will emanate from the messes caused by your mutual refusal of fiscal tasks. There is no future in fighting about it. Neither of you can win. Hire yourselves a good bookkeeper and (if you both hate housework as well) get somebody to come in and keep order at home. Your common energies are best spent earning and learning in the outside world where your talents are truly appreciated.

You both adore having sex. And, as luck would have it, you adore having that same sex with each other. Monkeys are the sex partners who put down their how-to book on newspaper origami or kite-flying in Tibet, cuddle their partner for a few secs, and get down to the business at hand. Then, of course, as Monkeys are notoriously healthy addicts of the gymnastics of lovemaking, they go at it for hours on end, leaping from position to position with remarkable and endless imagination. A tiny shadow of infidelity may lurk here. If one (or both) of you cannot resist the lure of some siren or other, have the decency to play your cards with the utmost of discretion.

If you have children (which I heartily advise you do), try to aim for their births in the Rat, Dragon, or Ox years. If you manage this complex feat, your family life will be full of just the sort of frolic and merriment mixed with hard work and serious problem-solving that you both are already so justly famous for.

♥ *Monkey with Rooster*

Although each of you is admirable in his or her own right, as a pair, you make an unlikely combination. Monkeys and Roosters are doomed, I fear, to remain very good (but fractious) friends after a brief, not-so-blazing affair.

First off; Monkeys are independent, freewheeling, and terribly clever at everything from making friends and influencing people to mastering skills and troubleshooting the most complicated of human endeavors. Monkeys are mostly jolly and upbeat. Monkeys don't like to be confined or kept in check. They also hate convention and deplore the very existence of show-offyness. Sometimes Monkeys can be also slippery, and they are definitely more libertarian than the average soul.

You, Rooster, are naturally vain and sometimes even bossy and supercilious. Despite an outward air of eccentricity or kookiness, deep down, you cling for your very life to the bounds of social tradition. You care a lot about how you look. You do not in the least mind being confined—in fact, it pleases you to feel secure in a safe relationship with a companionable mate who stays home when you do or who goes traveling with you in tow. You are always true to your word and firmly disapprove of anyone who is not.

When the two of you get down to the business of living together, the fireworks commence almost immediately. You are almost always of two minds on every issue. Rooster wants elegant furnishings from the latest showcase, a wardrobe of finery fit for the king or queen of formality, travel to wonderfully settled countries where people eat glorious victuals that take weeks to hunt and prepare laboriously over fires made of rare woods only found in the forests of northern Bulgaria. Monkey wants a showcase of gadgetry, an occasional work of art that gets hung crazily next to a child's crayoned scribble drawing, a wardrobe of comfortable, serviceable clothing that will go everywhere without wrinkling, and is happy eating snacks or fast food on the run.

If you two are attracted to each other in the first place, it is likely to be due to an extremely harmonious occidental compatibility. A Capricorn/Rooster male, for example, might be very turned on by a Leo/Monkey. Roosters are conservative in the extreme and can even seem a bit tight-lipped lipped and severe. But the rigidly ambitious Capricorn is naturally keen on the bright, shiny, summery Leo character—who, as a Monkey person, is unusually lighthearted. Here, the Monkey is charismatic enough to lift the Rooster's sometimes wintry spirits and save the day for the relationship. There are other exceptions akin to the Leo/Capricorn duo (see the Western astrology section) where the harmonious rapport between two signs can override all logical caveats and smooth out wrinkles before they get started.

We are now entering a sexual desert where the pair of you will cohabit in utter disharmony unless you manage to iron out your problems. Please don't imagine that having a child or two would help settle your differences. Where I come from, that kind of thinking is called "denial."

½ Monkey with Dog

Here is a real opportunity for long-term harmony. You, Monkey, are a born problem-solver. Given a dicey situation to ponder, a tricky contract to decode, or a nasty divorce to work out for someone, Monkey comes up with just the ticket we need to extricate ourselves from even the thorniest dilemma. Here are a few other things that Monkeys are famous for: neurotic behavior in crises, refusal to grow up, craving for an audience to entertain, need to be on the loose, and an ever-so-slight tendency to err and stray from the marital couch.

You, Doggy, are a different kettle of beans altogether. If you were a sailor, you would beg your commanding officer to put you on twenty-four hour watch. Guarding and protecting, keeping safe and detecting BS in any and all situations and people, is your forte. You just about never let down the sides of your own crib—even to let the mailman in. You trust nothing or nobody because you believe that basic treachery lurks everywhere in all of us—even yourself. You can be snappish too, growling about incidents of no seeming importance—just because you sense that something is fishy or you got a "tilt" message on your famous *crapola* meter. Of course, as a Dog, you are also dogged and determined, hardworking, mostly cheerful - loyal, faithful, and true.

The best thing about you two is that Monkey doesn't care much about causes and saving the world, but Dog cares intensely and wishes to engage in all variety of revolutionary activity. As it's all the same to Monkey as to who governs and wins or loses, he or she will gladly do much of the Dog's problem-solving. Monkey will let Doggy think up the schemes to overthrow Disneyworld or undo the Romanian adoption system, then leap into action untying the knottiest of problems and facilitating Doggy's path to righteousness. You are basically a great team—once you work out your differences.

When first the two of you come together, the attraction is likely to be physical. The somewhat awkward Dog picks up on the wiry Monkey's agility and is seduced by it. The Monkey gets turned on by Dog's natural sincerity and candor Monkeys and Dogs are equally attractive, yet not in the least artificial. A strong sexual tug is sure to be felt by both whenever they meet. So here, the romantic basis exists for at least the beginning of a passionate affair. However, later on, when the plot begins to grow dense with the realities and vicissitudes of coupledom, you, Monkey, begin to notice an occasional baring of teeth in your regard. Whereas you, Doggy, cannot help but regret the occasional absences of a frazzled Monkey mate who "needs some space." In real life, Monkey people are Cat fanciers—not Dog lovers. So your issues lie the fact that Dog rather enjoys the joined-at-the-hip type of relationship that many successful couples often aim for, and Monkey deplores the very idea of being tied down, caged, or clung to by anybody at all—especially a Dog!

But these problems can be worked out with some good therapy and a lot of mutual honesty and support. Monkey must learn to tolerate the Dog's need for constant companionship, and Dog must try to understand that just because Monkey races all over creation he or she is not running away—just taking a break.

Finances ought not to cause you trouble. Monkey might be on the frivolous side for Dog's taste. You will have vastly different tastes in furnishings and clothes—but you can compromise so that everyone is satisfied. As you grow more mature, your friendship deepens and ages gracefully. Compassion becomes strongest between you with time.

Sex, as I said above, is terrific with Monkey and Dog people. There's a lot of purely physical mutual attraction to start with and, as this relationship develops its own seasoned personality you that your kind of high-quality sex, like good wine, improved with age. Besides, the lithe Monkey's body always appeals to the somewhat chunkier Dog, who (if you recall) was attracted by those long muscles in the first place.

Oh yes. Do have some kids. Monkeys love entertaining and being entertained. Dogs make order wherever they live. The best choices children's birth years will be dauntless Dragon, fearless Tiger, headstrong Horse and—why not a sweet-natured Goat child to add artistic flair?

❤❤❤❤ *Monkey with Pig*

Lively and cheerful together, these two people simply adore each other's company. Monkey serves as guidance counselor/sweetheart, while Piggy trots out and earns them a handsome small fortune so they can both travel, buy real estate, invite all their friends to dinner, hire servants and nannies, accumulate oodles of jewels and artwork, build a rare books collection and fill the shelves in the music room with hordes of classical

CDs, stock the fridge with the finest champagnes, and drive cars fit for the most elegant of fat cats. Monkeys admire Pigs and vise-versa. Hand in hand, they jog through their life together, having a glorious time lavishing love and affection on one another and letting the good times roll.

Monkey and Pig are well aware that every day is not Christmas. They are both industrious and clever-minded. Portly Pig is less physically active than the agile Monkey, who never stops rushing through the day, exercising to keep in shape, ordering the help about, and making certain that not a single film or theatrical production goes through town without Monkey's attendance at least one performance. Pig is more culturally occupied. Pig likes to sit quietly in a comfortable room with a glass of excellent cognac or vintage Bordeaux and maybe some Belgian chocolates, absorbing the music of Vivaldi or Mozart, while musing about his or her next huge financial coup and contemplating a recent art acquisition.

Luckily, neither the Pig nor the Monkey is a clinging-vine type. Pig is content to lead his or her own existence, wheeling and dealing over gargantuan meals, playing at farming in the country château, or rebuilding a wing of the manor house they bought last year with the proceeds from that sale of that Renoir neither of them ever really liked. Monkey is a free-agent type, whose main pain is being confined or smothered.

Perhaps when this couple first hooks up, Pig will try to overdo the romance a bit—sending too many flowers, inviting Monkey to participate in every voluptuous occasion known to man and woman, and even flying him or her about in first-class air seats. But it won't be long before Monkey lets Piggy know (gently but firmly) that if Piggy sends one more remembrance or offers another freebie, it may drive practical Monkey away. Monkey wants not to be assailed by love. Pig catches on quickly to that fact and learns readily to let Monkey go on with the life on the side he or she brought into the relationship.

In business, you make fabulous partners. Pig smells a good opportunity. Monkey sniffs at it, turns it over, examines it, and then says, "If I were you,

I'd let this one go. Too complicated. The guy's not for real." Piggy, who is a genius at finding big money in business, is nonetheless often very naive. Monkey sets Piggy straight every time, As Pig is not one to carry around a burden of false pride, he or she learns early on to listen to Monkey's wise counsel and to take heed without passing Go or trying to collect the $2 million he or she just about lost shady character whom the credulous Pig never reckoned had a tricky bone in his body. Monkey can be trickier than any trickster. This sometimes bothers the scrupulous Pig. But when Monkey's craftiness serves both of their purposes, Pig learns to accept that a measure of guile is sometimes a necessity for their joint survival.

If Pig is careful not to lose his or her purest ideals and Monkey keeps them both out of real trouble, this duo is probably destined to cash in their art collection at age forty and retire to a glamorous estate in Normandy. Monkey won't have to do any paperwork in this marriage. Pig will have long since hired a full-time live-in accountant to handle the figures. Essentially, Pig lets the Monkey feel free to roam about and play at life while Pig stays in the barnyard reading up on antiques and collectibles.

Oh, yes. Do have children. Monkeys get along with everybody—especially Dragons and Rats. Pigs and Dragons get on well too. Pigs actually prefer the company of Goat and Cat people. For a truly harmonious household you really ought to try having a feisty Dragon first. Then you can try for a gentle Goat kid and a cozy little kitten as follow-ups.

ROOSTER

Taken to the extreme, all of our qualities can become frailties. Some of us are generous to a fault, which can be wasteful. Good communicators can also be blabbermouths. Nurturing parents can smother their children. Fortunately free will allows us to balance the positive and negative sides of our character. The resilient Rooster was born:

POSITIVE | NEGATIVE

forthright | belligerent

brave | foolhardy

enthusiastic | excitable

tenacious | obdurate

adventurous | fanatical

meticulous | picky

Rooster with Rooster

My feeling about the two of you trying to marry (or even to get on as a loving couple) is mostly negative because neither of wants to give an inch where imposing your will is concerned. If Rooster A wants to bake chocolate chip cookies, you can be certain Rooster B has decided to make fudge. If Rooster A chooses to see a movie about dancing giraffes, then Rooster B is going to seek out *Kung Fu goes to Hollywood* and insist on racing out to see that. Rooster A wants orange juice? Then Rooster B will develop a sudden craving for cranberry.

Two fertile and obstinate Rooster minds crawling with talent and creativity will not only think up varied and sundry occupations; each will firmly and resolutely believe that his or her choice of occupation is best. In a normally felicitous Rooster relationship with a sign whose character blends with the cocky ways of our feathered friend, the Rooster's choices almost invariably jibe with the other person's tastes. Why? Because Roosters mostly take up with people who let them rule the roost.

As friends, there's almost nothing better than a pair of Roosters. Mutual interest and synchronized teamwork help each Rooster to feel solidarity for the other. Moreover, Roosters are not very trusting—except with other Roosters. So if you are a Rooster, go right ahead and make friends with your fellow Roosters. But unless you are a *very* laid-back, passive, and unassuming Rooster, stay out of Rooster beds or you are liable to get "henpecked" to oblivion.

Of course, if you have taken up with a Rooster person and are even married to a co-Rooster, I suppose I should try to help you find a way to get along better. For example, you might see a therapist or go to a marriage counselor, try Rolfing or Reiki or identical twin running shoes—but frankly, I don't think any of the above will help. A pair of Roosters is more stubborn than one Rooster. A pair of Roosters is bossier than one Rooster. A pair of Roosters is doubly conservative, feistier, harder to please, and nitpickier than one single Rooster who has teamed up with, say, a slick and slithery Snake partner, an industrious plodding Ox person, or even a reckless but charming Tiger who takes the Rooster's snide remarks with a grain of sand and blithely tosses them back over his left shoulder. Roosters can also marry Horses because they admire their outspokenness and hardy work ethic. Roosters can even take up with Dragons occasionally or plod along with certain kinds of Cat/Rabbits. But forget about Rooster with Rooster love partnerships—they do not work. Roommates, yes. Long-lasting lovers, nix.

The sex will be tepid at best. You will notice that both of you are rather shy and also quite hectic about sex. Can you think of a worse scenario for the sex act than a timid quickie in the vestibule between the cheese and the salad courses? I can't.

Who should handle the money, how to decorate your home and what sort of kids you might want are irrelevant here. I advise against Rooster marriage because it's awful. *C'est tout!*

½ *Rooster with Dog*

I see you two falling easily in love and falling very clumsily right out when things start to get complicated. Roosters don't like to discuss their private selves very much. They prefer to move along in a kind of jet-propelled stiff-upper-lip British *carry on* way, plowing through life, getting stuff done, and being effective and efficient and successful or not—but they don't ask themselves or others too many probingly personal questions or wonder how the depths of their partner's psyche is faring. And Dogs never whine about what's going on deep down inside. Dogs may feel perfectly wretched. But they ain't gonna tell you about it until they are at the precipice suicide stage.

Dogs, as guards and watchers of the flock, like to be put to the test of just how hard they can work and slave and be loyal and faithful (and often feel very sorry for themselves in the bargain). Rooster and Dog get along.

Except about deep stuff. Each, for their own personal reasons, keeps secrets from the other. So, for a few years—while everybody is still on good behavior and only personality count, Rooster/Dog marriage can thrive.

But when one day Dog finds out that Rooster is not being honest about some extracurricular sexual encounters or twisty-turny business deals, the poop hits the ventilator. Dogs can put up with almost any pain—except disloyalty. Not only do they eschew disloyalty in their own lives, but Dogs hate seeing other people cheat on their friends, their mothers, dads—whatever. Dogs are forgiving about most things. But they cannot forgive treason. Dog mates are particularly critical about the superficial and can be downright hurtful when it comes to speaking their minds about how they feel you are treating an outsider. But the way *they* treat outsiders seems not to be one of their main considerations. And they certainly don't want any flak from their mate about their behavior. So there is a similarity of critical, acerbic style between these two that explains the original mad-about-you love tug.

Of course, the trick to staying together for this couple is obvious. It's called Talking Things Through. In fact, between Roosters and Dogs, therapy, talking things out, and getting all the cards face up on top of the table is the only solution. Neither of you is likely to fess up to his or her inner fears and tears without being forced to sit down before a third party and rap it out. So if you want to save this couple, do it.

Where money is concerned, should you find it possible to stay together, at first, you will both try to take over the finances and run them your way. That is, Dogs splurge when they're rich and budget when they're poor—being utterly successful at both and neither. And Roosters splurge when they're rich and then splurge when they're poor in hopes they will soon be rich again so they can splurge in peace. I advise you to keep all bank accounts separate except that one you use for household expenses. Rooster will want to buy the best-designed couches and spiffiest chairs to match. Roosters care a *lot* about how things look. Dogs will be happy with a simply designed couch they intend to have forever. And maybe some folding chairs.

How's the sex? Great. At first. Dogs are eager sex partners who really enjoy making the act happen. They can be a mite on the wham, bam, thank you ma'am side, but Dogs are teachable. Roosters? They love sex—period. Lots of sex and plenty more where that came from. Problem is ... Dogs and Roosters are both rather timid about baring their souls. As we all know, to maintain and deepen a long-lasting love relationship, it is urgently necessary to bare a bit more than one's incisors or prance eagerly about looking fetching. Here again, if you want things to get any better in the sex department, I advise counseling together to get some honesty going. Otherwise, soon Rooster will been seen in a darkened haunt with some unsavory character, and the Dog will be sniffing around for a good divorce lawyer.

How about kids? I would say yes if you have proven that you can open up to each other, stay together for over five years without separating, and have yourselves a pleasant cozy nest into which you will hatch these little Cockapooches. If you eventually do meet the above criteria, try to schedule your kids in Horse, Tiger, or Dragon years.

❤️❤️❤️❤️ *Rooster with Pig*

If you are the Rooster caught in the snuggly, warm, sensual hug of a Pig partner, I advise you to hang on with all your claws and never let go until death do you part. If, however, you are the Pig member of this couple, I advise you to listen up: Don't be too nice to this character you are about to promise your heart to, or the Rooster will take advantage of you. Roosters are fine people. They know how to work and are serious about their families' livelihoods. But they can be tough to deal with, irascible, and hard-nosed in business. Roosters are demanding as hell and they are extremely (no pun intended) pig-headed when it comes to changing their minds.

As you already know, Piggy, your biggest fault is your most valued quality. You really do not know how to say no loud and clear to anyone who asks you for a favor, a loan, a handout, a pardon, a cup of sugar, or a hand. Mind you, you are not too nice. You can, in fact, be very nasty. But you are too acquiescent. You surrender before you resist. You find excuses for any person who continually asks too much, who is always on the taking end of your kindly spirit. And then you give in some more. But you hardly ever defend yourself. Until it's too late. Then, before your warning light so much as flickers, you suddenly boil over, fly into a white rage, and scare the wits out of everybody in sight. Temper tantrums are your only method of expressing resistance to those who want too much from you.

Most Roosters not only demand too much of their partners, but they also despise witnessing fits of rage. Despite their occasionally outrageous appearance, Roosters are deeply conservative folks who do not like to make waves. Roosters sometimes admire outspokenness in others. But they are rarely, if ever, vociferous themselves. Imagine the fun when Piggy abruptly hits the ceiling because Rooster asked one more time if Piggy would mind cooking Thanksgiving dinner twice this year instead of once because Rooster's ex-mother-in-law is showing up. Fireworks! H-bombs! Exploding pumpkins! Piggy goes berserk with anger and throws the neighborhood into a public tizzy.

So, Pigs, take heed. Don't let Roosters get away with too much murder. And Roosters, take heed back. If you push a Pig too far, you are very likely to witness the outbreak of the third world war in the living room. Otherwise, the two of you get along swell.

Finances will not be a Problem as long as Pig gets to manage the money. For starters, Pigs attract wealth. Roosters have a way of scratching out a handsome living through awful hard work and subsequently losing their shirts through just as much hard work. Roosters always get back on their feet. But Pigs usually stay on their feet. So everything this pair of you own should be in Piggy's name. Of course, Pig gives Rooster a handsome allowance to squander at will on all manner of beautiful *stuff* with which to enhance the already gorgeously decorated golden-ensconced home that Pig has adorned so lavishly and into which guests throng for dinner party after dinner party of joyful conviviality.

Sex? But of course. The sex is fabulous between you two. Rooster is rather flinty and quick, but Piggy's gentle nature and soft touch tame the savage bird. One thing about Pig people is that they instinctively know how to smooth ruffled feathers. As Rooster's plumage is frequently a lot more than fluffed the wrong way, the physical comfort side of your relationship really works well. Pigs are rather greedy sexually. But then Roosters are Roosters, so it all proceeds without a hitch.

Babies? Oh, yes. Do have babies. Especially if Pig gets to be the mom. But even if Pig is not the female, Pig will be the mom anyway. Have yourselves an Ox child first. This behemoth of endurance and strength will be a terrific firstborn. Later on, when you have settled in with each other, have yourselves a Goat or a Snake child. These last two will be spoiled by both of you. But their sweetness will match your happiness to a fare-thee-well.

DOG

Taken to the extreme, all of our qualities can become frailties. Some of us are generous to a fault, which can be wasteful. Good communicators can also be blabbermouths. Nurturing parents can smother their children. Fortunately, free will allows us to balance the positive and negative sides of our character. The disquiet Dog was born:

POSITIVE | NEGATIVE

attentive | paranoid

well-meaning | intrusive

warmhearted | clinging

devoted | slavish

dutiful | servile

persistent | dogged

Dog with Dog

This relationship is shaky. Human Dogs are not classically attracted by other human Dogs because of their mutually abrasive personalities. One barks out snappy remarks at the other. The other replies with some caustic comment, and the fight is on. I truly cannot advise you two to go trotting off hand in hand into the sunset where you will build yourselves a household and family to live in perfect harmony forever. No way.

You can, however, be great friends and associates. Two Dogs will be twice as efficient, twice as wary, twice as loyal, and twice as humanistic as one. You two might open a business together, as one of you could always be counted on to watch over the store while the other travels or goes out selling or whatever. Working in tandem will build a tremendous trust between you. Neither of you will consider any task or any chore too drudgy, so sharing work will be a pleasure rather than a drag. Moreover, Dogs usually say what they feel like saying (*blurt* is the better word), so there will not be much pent-up emotions to create tensions and silent wars between a pair of working Dogs.

Where money is concerned, the pair of you will be equally reliable and honest. Whichever of you prefers to handle the finances should be elected do so. But if you would rather have joint custody of the business, then do that. Loyalty is everything to each of you. You are both faithful to the same cause, so it is unlikely that one of you will run off with the profits. Also, as a pair of devoted Dogs, your association and your business too will be capable of riding out the worst setbacks. You people are nothing if not dogged in your pursuit of a better life.

Your home will be cursed with that same sameness. Minimal furnishings and strict lines being the Dog's signature trait in decoration, I cannot promise much in the way of coziness or softly cushioned, charming households if they have been furnished by a pair of Dogs. Maybe Dogs who want to be married to each other should live in hotels—there would be less to bicker about. To be quite frank, disquieted Dogs are better off with anyone else than with more of the same.

It might happen that two Dog people would be attracted to each other for a purely sexual, genuinely passionate encounter. This would no doubt happen because your Western astrological configurations pulled you strongly at each other, so that the sexual need for each would override the customary nipping and growling that goes on between Pooches. For example, a Pisces/Dog who meets up with a Scorpio/Dog might well create some very strong sexual longings in the latter—especially if there is a broad generational difference. Or take a Capricorn/Dog who meets up with a Leo/Dog. Sparks? Yes. But attraction as well.

So lots depend on the individual charts here (see the Western astrology section for highly compatible signs). But whatever occurs (even if you do get married), it won't be an intensely happening sexual thing for the rest of your lives. If ever the sex is good between two Dogs, it's temporary. Otherwise, if you are to stick together for life, the sex will probably be quite boring. There is too much mutual criticism and inherent paranoia in a Dog/Dog relationship to keep your love affair afloat for long. A two-Dog marriage would drown in its own gloom and worry. Your native pessimism might be contagious to family and even to the whole entire neighborhood. I advise against this marriage because it's very difficult to succeed at.

Children? You must be joking.

💘💘💘💘 Dog with Pig

Dog and Pig are soul mates. They have many of the selfsame ideals: scrupulousness, hard work, belief in the value of family, and the nurturing of good solid friendships.

Both Dogs and Pigs hate lying and cheating and will gladly give up a job, or even a love affair, if it demands they engage in any shady dealings. The Dog sincerely believes that everyone is rotten to the core and must be watched carefully so they won't jump you in a dark alley. Pigs, on the other hand, are so credulous, tolerant, and indulgent that they often get snookered by people less pure of heart than they. Dogs rarely get snookered because they are on their guard up front about any and all people, old or new, who come down the pike.

So while the Pig is out hunting truffles, the Dog is watching over the home. What's more, the anxious, paranoiac Dog will snarl and even bite anyone who comes within a mile of the good Piggy. In fact, no matter their mutual pursuits, the Dog assumes the role of protector and never ceases reminding Piggy of all of life's pitfalls: "Mind that step. Pick up your feet now. Wear your woolly sweater." Of course, constant criticizing, nitpicking, and analyzing can drive the easygoing Pig a little bit bonkers. But then we did say that Pigs are tolerant, didn't we?

Somewhere in the bargain, Piggy has to take up some slack for the Dog. Pig does just that. Pigs know instinctively how to jolly up down-in-the-mouth, pessimistic Dogs by giving them delicious things to eat or taking them to a funny movie or inviting them to go dancing or help stomp some grapes for next year's wine. All of these activities delight the Dog, whose morbid preoccupations are never few and who appreciates all that Piggy does to make him or her laugh.

You can see for yourself that the easygoing, tolerant, yet strong-minded intellectual Pig character and the cynical, grouchy, meddlesome but adorable Dog character were meant to combine to create a fabulously balanced, loving couple. My advice is, go for it.

Who should handle the purse strings? I think either Piggy or Doggy can do that well. Dog will be much more practical-minded and even sometimes cranky about spending on frivolities. Besides, although Dog is teachable, the pooch doesn't care a wishbone for all those bronze sconces and gilt candelabra for which Piggy would kill. Dogs like to keep decoration minimal and spare of line. There will be much discussion about what gets spent on which piece of furniture and who gets to choose the color for drapes. Just look at it this way. The Dog will always want safe colors like beiges and grays, and organic materials like wood and stone. The Pig will invariably prefer peachy satin tones and rosy glow moiré wall treatments. Pigs like marble bathrooms, too. And you know those golden dolphin faucets? Those are definitely Pig accessories. Nice bit about these two is that they know how to compromise and will basically agree that finally authenticity is the most important aspect of any item of furnishing or clothing. So, bottom line, between the Pig and the Dog, money will be a mildly iffy issue, but as neither of these characters is dishonest or spendthrift or ruinously gamble-prone, finances can be managed between them.

Sex? Oh, the sex will be splendid! First of all, the bedroom will become a shrine to the act of love. Pigs simply adore everything trimmed and baroque, ruffly and curlicued. They often have canopy beds trimmed with the best lacy bedspreads and antique linens with satin pillows. How does Doggy take to this scrumptious sumptuousness? Well, we already know that Dogs are faithful to a fault. But they can also be extremely horny and eager to get down to the business of lovemaking. They might find Piggy's suffocating splendor just a tad overdone—but let's face it, what self-respecting breed of Dog would resist the chance to leap upon his or her lover in a huge comfortable love nest of a bed? Dog may think the whole thing a bit silly, but will probably keep still about it.

You may be so happy and peaceful as a couple that you will not want to tie yourselves down with kids. You are sure to have lovely homes, an excellent cultural life, and plenty of love to go around. If do have kids, your family harmony will be best served by a Goat child, a Horse, a Dragon, a Tiger cub, or any combination of the four.

PIG

Taken to the extreme, all of our qualities can become frailties. Some of us are generous to a fault, which can be wasteful. Good communicators can also be blabbermouths. Nurturing parents can smother their children. Fortunately, free will allows us to balance the positive and negative sides of our character. The compliant but stubborn Pig was born:

POSITIVE | NEGATIVE

sensible | hardheaded

sensual | raunchy

ingenious | naïve

caring | possessive

self-sacrificing | wimpy

virtuous | sanctimonious

❤️❤️❤️❤️ Pig with Pig

Here we have a felicitous match between two people whose mutual modus operandi is as similar as they are compatible with each other. Moreover, despite their similarities, there is sufficient variety of purpose and manner between two Pigs to provide them with a fine basis for a sound marriage complete with home and children, pets—the lot.

Mind you, Pigs don't have to fall in love with each other. They can also work well together in associative endeavors or charitable projects. They can initiate businesses or simply help each other out with their lives. But whatever they do, Pigs in tandem are dynamite—congenial, well-adjusted, and fun to be around.

Unlike other signs, where twinship often compounds difficult character traits, the blending of Pig with Pig somehow helps to round out angles and sand off some of life's sharper corners. With Pig couples, all is compromise, deals, concession, and tolerance. Each Pig allows the other to breathe. But then each Pig also knows very well how to get on the other Pig's case (gently, of course, but firmly) when he or she feels misused.

Also, in other couples where people are of like signs, life can become dull and predictably routine. I mean, stumble into a double-Oxen household and you'll see *tout de suite* what I mean. Double plod plod plod and drudge drudge drudge makes Ox a very dull boy indeed. But not so with Pigs. Pigs have a pleasant sort of life where things get done in an atmosphere of complicity and joy—yes, I said joy. Just writing about this coupling makes me want to be a Pig married to another Pig so I might wallow and roll about in the charm of it all.

Now, Pig couples are not perfect. Far from it. They have some major troubles with temper tantrums, wherein one or the other or even both can manage just fine (without the Wolf's intervention) to huff and puff the whole house in. Pigs are ordinarily tolerant, loving, kindly, and giving. Pigs even have a hard time saying no to each other. When one Pig partner decides that he or she has had enough and will no longer surrender every last morsel of praise or compassion or indulgence to the other—those little Piggy eyes squint up tight, the mouth turns down, the voice grows shrill and louder until—thar she blows! The world is suddenly full of molten white Piggy rage of the purest sort. If you have any sense at all, you take shelter under a rock until it passes.

The second big Pig family problem is overeating. Pigs like to grow and buy and prepare food in large quantities for friends and family, which they then very often consume in just as large quantities themselves. In this particular instance, two Pigs are worse than one because if they are both enjoying the act of fattening up, there is nobody to ride herd on their caloric intake.

Money will never be a problem two Pigs. They both know how to work hard, make money, and invest it too. Moreover, a single Pig will attract wealth. Hence two Pigs magnetize twice as much cash. They also like the same things. Pigs accumulate art and art objects. They adore luxury and will surely have a silky, cushiony, comfortable home lined with books, full of the sounds of music of all types, overflowing with laughter and guests and cozy fireside chats. Pets will be more than welcome as well.

The sex, of course, is divine. Pigs are sensualists. Watch a Pig eat sometime. It's like dining with wolves. They dig in with their paws, and slurp and just *love* the very act of ingesting food. Same goes for sex. Pigs adore the act of love, know very well how to laugh and play at lovemaking. They are earthy lovers, unafraid of digging right in with both hands and feet for a good funky messy time of the whole shebang. At this part of life as well, two Pigs are definitely better than one.

Having children is a Pig's paradise. This couple should have as many as they want and can afford. Pigs are nurturing parents who know how to care for and educate their beloved offspring. But they also know about not smothering them too much, leaving them to their vices, and taking a backseat when the child needs to be first. Pig couples should have Goat kids, Cat kittens, and puppy Dogs. Pigs are so flexible that they can even learn how to calm the feistiest of Roosters and tame even the terriblest Tiger cub alive.

PART 2

Western Astrology Signs

ARIES

Taken to the extreme, all of our qualities can become frailties. Some of us are generous to a fault, which can be wasteful. Good communicators can also be blabbermouths. Nurturing parents can smother their children. Fortunately, free will allows us to balance the positive and negative sides of our character. Aries, the aggressive innocent, was born:

POSITIVE | NEGATIVE

brave | reckless

prominent | tyrannical

sincere | gullible

enthusiastic | overbearing

plucky | willful

curious | suspicious

Aries with Aries

A pair of Aries? In a poker game, maybe. But hardly in the same house. The full-tilt noise, conflict, and intense activity generated by the pair of you pioneering fire-sign creatures would demolish even the strongest of tethers. Let's say there is hope. But not much.

To ensure that your double-Aries couple will last more than a week and a half, you had better make certain at the outset that at least one of you has a gentle, good-natured Chinese sign to mitigate the harrowingly argumentative dynamic produced by your cohabitation. Aries don't like to be countered. They are *always* right. If both of you are born under this critically incisive sign, how can dissension not set in? Who is going to be the hero? Neither.

What's the trouble with two Aries falling smack in love, getting married in a roadside chapel by a quick-fix judge, and deciding to live flamingly ever after? Not only do Aries share a tendency to indulge in instant burning passion, they are both equally hotheaded. Tempers flare readily between two Aries. No matter how polite they may manage to appear, each will ultimately accuse the other of stepping on his or her territory, of vying for attention in social situations, of meddling with the tools in "my" workroom or messing with the paints in "my" studio? The Ram (get it?) butts in where less frantically eager signs would not dare to tread. And although Aries is a charming and generous character, he or she does not necessarily adore sharing toys.

Basically, you two Aries know that you are essentially selfish by nature and that each of you wants to be the one who shines in most relational situations. The competition for spotlights and hurrahs may very well spoil things early on. Take my advice. If you absolutely cannot keep your impulsive little hooves off each other, take the experimental road. Live together. Keep separate accounts and don't anyone give up any jobs just yet. Get a pleasant flat with space for both of you to work on your myriad projects, move in, and wait. Give yourselves a year. Make a pact to reassess at the end of twelve months. Then, if it seems to be working and both of you are happy, write yourselves another year's contract. After three years of relatively harmonious living together, I'd say you can safely take the marriage leap.

Money could become a problem between two Aries in love. If one Aries is a tolerant, easygoing, multitalented, and compliant Aries/Pig and the other is a tradition-bound Aries/Cat who flees conflict, the double-Aries match could bounce along nicely. Pigs and Cats love refinement. Aries spunk will help these folks move along rather than sit around in their châteaux eating bonbons and admiring their Louis XV armoires. (See the Chinese astrology section for some more feasible combinations.)

As subtlety and nuance are unknown to Aries, there will probably not be a moment's hesitation on either part about leaping into the hay when first you first meet. You are decidedly sexy people. But you are usually not inspired by the anticipation of recital lah-dee-dahs such as candlelight dinners or long-winded romantic palaver. Foreplay, for Aries, is of the "Me Tarzan, you Jane" school of seduction. Mind you, most of Aries' previous partners will, at some time, probably complained about their brusqueness and resisted the Aries' bam-over-the-sink-you-go-m' love approach. So when two Aries do find each other attractive and blast off without so much as a weather check, it may seem somewhat of a relief to both not to have to suffer the *longueurs* of endless planned sex with moony, emotional Cancers or deep, dark Scorpios.

Children? Maybe. But only after five years of life as a couple in a home with all the necessary harmony for raising a family. When you do it, make yourselves a cuddly Gemini baby, whose sunny jokes will keep you in stitches, or go for a sunny Leo child, whose pure majesty will thrill you both for life. Steer clear of Aquarian children … you will make each other miserable without half trying.

Aries with Taurus

Aries sails freewheeling into Taurus's life out of practically nowhere, instantly sleeps with him or her, and before Taurus can ascertain which variety of lightning has struck, moves bag and baggage into the Taurus's cozy comfortable household and world.

At first, the reserved, somewhat countrified Taurean is struck dumb, amazed by Aries' dispatch, dizzied by Aries' incessant activity. How, Taurus wonders, still reeling, am I to deal with this invasive yet charming human who values action over any other human endeavor? You, Aries, will be content to note that the Taurus you have fallen in with provides exactly the sort of security you have been seeking. Didn't you always fancy living in a solid house with an earthy soul whose ability to create a real *home* makes you feel safe? (And who can perhaps even keep you from wandering off?) Taurus is a homebody. Moreover, he or she makes glorious love to you and seems content with your brand of instant intimacy. Taurus can cook, which leaves you free to tinker in your workshop, invent new gadgets, and refinish the bits of old furniture you find in the dump.

Next comes the hard part: the part about freedom of movement, range of friendships tolerated, and the especially dicey part about who gets to spend whose money on what. Aries wants to fly about the world at will and whim, without explanation. Of course, Aries is not plotting to run away. Aries hardly ever plots—about anything. Aries acts. Aries moves. Aries reacts. Taurus, however, is a static, introspective type who does ponder every tiny centimeter before setting one foot ahead of the other. In the end, Taurus wonders how Aries can be so *doggone* impetuous, thoughtless, and lacking in depth. Aries, irked by Taurus's deliberate ways, sighs in exasperation, "Why does my Taurus lover have to plan for forty days and forty nights before driving to the corner for hamburger?"

What's worse for the Taurus side of this duo is that Aries drags in strays. Aries has a million *friends* and Taurus wouldn't give you so much as a stick of gum for one of them. Taurus, on the other hand, will be likely to have three or four very dear, very old friends who spend evenings at home chatting, watching TV, and telling old jokes that everybody has heard a hundred and six times before. Aries, always generous, may invite the crowd along for a barbecue, and when the hot dogs run out will not hesitate to invade the Taurus's larder *de luxe* and drag out the smoked salmon, caviar, and champagne that the Bull was saving for a future joke-telling session with old cronies. Aries' pals may be in paradise. But Taurus is not amused.

Because of these basic differences of rhythm and style, bickering ensues. And one day, when Taurus is fed up being called *stodgy* by the airily confident Aries, the Bull simply leaves quietly by the back door, having plotted well ahead with a crusty old lawyer friend all the details of who will get what when the divorce comes through. Aries, never a master of foresight, stands gaping at the shipwrecked union, confused, misunderstood—and very broke.

In this relationship, Taurus is definitely the more passive *lovee*. A laid-back Taurus enjoys the spontaneous passion, revels in the rapid-fire sensuality and gobble-you-up approach of the Aries. Basically, Taurus is conservative and prefers not to have to make advances or seduce possible partners. Taurus doesn't mind doing the cooking or tending the flock, but prospecting for love is no self-respecting Taurean's idea of fun. On the strength of initial passion alone, these two may take up residence together. But the long run is really quite a long shot.

Having kids together might be fine for this couple, so long as they have proven they can live together in harmony for at least five years previous to giving birth. I advise Gemini children to help to lighten the sometimes fraught atmosphere in household. Or they might try having a Sagittarius or even a Scorpio baby. Throwing a bit of crisp wintry spirit into this excessively spring-like marriage wouldn't do any harm at all.

Aries with Gemini

I always used to give my unconditional blessing to Aries/Gemini relationships. There is something playful about their banter. Gemini and Aries have similar senses of humor and equally like to flirt. Their agile minds criss and cross, teasing each other's wits in a generous, antic way. My fellow astrologers do not, however, always agree with my enthusiasm for the couple's fate. Many claim that Aries' methodical, practical side eventually bores Gemini. Or else they say that Gemini's wild mood swings drive the straight-arrow Aries to distraction. To me, these do not constitute real hindrances to the Aries/Gemini couple. But they must surely be openly dealt with for the initial attraction to survive the rigors of a long-term live-in relationship. Cards on the table—openly and candidly discussing feelings—is paramount if this union is to succeed.

Nobody can influence an excessive Gemini, who often eats too much or too fast, rampages through parties playing the fool, or talks a blue streak when everyone's ears have been plugged by overkill for five full minutes. Aries, bless his or her innocent little heart, will certainly try to talk sense to a Gemini partner. But Gemini will always balk at Aries' attempts to civilize or tame his or her exorbitant behavior. But "Off my back!" is not a Gemini's normal riposte to Aries' kindly remarks. More likely, the wily Gemini will launch into a diatribe of denial worthy of a master neurotic. "Haven't you noticed, honey? Lately, I haven't been happy. I get these panic attacks and desperately need a chocolate éclair? It's like I cannot live without sugar these days ..." Gemini's excuses are so numerous and fanciful that Aries often ends up believing them. Nobody ever accused a Gemini of excessive candor.

In other areas, such as finance and business, this couple might make themselves a bundle of loot—providing Gemini accepts Aries' superior management talents. Aries is a go-getter, more focused and directed than Gemini. But that old Gemini definitely has a genius for communication. Geminis are born actors and actresses. Their psyches zip along a mile a minute while their tongues wag apace. Without the good sense to let each one do what the other is not particularly gifted for, this couple's joint career plans are doomed. Yet, providing that Aries sits solemnly behind the ledgers, copying all the numbers in a big round hand, and allows Gemini to meet the public, handle the sales, and do the public relations, they could do a land office business in just about any endeavor.

Sexually, the picture is a bit testy. Aries is a hop-in-the-sack sort of person. Gemini is up to all manner of mind games and theatrics as play. Geminis are usually in love with the brains as well as the bodies of those they are passionately involved with. Gemini craves the cerebral type of sex that lasts for hours, interrupted by conversation, snacks, musical interludes—you name it. Orgasm can wait. And Aries? Well, Aries is more of a frequent-flyer in bed. The act itself takes priority over either conversation or syrupy sentimental romanticizing. Aries needs and wants to get down to the nitty-gritty right away so they can get on with their projects, businesses, wars, or inventions.

So, despite excellent chances for social and personal success between these two signs, intimacy can be a problem. On the surface, everything looks (and is) peachy fine. But underneath there will always lurk a gap in the sexual understanding. As a result, one or both may stray. Without considerable joint therapy, and intensely compatible Chinese signs, the Aries/Gemini bedroom rapport may leave much to be desired.

Children? Well, as long as you have proven that you can live a few good years together successfully, develop ego control, and not sabotage each other's area of prowess, I highly recommend you go ahead have some kids. You do have that terrific, shared sense of humor. And you carry off a very convincing marriage façade. Your home should be a pleasant place to grow up in. Choose your children from among Librans (to help keep the peace), Aquarians (to stimulate Gemini's active cerebellum), Leos (to teach the pair of you how to be king or queen of the world), and Sagittarians (to keep the whole family on its collective toes).

Aries with Cancer

Feisty Aries, the dynamic do-it-all, meets Cancer, the slower, more sensuous lead singer of the Moody Blues. Nobody's perfect. And no relationship is ever quite all right in its every aspect. But unless you have ultra-compatible Chinese signs and harmonious rising signs, I'd suggest you make this passion into a short subject rather than a feature film. So long as you don't set up housekeeping for the duration, you will probably remain good friends.

The major emotional barrier between Aries and Cancer stems from Aries' indifference to Cancer's lush sensitivities. You, Cancer, go through stages where you face each day in a funk. It is frequently hard for you to get going on a project or even to show your enthusiasm. Black moods threaten to overcome you at every turn. If somebody speaks to you sideways, you can be crushed or baffled or even confused and afraid. Your self-image needs quite a lot of propping up—especially in matters of the heart concerning family ties or lovers—and sometimes, rather than bawling your nose off or ranting and raging, you retreat, sulk, and look increasingly grave.

You, Aries, have the sensitivities of a Mack truck. All you think about is results. Feelings? Oh, yes. You do recall having one or two of those somewhere. But who has time to take such frivolous matters into consideration when there is so much work to be done? Certainly not you. You are the Ram, the enthusiastic character whose aim in life is to work hard and achieve and buy more stuff and experience lots of adventure. Your Cancer partner's languor and exaggerated attachment to the intangible and the romantic exasperates you. At first, of course, you are quite naturally attracted to your Cancer friend because he or she is so opposite to you. It's fascinating for you to watch this slow-moving, deep-thinking creature operate. Invariably, you both discover that you are not only stylistically mismatched, but your values don't jibe either. Aries wants action and results.

Cancer wants a solid basis for family and acres of time in which to read books, write poetry, and perhaps even ponder his or her navel.

If you already have such a relationship, you may be able to salvage or repair your rapport by making individual efforts to better understand your partner's needs. If you are the Aries, you have to work at becoming more flexible and gentle. You will need to slow down and learn to love listening to the mere rustling of the leaves in the trees, enjoy just looking at a lingering sunset, to sit perfectly still and not be selfish about who gets what first. Try meditation. Or yoga.

Cancer, you will be harder put to alter your ways. If you want to be happier living with an Aries, you will have to be willing to surrender much of your precious inner privacy, appear more eager to socialize and mix it up with friends for a rollicking good time, and not cringe every time Aries' clear-pitched voice hollers, "Hey, honey! How about showing the folks how we learned to dance the hula in Hawaii last winter?"

Problems in bed. Cancer is profoundly sensuous and sexy, while Aries is more gymnastically gifted for the physical act of love. Aries' therapeutic approach to lovemaking ends up .boring the complex, densely sentimental Crab to extinction. Who, thinks Cancer, wants to be in bed with this disinterested and unimaginative person whose aim seems to be limited to jiffy orgasms for the sake of keeping away crankiness or of calming one's overwrought nerves? Cancer simmers away imagining baroque fantasies and new methods of approaching the issue, while Aries is just anxious to get the job done right and get to the supermarket before it closes.

Children? It's iffy. But if you must procreate together, then be content to raise a nicely balanced Libra or an easygoing Pisces. Steer clear of big, tough-guy signs like Leo and Scorpio, whose self-importance will upset your already lopsided parental relationship.

💘💘💘 Aries with Leo

A Leo friend of mine always says that Aries take a vivid interest in seducing Leos with intent to destroy. She has had her share of near-death experiences with a few-Aries lovers. Still, I cannot agree. To me, Leos and Aries are well-matched both in bed and in company. They enjoy socializing, entertaining generously, and giving of themselves for the pleasure of others. The childlike and naive Aries sometimes exhibits clumsy or ungainly manners, but indulgent (superior) Leo actually enjoys correcting the rampant social faux pas for which Rams are so famous. If these two can just manage to keep their spheres of activity separate, they have a good chance of loving together for a long time.

One thing that can cause heroic battles to erupt in this couple's life is a major clash of wills. Aries people personify willfulness. They are not subtle, nor are they able to surrender either authority or control. Whether it's business, a household, or a jaunt to the mountains on a fifty-speed bike, Aries must seem to be *in charge*. With partners such as Pisces or Gemini, for whom relinquishing power is second nature, Aries feels no threat of takeover lurking under the covers, in the car, or in any of the other playing fields of life. But side by side with a thoroughly self-possessed Lion, Aries' control center feels itself constantly under threat of takeover.

The difference in character here is that Aries embarks on each new endeavor with the sole objective of taking the helm. Leo, lucky devil, is born to the crown. The King or Queen never embarks on any endeavor without knowing full well ahead of time that he or she will be in power. Leo is a born ruler. Aries must aspire to leadership.

Aries cannot seem to be the boss here. The Ram will have to ride shotgun while Leo drives. Aries' secret will be to keep a second set of controls on the passenger side. This way, Leo gets. to appear to own the Mercedes in which they are both riding, to give the impression of dominion over partner, while Aries secretly runs things from behind the throne, all the while protecting Leo's image of grandeur. An Aries who wants to couple with a Leo for life must accept basking in the light of reflected glory.

Essentially, if you want this speedy, romantic, fun-loving relationship to survive for any length of time, you must try to avoid competition. Keep your individual lives and friendships very separate. Enjoy each other for the qualities that you do appreciate. Don't try to melt together as one for much more than your sexual pleasure. When Aries gives a dinner, Aries cooks. When Leo invites friends, Leo cooks. Keep things clear between you as to whose department is whose and stay out of the other's fiefdom.

With regard to money, Aries is tough-minded yet sentimental. Leo is firmly purposeful yet munificent, giving easily of good cheer and readily sharing with others. Aries, by far the thriftier of the two, is well-advised to keep the couple's purse strings under close scrutiny. Leos like to be magnanimous as well as magnificent. They may tend to run up bills, flaunt what they have when they have it, and spend more when they're broke than most of us do when we're drowning in expendable income.

Taming Lions for mating purposes is child's play for the sexy, open-handed, easy-to-read Aries. So caught up in self-image is the average imperious Lion that the great beast hardly budges a whisker when Aries, the blatant, soldierly initiator, comes bopping along looking for some serious love action. In Aries' capable hands, proud Leo becomes a willing pussycat, snuggly and ready for the joys of some brilliantly dynamic lovemaking.

Also, despite your reciprocal willfulness, you are both extremely capable people. In my opinion, you ought to consider marriage and children. The twin forces of Leo the King or Queen and Aries the pragmatic go-getter is sure to create a sound basis for making a home or a family. The best signs for your children would be Gemini or Libra—flexible people with plenty of whimsy will lend a dash of sparkle to your purpose-oriented household.

Aries with Virgo

An emotional seesaw. Virgo is a born critic, a finite sort of person with serious, almost puritanical, ideas and ideals to match. Aries always wants to dash ahead, seeks change and adventure, and is a sexual free-thinker. Their lifetime union would, at best, be problematic.

You, Aries, are vivacious, vituperative, and vehement about getting on with the practical in life. You give off enthusiasm rays, are mostly cheerful, hopeful, and even a tad devil-may-care about money. Moreover you don't take any guff. Very little (even hard criticism) can discourage you from pursuing your goals. Your sexual appetites are constant, keeping you almost always ready to get into the act. Failure, to someone as enterprising as yourself, is always a possibility, but you don't fear losing. You always believe that somehow conditions will change, that you will adapt, and that success will be assured by the time the very next phone call or board meeting is through. Analyze? You do indulge in a sort of head-on-collision form of analysis. But your swift and headlong methods are crude. People tease you about being naïve. That's because you are.

You, Virgo, are the more inflexible member of this duo. You don't make friends easily. You give and demand loyalty in return. You keep your finances shipshape. You hate to squander your energies. You analyze and plan everything well in advance. In some ways, you are even more practical-minded (but less concrete) than Aries. Yet, despite your tendency to rigidity, you willingly caretake when your Aries is ill or in need of support. You don't mind sacrificing your time to your partner's social or career needs. You are tenderhearted and helpful to one and all in your limited entourage. You give your love completely, put up with a ton of annoyances, and tolerate many of your Aries partner's idiosyncrasies.

Thus far, it sounds almost as though you two might complement each other. Alas, you don't. Aries wants to party. Virgo prefers staying home. Aries urges Virgo to make some new casual friends, but Virgo hasn't the tiniest desire to commingle with strangers. Virgo is driven by a desire to keep life manageable, size up circumstances, and remain in control. Too much jarring static interference from without can cause even the jolliest Virgo to lose it. A *place for everything and everything in its place* is Virgo's safety slogan.

Also, Virgos are thrifty. Aries like to spend money till dawn, then wait for the shops to open so they can spend more. Virgo lives cautiously, sensibly glued to an orderly environment.

The sex?

What sex?

In light of my above comment, procreation between Aries threatens to be dicey—if not impossible. But I am being facetious. Aries, as I mentioned, is a sexual EverReady battery. Virgo is a thinker, a muser, an analyst, and is often perceived by partners as a sexual cold fish. Unless the Aries person here finds new and unique ways to entice the modest Virgo into a more frequent, steadier sex pattern, the chances are high for Aries straying. After a few disappointing months repeating, "Come on sweetie, warm up, snuggle over here with me, let's get cozy," and eliciting only resistance (and not even coy resistance at that), in return, any right-minded Aries would leap out of those covers and bolt over to the next mountaintop for a little cuddling action among some warm-bodied Leos or Gemini

If you are already an Aries/Virgo couple and are getting along well, you are lucky—and undoubtedly were born under ultra-harmonious Chinese signs. If and when you do have a child, I hope it's a Leo or a Capricorn—or both. Rest assured. Even if you parents don't get on well, they will.

💘 💘 *Aries with Libra*

This relationship, which starts out as an intense mutual attraction based largely on sexual magnetism, can turn out to be a long-term major mistake. Quarrelsome Libra will constantly be tempted to goad the innocent, spirited, opinionated Aries into taking a strong view on some issue or other, then drop the discussion, call it *futile or silly,* and walk away, laughing up his or her sleeve. Aries does not take kindly to being made fun of and ends up confused and angry at Libra's nasty little game. Basic difference here? Libra is indirect. Aries is direct.

Aries, the first sign of the Western zodiac, is often born naive. There is not a lot of deep soul-searching here. Libra is the seventh sign. Lots of psychic water has flowed under the bridge since feisty, energetic Aries' time. Libra is also cool, beauty-loving, equity-seeking, and fair. Things psychic delight and amaze Librans. They leave many Aries cold.

Bohemian, artsy, yet bulldozer-like. Libra is gossamer, fair-minded, and intellectual. These two characters in the same living situation make for strange housemates. Their home will reek of the higgledy-piggledy: Patchwork quilts thrown over sleek leather couches. White cats coiled up on black velvet settees. Ultra-relaxed housekeeping habits compete with carte blanche refrigerator privileges and forget-about-it-till-morning dishwashing patterns. Even full-time live-in help cannot stem the tide of clutter and mess we find in the Aries/Libra lair.

This couple gives off an air of eccentricity. Aries dives headlong into thrills. Libra looks for perfect stages on which to build up gorgeous plans. Aries is manual. Libra is heady. After, the initial sexual excitement, time erodes some of the enchantment. The picture looks like this: Aries stomps about the house in grubby work clothes, permanently annoyed at Libra's resistance to practicality. Libra lies around reading a superb novel of rape and rampage, waits until Aries' back is turned, hides the tool kit, then insists on going to the theater *tonight*—in full formal dress.

At best, Aries and Libra make excellent friends. Without the onus of marriage or commitment to weigh them down, they can expect to have a good deal of fun. They might even go into business together. Aries might create merchandise while Libra mans the store, greeting people and selling up a storm. Or they might simply be good neighbors and give out free advice on gardening and the joys of redwood lawn furniture.

Libra likes money and often has plenty. Libra will not mind giving some of that loot away to a beloved Aries. When and if Aries is spoiled by a partner, he or she becomes greedy and snooty about it. If this pretentiousness persists, Libra may tiptoe out of the room, vacate the premises, call Aries from Hawaii, and ask for a divorce. Long and short? Aries may squander, but Aries is not lavish about spending. Libra is.

This couple's potential for sizzling lovemaking is high. I call Aries' sexual approach exceedingly *direct*. Lovemaking for Aries is often a hasty matter carried out in an athletic or therapeutic atmosphere of "Whew! That was great, honey. How'd it go for you?" 'Low lights, musky perfumes, bath oils, and lacy nighties or silk pajamas characterize the Libra's romantic bedside manners. Moreover, Libra wants a sexual partner, a conversational chum, a lover to work next to and share a lovely day with. As well, Libra is often engaged in sexual window shopping. Aries could no care less about creating a setting for sex. Aries is a randy, playful partner who tends to be mostly loyal to a main squeeze. Oh, Aries is certainly not above some straying. But if the sex with one person is good, Aries prefers not to complicate matters. Aries is practical. Libra a dreamer.

Because the couple-for-life prospects are not excellent with Aries, I frankly advise against you two having babies together. A good time in bed is one thing. But kids demand deeper commitment and necessitate staying power. No matter how terrific this relationship may seem at first, it doesn't bode well for the long haul. You are both happiest in unconventional surroundings with an unstructured lifestyle. Kids need solid. Not weird. Abstain unless and until you have proven to each other that you can live in harmony for at least five good years.

½ *Aries with Scorpio*

The sex may be fantastic. But to my mind, Aries/Scorpio is the original combination of two ego-centered personalities from hell. Here, we have a true-life battleground relationship, tumultuous, sexual, and insufferably action-packed. Aries cannot keep that big, innocent mouth shut. Scorpio pummels Aries back with left-handed insults. Aries moves in for the kill, innocent as Cupid on a cloud, arrow drawn in the thrall of hoping for even one moment of the delicious tenderness that lurks under the carapace of Scorpio's sneering. But Aries is clumsy. Clumsy annoys Scorpio, who shows disdainful disapproval: "For Heaven's sake, put your pants back on." Does Aries get insulted? Yes of course. But Aries doesn't mind. Aries is in love. And Aries/Scorpio sex, as I said before, is unusually fantastic.

Being upbeat and sunny is Aries' nature. In fact, Aries is either pleasant and charming or off to war, weapon in hand, fully prepared to kill. But with Scorpio, pleasant is never enough. Scorpio lives for mystery, intrigue, and fascination. So when Aries is charming and warmhearted to a beloved Scorpio, the Scorpio might say, "What's that grin for? Are you drunk? Or just in stupid mode?" To put it mildly, the Aries feels rebuffed. Yet Aries keeps coming back for more. Why? The Ram is lovesick and does not know the cure. Besides, even if Scorpio plays nasty guy, he or she is hooked on the sex too. This relationship is based on passion ... base physical need and addiction to each other in the sack.

As for you, Scorpio, you love your Aries in your own way. But being stuck in love makes you grumpy. You may enjoy Aries' proficient lovemaking and manual talents around the house, but underneath you grumble: "Why must that Ram always talk so loud? And boast so much?" That flat-out Aries happy-face-in-the-morning style grates on the subtler Scorpio's hypersensitive *crapola* zone. To a Scorpio, Aries is too nice. Too open. Too available. To an Aries, Scorpio is a pain in the butt. But loves knows no frontiers of humiliation. So Aries stays around.

Aries *is* mostly noisy and direct. Scorpio is inward, sullen, and unforgiving. These two are competitive. Both subjects believe they are right about absolutely everything. The Aries/Scorpio couple is a kind of push-me pull-you vaudeville act, wherein the audience cannot decide who is the victim of whom. Scorpio tugs on the reins, trying to keep Aries in check. Aries dashes flirtatiously about trying to please everyone, which often infuriates a cranky Scorpio mate whose lack of trust and intense jealousy only compound the problem

Should you already be blessed by this type of love relationship—married or worse—here's my advice: Keep things moving. No stagnant evenings without entertainment. Flatter each other a lot. Your egos are both enormous. Have separate bedrooms and different friends—perhaps build twin houses so as not to get in each others' way. Undertake mutual projects—political, educational, sportive, or household. Scorpio, let the Aries boss you for all handwork. You take over when it comes to dealing with the subtleties. You can both handle money. But to avoid giant fights, I suggest you each manage your own stock portfolio.

An Aries partnered with Scorpio is simply smitten by the steaminess of it all. Sex, you will recall, is *very* important to Aries. Subterranean, subtle, magical sex like that which Scorpio knows how to deliver drives the Ram bonkers. So naturally, being practical, Aries tries Scorpio's every whim and dictate, and attempts to anticipate and satisfy his or her desires.

But no matter how mad Aries is for Scorpio's sexual favors and vice-versa, Aries remains flirtatious. Because Scorpio is intolerant of such disloyalty, Aries perceives him or her as intolerant. The deep, dark Scorpio perceives Aries as a nuts-and-bolts lover with about as much philosophical depth as a cuckoo clock Yet Scorpio doesn't make a move to leave either. Scorpio is addicted to Aries too. Harmony-seekers abstain from this stormy union. Enjoy each other if you must. But don't get married if you don't have to. And whatever else you do together ... don't have children.

Aries with Sagittarius

An A+ relationship designed by destiny to last and last, provided Aries learns not to be so possessive and allows the Sagittarius partner to flirt and even (on occasion) stray from the sexual straight and narrow. Sagittarius will be obliged to learn to be more discreet about petty infidelities, or else stop cutting holes in the marital contract altogether. But in general, this pair gets along swimmingly with very little effort.

Aries, you know how you are. You dashed headlong into this love affair, attracted mainly by the Sagittarian's questing spirit and relentless desire to be free. Sagittarius piques your interest also because of Sag's unique ability to tease out the barest truth from life's eternal barrage of BS. Nothing annoys the Sagittarius more than obvious falseness or sniveling from people who don't seem to take his or her advice. So fortunate indeed is the Aries lover who, despite several glaring faults in other areas, is not often accused of dishonesty. Aries can be credulous, childish, possessive, and entertain certain ideas of grandeur. But Aries are rarely liars.

You were both born with a strong yen for fresh air and outdoor sports, so you will share many activities and hobbies such as camping, biking, boating, and hiking in the wild. Householding should go well too. Aries and Sag both like the simple things in life. You may furnish your houses sparingly or cram them full of beautiful antiques, but either way the result will look clean and neat as you will each contribute your share to caring for the grounds and fixing up chores. Sagittarius doesn't require masses of creative projects to feel fulfilled. Aries often does, and is decidedly the better craftsperson. Sag doesn't mind running out for more nails or ringing up the catalog houses to find the cheapest, best-priced sofas or peach-colored bathroom fixtures, but this doesn't bother Sag as he or she not usually the one to make the decorating choices. Aries doesn't mind the truth. But does Sag have to be so cutting? So mean?

To make a long story short, Sagittarians have no patience with naiveté. The danger, of course, is that Sag will cow poor Aries into handing over the family finances. This would be a disaster. Nobody is more glad-handed than Sag, who gambles, takes daring risks, or spends all the money in the till, then sets about gaining it all back with interest. In the void between spending the booty and rescuing the family ship, the Aries will no doubt experience plenty of fear and anxiety. Sag may sulk too. Or disappear into the ether for a few days. Aries will need all the resilience he or she can

So you share a healthy measure of mutual admiration. You are able to be perfectly honest with each other about most of life's important business. Oh, maybe one day when Aries is puzzled about what Sag sees as a transparently simple bad deal wherein Aries ought to have been more clever than to become involved, bam! Sag cuts the air with, "You were completely stupid to let yourself get dragged in by those lowlifes. A babe in the woods. Now what are we going to do?" muster to ride out Sag's blank periods. Basically, Aries ought never to relinquish the purse strings, but rather should put Sag on a budget so he or she feels free to play poker, go skydiving, and buy out the town within the family's means. Here, Aries will need to learn more strategy, subtlety, and finesse.

The sex. is delicious as well. Both of you are simple and direct in bed and don't bother much with fantasy frills or initiate outrageous, perverted behavior. Sagittarius, however, has a lusty appetite and may use far more than the basics to arouse an Aries partner. Here, Aries' innocence turns Sagittarius on. Sagittarius plays the well-traveled sophisticate and Aries gets to be the wide-eyed child. Yours is a good, down-to-earth, *normal* sexual entente.

When all is said and done, you two make a fine match. Naturally, there will be many ups and downs. But just as naturally, you ought to be able to put your egos in your pockets when the going gets rough, pull yourselves up by the proverbial bootstraps, and get on with righting the ship together. You set a fine example of how teamwork can make a marriage last.

For children, if you have your choice, hatch yourselves hardy babies born in sunny Leo, brilliant Aquarius, and/or a purist Virgo, whose critical talents will always help shed light on family difficulties.

Aries with Capricorn

Oh, my gosh. The headstrong, horny Ram meets the ponderous, ambitious, social-climbing mountain Goat! I think maybe we're in for some peaks and valleys on this pair's long climb to marital bliss. Aries the Ram is so direct, so overly enthusiastic about the new, the attractive, the shiny parts of life that hesitant Capricorn may instinctively back away. Capricorn is security-conscious in the extreme and has little taste for recklessness. Capricorn also has a deadly fear of being dragged into ambitious schemes freighted with risk.

For Aries, security is secondary to novelty. If a Ram sees an opportunity to move about from city to city, or hie the whole family from country to country to live in a more daring or adventurous fashion, he or she can easily subjugate any need for security. They either pack up and store, or they sell everything and start over. And although they are sincerely involved in the present, once they are off on a new life, they don't look back.

Capricorns are not comfortable gamblers. They like things to feel sure before they move ahead. They want rock-solid ground under their hooves each time they move up in the world. Because of their need for each new step to be granite sure, they may be slow to achieve and not reach the summit of success before middle age. But, although that may depress and irritate them, they are not usually willing to take chances in order to reach their goals sooner. Making their own security is one of their best gifts. They do not enjoy living in a nomadic fashion.

Bottom line, Capricorn and Aries are not really well-suited to an extended live-in love affair or marriage. Aries wants colorful, comfortable, durable furniture with plenty of pizzazz. Capricorn likes purity of line, decorating with off-white couches on white carpets highlighted with smooth blond woods to lend a starker quality to an already near monotone scheme. No frills is the Capricorn notion of chic. Capricorn wants an upscale four-wheel-drive vehicle that serves both as a status symbol and a practical means of transport. Aries will prefer a small red convertible that not only looks smart but goes like a bat out of hell. Capricorn is low key. Aries is brazen and bold.

Also, poor, sweet, drudgery-laden Capricorns frequently suffer from depression, sometimes emanating such seriousness as to pull a cloud of gloomy fog over the entire breakfast nook. They are not exactly pliable; they tend to rigidity of both thought and deed. They are also accident-prone, sometimes falling down in the street or getting hit by errant automobiles. Capricorns don't have a reputation for being sex maniacs, either. Trouble is, they hold their emotional responses to a minimum. This reserve then creeps into the bedroom and under the sheets, where it often causes sexual impulses to seize up at the wrong moment.

Aries, you are initially attracted to the Capricorn's work ethic and dreams of success. (Capricorns carefully stash money in one envelope for the taxes, another for home repairs, and a third for the kids' school fees.) But you soon discover that your Capricorn's ambition takes precedence over time spent with you, over attendance at Little League games and ballet recitals for the kids, and even gets in the way of an active sex life.

As a highly-charged sexual type, Aries wants to have a lot of lovemaking at all times and will stop at nothing to get it. As a result, forgets that Capricorn needs to be approached in a specific manner, cajoled out of pessimistic notions, massaged into submission to your playful little physical games. Aries, beware! In your characteristic Aries impetuousness, you may shock the nervous Capricorn out of your bed and back into the office. The workplace, for the Capricorn, is an acceptable way of avoiding intimacy. You, Aries, are too superficial to grasp the significance of Capricorn's profound drama of the inner soul. When these carnal crises arise and finally linger, Aries may grow impatient and ultimately find an excuse for descending from Capricorn's chilly mountaintop in hopes of colliding with some warm-blooded creature who promises more productive sacktime.

Having children would be a mistake. But if you must, I highly recommend the softer signs for your offspring. Take a sweet-natured Taurus or a strong-minded Scorpio, for example. No overly structured Virgos or densely emotive Cancerian kids.

Aries with Aquarius

Here's a rocky one for you! The self-propelled Aries and the aura-propelled Aquarius, each accusing the other of being the more selfish of the two.

Frankly, I don't see much beyond the initial attraction. You have polarized goals. You don't like the same sorts of people. Aries wishes to be *someone* and therefore needs the company of others. Aquarius is born thinking he or she is *already* someone and so requires only the company of a select few cronies who "understand" the lunatic-fringe approach. I don't see you entertaining together. But I can conjure an image of Aquarius and friends lolling about the drawing room speaking of Anglo-Saxon poetry's effect on the lower classes during the Middle Ages, while poor Aries attempts to prepare a posh, snooty, gourmet dinner for the lot of them—who, it turns out, only eat porridge and gruel.

For a straight-dealing, down-to-earth Aries person to survive in the Aquarian's cosmic intellectual aura would be *iffy* at best. Aries is far from stupid. He or she may even be brainy in the extreme. But Aries is decidedly not ethereal. Like a punchy young stripling, Aries likes to get things done, take on new projects, grab life while it's happening, act now before it's too late. Aquarius admires this get up and go, but doesn't fancy being obliged to get involved in too many tangibles.

Interestingly both of you are quite power-hungry. Aries would love to be the king or queen of the world. Aquarius has big eyes for top position as well. Aries wants to make everybody behave. Aquarius wants to make everybody stop behaving. Imagine the battles over everything from politics to who gets to decide on children's bedtimes. Couch colors. Movies to see. Aquarius wants to live on a free-floating barge. Aries wants a big impressive house overlooking the valley. Two stylistically opposite power freaks living under the same roof?

I don't think so.

If you insist on trying to make this relationship into a marriage, I suggest you consult each other's charts long and hard, pore over your Chinese sign descriptions, and check out family similarities before becoming engaged. Then try living for six months together on a desert island. If Aries revels in nightly abstract conversations around the campfire that Aries builds, perhaps this odd couple can survive. Aquarius must be the star genius of this duo and will rarely move over for a partner to take the limelight for a spell. If Aries can keep the applause meter at full tilt while managing budgets and juggling jobs and kids and everything else, this lopsided marriage might have a chance.

Not surprisingly, as far as money goes, it's go-getter Aries who slaves at boring, routine tasks in order to keep the larders filled. It's up to Aries as well to supply the couple's bank account with enough money to keep a roof over the genius Aquarian's head.

And then there's sex. Aries, need I remind you, needs sex. And often. Regular old straight-ahead sex. Aquarians have eccentric, if not altogether missing, sexual habits. They are heady people whose physical needs are easily abstracted in favor of the joys of anything from reading philosophy to listening to eerie ethnic from the untrammeled cultures to which they dream of escaping. "Sex? Oh, yes? I was just thinking about sex. Did you know that there is a tribe in New Guinea where the young boys cannot have sex until they kill a wild boar?"

Kids? Only one, please. Make it a saucy Gemini, a glowing little Leo, or a damn-the-torpedoes Sagittarius child. The kid will need to be strong to survive the thorny dysfunctions of its parents. Moreover, the Aries parent will need an ally to help take down the tent while Aquarius is busy tapping out the great American novel on a special computer she or he designed to compose simultaneously in Sanskrit and Tagalog for the benefit of the New Delhi and New Guinea newspapers' bestseller lists.

½ *Aries with Pisces*

Aries the first sign of the Western zodiac, hitches up with Pisces, the final sign. The result? Although in some ways it seems like polarization, in other ways you are surprisingly well-suited. Aries, you charge ahead like a benign storm trooper. Pisces, you shilly-shally along behind, lyrically imagining solutions to problems you have only just dreamed up. The two of you could not be more different. Yet, as a couple, you might just make it. A long-lasting relationship is a challenge for both parties and will require work and real effort—especially on the part of Aries—to attempt to fully understand the others' motivations.

Why, for example, does Pisces always weigh each move: deciding to take one approach, then undeciding that method, and redeciding a new way? Obviously, this Piscean wishy-washyness drives a decisive Aries partner mad. On the other hand, the softer Pisces wonders how Aries can be gently advised to hush his or her piercing voice, rein in the aggressiveness, and take more careful stock of the weirdo schemes that constantly tempt this naive Ram?

When first you meet, the physical attraction is obvious. The straight-ahead Aries stalks into the room, turns on the overhead light full blast, and bellows, "Hi there, kid, you are really terrific to look at! What are you doing for dinner?" Unfortunately, the Ram's open declarations about how *terrifically good-looking* the Pisces is could cause Pisces to shrink back in fear and swim away to watery depths. Dual-natured Pisces lives part-time in a fantasy netherworld, and spends the rest of the time being congenial and easygoing. Unlike Gemini, who openly wears two personalities, Pisces keeps the second nature under wraps, retreating into an altered state whenever shocked, hurt, or awakened from reverie.

How can Aries be persuaded to cool it? What can convince Pisces to leave behind fear and take one or two plunges alongside Aries—jumping in for a cooling swim in the present, if only to go along for the Aries' ride?

Therapy. Discussions. Intimacy of exchange in and out of bed. Vacations for two that include an afternoon's worth of conversational interchange as part of every day's activity program. You two need to talk things out, chat each other up, practice mutual romanticism, seduce and re-seduce each other endlessly, if only for the survival of the relationship. Cultural sharing will serve as excellent cement. You both adore music, art, theater, the cinema, and dance. You might sing in choral groups together, form a local movie club, or study abstract painting with the same teacher. All of these (or others you may think up together) shared activities will draw you closer and make you better able to comprehend your partner's actions.

All in all, I like this duo. You seem very different. And you are. But you are both rather childlike, innocent, and naive. Pisces will soften Aries. Aries can learn to put starch into Pisces' sails without hurtful scoldings and reproach. Aries can handle the tough outside world. Pisces will be able to take care of the family soul.

Some aspects of your life together can be made clear from the outset. Aries ought to handle the money. Pisces should be given plenty of loot to play around with. Aries is crafty, talented, and sometimes artistic. But nobody is more innately creative than Pisces. Ideally, time, money, and marketing skills should be provided for the Piscean. Aries manages. Pisces invents. Aries sells while Pisces muses.

If you have kids, try to bear them in the signs of Scorpio for ballast, Leo for challenge, Libra for balance, and Gemini for fun. Both of you love children. Pisces enjoys being down on the floor with the little ones, adores animals, and enjoys the loving chaos of family life. Aries is a fine provider, a kindly disciplinarian, and a hell of a responsible soulmate.

TAURUS

Taken to the extreme, all of our qualities can become frailties. Some of us are generous to a fault, which can be wasteful. Good communicators can also be blabbermouths. Nurturing parents can smother their children. Fortunately, free will allows us to balance the positive and negative sides of our character. The tough but tender Taurus was born:

POSITIVE | NEGATIVE

ardent | lustful

determined | obstinate

industrious | drudging

patient | obdurate

sensual | ribald

acquisitive | greedy

💘💘 Taurus with Taurus

In this earthy configuration, terra meets firma. Overall, this is a positive combination. You like each other as friends. You are sensitive, warmhearted lovers whose similar point of view on life shines the light of harmony on your lucky couple. The bond between you, if allowed to flourish where enough money and goods are available, should be not only positive but long-lasting. Having identical Sun signs endows you with the luck of a similar energy vector. Both of you are basically willing to strive for a stable, healthy lifestyle: a home, children, full employment, ownership of land, music wafting through the air, a garden where all four of your hands can be busy at once, tilling and planting, hoeing and harvesting. In short, you both want to go in the same direction at the same speeds. So far, so good.

In twin-sign relationships, we invariably recognize ourselves in the other person. You see your own little faults being repeated before your very eyes. You understand the other's whimsy and sympathize with his or her woes. If both of you are comfortable with your own little quirks then the way you mirror each other is likely to improve the entente between you. However, if one of you harbors a too-long-cherished-neurosis and fairly drips excess guilt, the other partner will undoubtedly be the first to sense it and wish to uncover the façade. Unless you both work at it, drag all the truth out of the crowded closet, and lay it on the carpet, the relationship will always suffer from lopsidedness.

Taureans are usually mellow, loving, and gentle, but on the underbelly of those sterling Taurus qualities lives a manifestly stubborn and willful creature. Because you are born in the same sign, at any time one of you could be representing one end of the Taurean behavior spectrum while the other one is acting out the other side. Talk about excessive! If you folks allow the seesaw effect to get a foothold in your emotional life, you may one day be very, very sorry you ever met. The battles could be monumental, epic, and unremitting. Obstinacy rarely leads us beyond the battlefield and into the light of reason.

The Taurean way of achieving is steadfast and persistent. Bulls have the patience and perseverance to wait things out, knowing instinctively that time will often rule in their favor. Yet this waiting game itself can be their undoing. Trusting blindly in the wisdom of the future (as we know) is tricky business. But Taureans are generally peace-loving creatures. As a couple, you will both love the steadier things in life, money in the bank, a safe and sturdy home, excellent food and wine, fine yet casual clothes, and every sort of the finest art. Most of all, you both need security—emotional and financial. And with any luck, you will be able to provide it for each other.

The downside? You Taureans are possessive, which can, of course, cause jealousy. But the, sort of jealousy that stalks the Taurean mind is not always of the sexual "You must be sleeping with So-and-so" type. It's more of the "You (and everything about you) belong to me and are an integral part of my assets" type. Being the mate of a Taurus is difficult enough for an easygoing, flexible sort of partner who can stand the Taurean need for reassurance about "possessions." But for a second Taurus, who is also obsessed by the ownership aspect of love, the feeling of being taken for granted might escalate—big time!

You are both very sensual. With Taureans, the material part of lovemaking has to feel right. Taureans are frequently turned on by a cashmere sweater, a silk dress, or a bubble bath and a tender embrace. Tauruses adore being touched. They like getting and giving massages. It may take you Taureans a little while to really commit to each other. But if you decide to make that decision to marry and raise a family, you will most likely both stay in the relationship to the bitter end. No other sign has so much loyalty and dedication to partners, associates, and friends.

You definitely should have children. If you marry young, have yourself a few. You are co-responsible and will do a good job once you are confronted with the little darlings. Try filling your home with a moony little

Cancer, a feisty, deep Scorpio, and maybe even one or to Libras to round things out in the love department.

Taurus with Gemini

I am not much on adjacent signs pairing up for life. Usually, the risk of boredom over the long term is high. But here, with Taurus ruled by stick-in-the-mud, fixed earth, and Gemini as mutable as springtime weather, boredom is not the problem. In this couple, persistence tries to slow down mutability and mutability longs to put at least one firecracker a day under persistence. It's the tortoise and the hare—only the moral of the story is not necessarily *steady plodding wins the race*. It's more the reverse. At best, this match is a curious and challenging combination. At worst, a war.

You Tauruses approach things in a practical, terrestrial, heartfelt (if stodgy) manner. Gemini partners know how to use their heads more than their hearts and have a hard time staying grounded. A landlubbing Taurus, despite dreams of roaming the world with only a string bag for company, usually stays in one place forever. Gemini needs to move. Tauruses resist change and are not famous for their flexibility, while Geminis race about networking, social butterflying, and slipsliding away.

Taureans move slowly and take their good old time adjusting to things. The communicative Gemini can do three things (yammering on the phone, gaping at the TV, and playing computer games) at the same time. Taurus is a one-task-at-a-time sort of person, happy pruning the yard or doing the dishes, eating a hot dog, or playing with the cat. But Taurus cannot do more than one of those things at a time, thank you very much.

Luckily, even at their worst, Geminis possess a keen sense of humor and can practically always make Taureans laugh. Warmhearted, mellow and loving Taureans are able to create a comfortable, cozy, and beautiful home, and love to dress well. Geminis couldn't care less about color combinations. Gems feel cheerful as long as they have their cellular phone, latest-model computer, and the fanciest fax machine. Taureans need to give Geminis space to roam around, be with people, talk on the phone for hours.

You can be a good match if you can learn to tolerate each other's polarized views. Gemini might actually help a Taurus partner out of an old rut, urge him or her to try out some fancy new adventures. Taurus might try to teach the Gemini how to become more physical and sensuous, enjoying good food instead of jabbering aimlessly, entertaining the dinner guests and forgetting to eat. Gemini, in turn, can inspire the beloved Taurus to mix with more people, communicate, read a book or scan the newspaper, go on short trips, hang out in coffee houses, connect with the neighbors, and find out what's going on besides the grass reproducing molecule in the home pasture.

The Gemini partner will derive stability and financial backup from the steady, economy-conscious Taurean. Tauruses sense and know how to make money. But they hesitate to take risks and venture into something new. Geminis are the jugglers: they have the knack of picking up information, grabbing opportunities, wheeling and dealing. A crafty Gemini can not only present the Taurean with new business ideas, but might even inspire Taurus intellectually.

Money should not be an object in this duo. Taureans earn and keep money. They can become realtors, landscape architects, farmers, or even bankers. Geminis are born journalists. They also make excellent talk show hosts with their quick wit and gift of gab. I would advise that Taurus be the treasurer of this marriage. Geminis are not too terrific at keeping either books or money.

The Taurean Bull and the Geminian Butterfly form an outstanding couple for having kids. Half the time Gemini acts like a kid anyway—and the other half he or she can be out hunting the means to put the poor devils through college. Taureans are delighted to stay at home with their offspring as much as possible, caring and tending, singing and teaching them the ways of nature. Try to have your kids in Scorpio for depth, in Aries for get up and go, and possibly even in brainy genius Aquarius, whose far-reaching mind games will serve as a challenge to get you off of your intellectual duffs

Taurus with Cancer

This is a binding combination of fixed earth and cardinal water. Muddy? Not really. You two are very compatible, because you both need stability. The Taurus is attracted to material and financial stability, while Cancer goes more for the emotional security afforded him or her by this team.

Cancers are sensitive. They are easily hurt. This can puzzle Taureans, who think they are doing admirably in terms of reliability and providing for their family. But being stolid Bulls, Taureans do lack openness. They have trouble sharing their emotions. Rather, they take their feelings for granted, hoping that routine and stability will keep them from getting out of hand. In fact, ruts are where Taureans feel most at home. So impenetrable are some Taureans that even their lusty lovemaking can grow flat and lose its fizz.

Cancers, poor babies, need a lot of emotional recognition. If they are lacking sentimental stimulation, Cancers often become moody and withdrawn. They have a tendency to be in love with love itself and long to hear slavering, romantic incantations and blandishments, such as: "I love you so much that if I perished right now my life would be complete. Your eyes light up my heart. We are entwined in this love odyssey forever, my darling heart." Cancers live to be surprised with bouquets of flowers and boxes of Valentine's chocolates. Many times, however, Cancer's way of expressing desire is a shade too subtle for our rustic Taurean. Not to worry, however. If things don't work out the way they want to, Cancers understand the myriad uses of self-pity. They simply turn up the volume on the sobs until Taurus gets the full picture.

Despite their soft centers, Cancers have a lot of imagination, are talented at initiating projects, and can be quite shrewd in business. Taurus is more concerned with preserving and stabilizing. The Taurean way of doing business is practical, down to earth, and straightforward. With Taureans, what you see is what you get. Cancer is wilier and doesn't shy from using a little salesmanship or manipulation to achieve a goal.

Taurus is the preserver, Cancer the nurturer. Taurus goes out into the world (never terribly far, mind you) and brings money back to the nest, where Cancer plays the nest builder. This relationship grows more solid, too, because Cancer enjoys cooking and homemaking for the Taurus, who in return loves to eat well and delights in the physical pleasures, a comfortable, cozy home, and a stable family situation. Both Taurus and Cancer need some time to open up to each other, but have no problems in totally committing to a relationship once the partner has been found worthy of their love and devotion. Overall, the combination of Taurus and Cancer is a dandy one, especially if you want to have children, build a home, and leave gray hairs on the same sofa you bought when you were still shedding brown or blond ones.

There is one downside in this match: Neither the Taurus nor the Cancer can let go easily. Relationships as well as material goods get saved up forever. These two may stick to each other even when it has long since been time to move on. Taurus can be possessive and jealous, and Cancer can be smothering and suffocating.

If you have kids, try to have a creative Pisces child whose adult success depends greatly on parental guidance and understanding. The luckiest kid in the world would be your Scorpio only child. Scorpios love to be spoiled rotten, hugged all the time, and encouraged in their weirdo schemes. What could be better for the little Scorp than a protective Cancer/Taurus household to grow up in? Libras and Capricorns would be happy with you as well.

❤ ❤ ❤ *Taurus with Leo*

An immovable, earth-sponsored Bull and the luscious Lion fixed in forever fire? It can work. Here we are confronted with two powerful signs whose life together will be a full-time creative experiment. Even though they are both fixed signs, Taurus is earthbound and Leo is very action-bound. This very fact allows for sparks to fly—often in the right direction.

Although their individual approaches are quite different, Taurus and Leo are both artistic people. Taurus's art can be self-generated and is usually tangible: pottery, sculpture, crafts, and so on. Further, Taurus loves to acquire, possess, and savor masterpieces. Fiery Leo needs to create, be expressive, or at least make up brilliant stuff that says lots about some other brilliant stuff and then be applauded for it. Leo yearns for the limelight, likes to play the leading role in the big exciting game of life. Every activity must be full of color, packed with fun, and rife with activity. Leos paint their canvases with big, powerful strokes, and usually forget to clean up after themselves. Recognition is a key issue for Leo. For self-validation to exist at all, Leo must be made to feel special. The spotlight's piercing glow refills Leo's creative fuel tank.

Leos are the Prince and Princess Charmings of the zodiac. They often inspire the people around them with their straightforward charm and radiance. They can also be intensely self-centered and arrogant if they don't get what they think they deserve. But for the Bull to be involved with such a livewire can cheer a Taurean up and improve an otherwise routine lifestyle.

The mellow, peace-loving Taurus needs low-key, low-profile privacy. Tauruses are hard workers, disciplined, organized, modest, and will persistently pursue a career or any other objective they desire. Slow but steady, Taureans are always playing it safe. To a Leo, the Taurus workaday life may appear boring or uninteresting. But smart Leos will recognize that even if they love parties, sports, risk-taking, excitement, gambling; and romance, have a magnanimous, generous heart, and tend to shower their love partners with lavish gifts, hitching their wagon to a stolid Bull person may be just the settling agent they need to ply their own splendor with more ease and in perfect luxury.

Here comes the rub. Both of you have a stubborn streak. The Taurus is attached to habits set in cement. Leo needs action at any price. These differences in style will lead to conflict. To nip these incipient battles in the bud, take my advice: Taurus, take up race car driving or some other Leonine breakneck activity. Leo, stay home once in a while with the kids, wash the car, and make popcorn around the fireplace. With you two, harmony is only a question of balance. If you keep plugging away at it, you will get it right.

So what makes this couple tick? The Leo lightens up the Taurus through creative lovemaking and intensive passion, and teaches the Bull that money and work are not everything in life—and that in fact, we are here to have a good time and make the most fun of our existence. The Taurus can help the Leo to hold on to capital, stay more grounded, be more disciplined, turn those multifarious projects into tangible reality.

Let the Taurus handle the money. Tauruses are masters of the savings account and balance their checkbooks regularly. Leos love to max out to the limits on as many credit cards as they can fit into a wallet at one time. "What the heck, I'm worth it! I deserve only the best! Who cares about tomorrow?"

Leo is not gifted for life on a sexual treadmill. Leo will challenge the plodding Taurus to a more gaudy and expressive sex life. Taureans, of course, adore the sex act and are no slouches in the sensuality department. But they cling to tradition and hanker a after the sameness of sex "the way we used to do it." Leo has no time for such drudgery in sex and with winning Leo charm will undoubtedly seduce Taurus into sexual fore and after play sessions designed to loosen the characteristic Taurean reserve—big time!

Leos love children and jolly them along. Tauruses are keen to play the role of the responsible parent. Whatever the differences between the Leo and Taurus may be, there is a lot of love, fun, warmth and loyalty between the two of you. Have scads of kids. Choose Gemini, Aquarius, Sagittarius, Capricorn, and Cancer.

💘💘💘💘 *Taurus with Virgo*

These two signs—Taurus, fixed earth, and Virgo, a mutable earth sign—are very compatible. You feel naturally at home with each other and enjoy a flowing, quiet understanding. You support each other's goals, ambitions, and needs for self-expression. Being a pair of earth signs, both of you are practical, disciplined, down to earth, and don't shirk from hard work. This is one of the zodiac's great matches.

You will, of course, discover some differences. Virgo will be more interested in keeping the house neat and tidy, while Taurus prefers sorting out the garbage or puttering around in the garden. But you like each other, so you can easily empathize with the other's needs. Besides, whatever the method, you both insist on keeping your life and your affairs in order and are concerned with creating a sound public image.

The Virgo has a tendency to overwork in a relentless effort to create a perfect home environment. This compulsion can cause Virgo to become very critical and fussy. Taurus likes a nice home, but is not going to pick crumbs off the carpet during dinner just to make sure everything remains immaculate. Virgo is a driven sign. Virgos stop at nothing to see a job done perfectly and on time. The good-natured Bull finds it much easier to kick back and take a little nap to rest up before going ahead with a task. Virgo may have to fall ill before realizing that it's time to take a break or grab a cuddle.

There are some even bigger differences. Taurus is basically interested in securing a pleasantly cozy and comfortable lifestyle. Virgo lives inside his or her head and requires a lot of intellectual stimulation. While Taurus may be stretched out on the cushy settee watching a favorite inane TV sitcom, a Virgo partner may be spending evening hunched over a hot computer, painstakingly analyzing all the different possibilities for investing in mutual funds or obsessing on finding out more about Tutankhamen's tomb. Virgos crave the written word and are very attached to their books. A Taurus may find books tedious and be more interested in contemplating a beautiful work of art, listening to music, or in simply relaxing under a tree.

Taureans love to eat and drink as well, and can at times overindulge. The Virgo is very health conscious and may also be intensely interested in alternative medicine, exercise programs, and oddball nutrition. Taurus can't relate to this, but can be tolerant. Taurus may never go on that cleansing fast with Virgo or drive the two of them to ashram for .a meditation. Nor will any self-respecting clumpety-clump Taurus put up with Virgo's perpetual analyses of their relationship. Taurus's advice to a beloved Virgo? "Reeelaaaax, Babe. Just chill out."

Virgos truly do not mind getting up first thing in the morning to serve their sweetheart coffee in bed, as long as they get recognition for it. The Bull adores being spoiled and is sometimes even accused of being a bit of a slob, but nevertheless Taurus does remember to applaud the slaves. Taurus's praise validates Virgo's efforts and spurs him or her on to more avidly picking up yesterday's panty hose, scrubbing harder, and getting those hard-to-reach sash window corners crystal clean.

Sound boring? Not for a Taurus and a Virgo. They both shine when everything is under control. Their happy little secret is in knowing exactly where the next paycheck is coming from.

Oh, yes, there is one other area of entente that definitely helps keep the Taurus/Virgo relationship juicy: The sensuous sexpot Taurus can help the anxious, hard-to-reach Virgo overcome prudish shyness. Taurus's kindly insistence on better communication in bed will assist Virgo in learning to get full enjoyment from the sex act. Virgo needs to trust a partner. Taurus knows how to build that confidence.

You have a good marriage on your hands, folks. Work hard to stay together. Learn to understand each other's special needs and then manufacture yourselves some kidlets to nurture and play with. You might want to try a Capricorn baby first. You will both find harmony with an ambitious little mountain goat. Or a sweet little Cancer kid, whose emotions will teach you both (especially Virgo) more than you ever thought you knew about cuddling. A Scorpio baby will provide a special challenge for you both—a joyful if complicated one. If you are so inclined, have yourselves a trio of kids. Your sound marriage can handle at least that many—if not more.

Taurus with Libra

The Rock of Gibraltar and the Social Butterfly. Here we are dealing with the fixed earth, yin, personal Taurean and the mutable air, yang, intrapersonal Libra. You are different. But complementary. Taurus might be a real estate developer. Libra might then be brought in as interior designer. With this couple, we encounter both strength and beauty, prosperity and social status, sensuality and a gracious environment.

What did you two do to deserve this (almost) perfect match? Both your Sun signs are blessed by the same guiding light—the planet Venus. You have oodles of things in common: a need for solid relationships, taste, love of art and beauty, and the inimitable ability to attract people and bounteous wealth. Sounds like perfect bliss so far.

Well, it almost is. But there is one thing that could cause discord in this dedicated twosome: Idealistic Libras filter everything through their intellect. Libras are gregarious and have a strong urge to be included on the party circuit, to harmonize with all of their acquaintances, and to balance everything and everybody in their surroundings. Adorned with their favorite accessory, the cordless telephone, Libras are forever discussing relationship problems with their cronies. They hash through the pros and sniff out the cons. They love to entertain their peers and to play matchmaker for those they know best.

And what about their poor private, pragmatic, plodding, down-to-earth Taurus partner? Does he or she have a hard time relating to the restlessness of a Libra? I guess so. Taurus thinks, "What a waste and energy!" and comes along to say, "I'd rather spend some with you. Let's stay home and cuddle. I'll fetch up a bottle of my finest Bordeaux. I'll even make a nice fire in the fireplace. Come on sweetie, you can see your pals some other time." So, Libras, forget being able to lure Taurus into your social activities, unless you can make it financially worthwhile.

Libras like to work in cooperation with a partner. Both Taurus and Libra were born with some degree of creative talent, so you can very likely make a great team. When it comes to conceiving original ideas and concepts, you, Libra, are probably the initiator. And Taurus is more gifted for producing tangible results and managing your joint income.

Also, you both love luxury. Your home (which you own, of course, thanks to Taurus) is a designer's showcase. You both have excellent taste. Besides, for Taurus it isn't enough that things merely *look* wonderful—everything has to feel right too. Taurus wants to sink into overstuffed chairs and brandish the *real thing* brass fireplace tools. For Libra, the most important decorating elements are the perfect color combination and a refined sense of equilibrium about furniture.

But Libra is not usually content to settle down and play house. So you may both have to do some compromising here. For example, if you, Taurus, want to lure your Libra sweetheart into the bedroom, turn off all the phones in the house and prepare the terrain: silk sheets, purple flowers, perfumed candles, and romantic music. No Libra can resist romance. Librans adore the quest for the perfect love partner. So seduce them. Keep them interested. Ply them with romantic scheme after romantic scheme. For your Libra sweetie, finding and maintaining a fulfilling and harmonious relationship is the only thing worth living for. He or she will do anything to satisfy your murky emotional and physical needs, even if it means clamming up for a while and making love twelve times in a row.

You two would probably adore raising a sensitive Pisces child. Or how about a warmhearted Leo kid, whose imagination could benefit a lot from growing up in the atmosphere of your affluent, artistic, and stable home.

💘💘💘 ½   *Taurus with Scorpio*

On the great astrological wheel of fortune in the sky, Scorpio is directly opposite Taurus. Opposites attract. Hence, as Sun signs go, this couple really sizzles—at first. But think twice before signing a lifetime contract. This relationship is one of my favorite fixer-uppers. If you take the trouble to make the renovations, you'll have a doozy of a terrific marriage!

Scorpios are secretive, eccentric, and impulsive to a fault. They are always racing off in seven exotic, erratic directions at once in order to reach a goal that Taureans would take the shortest, most direct, route to achieve. Scorpios are often wanton types who long for excitement and crave change as well as solitude in large doses.

Not so Taurus. Taureans tend to enjoy the security of staying in the same place for long periods of time, meanwhile raising everything from vegetables to cattle to children and pets from cradle to grave. They love the company of their family and associates, their kids and their animals.

Communication can be a sore issue with these two. You, Scorpio, can be open, chatty, and jolly, but you are also capable of gloomy, sulky withdrawal. Tauruses, you also may keep a lot of emotion pent up inside your heart. Instead of processing feelings as they crop up, you Taurus folks often swallow hard, say nothing, and wait until your acid sentiments turn into ulcers.

The consequences of living *à deux* with such giant twin capacities for brooding and withholding may not be productive. Life inside the black hole created by your dual melancholias will be anything but a hootenanny. Between these two secretive ruminators is an unpleasant jealousy, violence, and manipulation. An enlightened Taurus/Scorpio pair will, of course, know enough to seek professional help when clouds roll into the house and refuse to leave.

My advice? Think twice before you try marriage. Make certain your Chinese signs jibe extra well. If it looks, dicey, why not live together for a few years till you iron out the wrinkles? You can always get married. But divorce is sooooo painful—especially for two such creatures as you.

Remember, Taureans are slow, deliberate souls, whose main goal in life is to stash and invest their hard-won bejillions in safe places. They're ponderers, not gamblers. To Taureans, credit card debt is worse than death. Taurus wants security, ownership, economy of gesture and purpose, and never to speak an unnecessary word or waste a drop in the honey jar.

The danger here is that the spendthrift Scorpio may initially be drawn to the budget-conscious Taurus, imagining that an involvement with someone with such opposite views on money will be just the ticket. Likewise, Taurus is fascinated by the wastrel spending habits of the Scorpio partner and considers such blatant openhandedness a miracle. How, wonders Taurus, can this magically attractive Scorpio survive while throwing caution and kopeks to the winds every single day? Answer? Scorpio can't survive without Taurus to put the brakes on the exorbitant squander factor.

Lascivious sex is the real glue in this hot relationship. Tauruses are down-home, straightforward sensualists. They adore softness and admire silks and squishy velvets and smooth satins in which to make love for hours. Taureans glory in gentle background music, and would not at all mind if pungent, herby smells of roasting quail were wafting through the bedroom. Scorpios, we know, also tend to favor elegant fabrics, heady scents, and titillating ambiance. They need sex (although they can do it on a roller-coaster as well as in silken sheets) in all of its forms almost all the time. Scorpios adore the rites of seduction—including days of subtle foreplay, exciting underwear, back rubs, massages, and sitting naked for hours in swirling hot tubs playing footsie before moving on to the act itself.

Plan some of your kids in Cancer, Pisces, or Capricorn. These three signs do harmonize naturally with you both. However, for a little pizzazz and an extra shot of fun, might I suggest a Virgo or Gemini or Libra baby or two? I assure you, they will teach you both all matter of special things about yourselves that you would otherwise never even guessed at.

Taurus with Sagittarius

Never a peaceful moment in this hectic relationship combining fixed earth and mutable fire. At best, this will be an interesting couple. The two Sun signs are thoroughly at odds with each other. Without the tolerance of a saint and the patience of at least one Job, I cannot imagine how you two would weather the outrages of a tandem long life.

Taurus, the Bull, is born fixed to the ground, hooves cemented to the earth. Taurus is a no-nonsense, right-here-and-now sort of person. Taurus refuses change and is only comfortable when everything stays in one place all the time. Taurus is placid, careful, and might be said to live for the love of money. Taurus has a serious, hardworking approach to life. Taurus needs constant loving reassurance and longstanding (if not long-suffering) relationships. Taurus is diplomatic and gentle. When occasionally Taureans unstick a hoof or two, they can be resourceful and productive. Then they will become interested in a safe investment in real estate, secure purchases on the stock market, and may even till the earth for profit. About as adventurous as Taurus ever gets is taking a safe hike in a nearby forest—and even then he or she is in quite a hurry to get back to check on the dog and cat, feed the bunnies, and hug the children.

Sagittarius, the Archer, gets up each day with an eye to aiming his or her arrow high into the air and shooting it far into the future. Sag loves to travel to faraway countries and experience new and ever more exciting adventures. Sag wants to explore mental horizons and reinvent the world. Sag is fiery and restless. Sag is cheerful and optimistic and loves a good risk. Sag has a hard time committing and may not always be there for a partner. Sag is scattered, idealistic, and wasteful. Sag can be tactless and arrogant. Sag is expansive and loves to entertain the universe at his table. Above all, in order to breathe freely, Sagittarians need tons of personal space and complete freedom. They crave the vastness of metaphysics and the expanse of spiritualism and peruse many tomes of text to find meaning in religion. Sagittarians are truth-seeking, open-minded, and openhanded.

In light of the above, do you two still want to live together and have a family? I'm afraid I cannot recommend this marriage. Why not have a trial separation? Right now.

Of course if you insist on staying together, let me remind you that you, Taurus, cannot and do not wish to learn to relate to the Archer's quest for metaphysical knowledge and learning on that far-out planet once removed from reality. Oh, it's true. Once committed to a relationship, you remain loyal and content and even willing to hang in there until the end of time. But hanging in there should not really require swinging by one hand from the left aileron of a hang glider, attempting to feed porridge to a wild-eyed Sagittarian high-flyer. Moreover, Sagittarians have the adorable habit of always imagining there could be someone better just around the next mountain peak. I see twisted wreckage afoot here. Brokenhearted Taureans can be mean-spirited, embittered, and depressed. Oh, gloom!

Your beloved Sagittarius will never be content with routine. No matter how benevolently I attempt to see this situation, I just don't see you two cohabiting happily ever after in a two-bedroom condo with a matched pair of nine-to-five jobs. To make this match work even a tiny bit, ideally the Taurus in question will create a solid, financially safe home base for the Sagittarius, teaching him to think and carry things through, to be more disciplined and connected with his senses. In turn, the Sag's piquant sense of humor, generosity, and optimism the Taurus's world more colorful and exciting.

Opposites do attract. Friction brings growth. There is enormous compromising to be done here. If you do stay together, I suggest you abstain from having kids. An atmosphere of trouble and heartache will no doubt appear and reappear throughout your relationship. Please don't inflict your topsy-turvy lifestyle on little ones.

❤️❤️ ½ Taurus with Capricorn

Fixed earth and cardinal earth. The builder and the banker. Sounds like a good match, and it usually is—especially for accumulating wealth. But there are some distinct differences. Imagine: the warm, affectionate, and pleasure-loving Taurus, whose greatest pleasure in life is to start the day cuddling with your Capricorn sweetheart in bed. Oh, those delicious back rubs you dream of. But what you get instead is a mere glimpse of your sweetie's back as it makes its way out of the bed in career mode with the question, "Where the hell is my Armani suit?"

Capricorns are very sparing in the expression of their sensuality. They are loners at heart, who always seem to wear an invisible protective shield against too much physicality. This Capricorn air of aloofness can drive the sensual, relationship-oriented Taurus to overeat. Or even to shop. All the way to the mall, Taurus hums over and over, "Love me, feel me, touch me" while fantasizing a different Capricorn than the one in the Armani suit who left so coldly at 6 A.M.

Tauruses, by the way, are born to shop. Connoisseurs one and all, Taureans search their world for the best of everything available. Whether food or fashion, you can count on Taurus to acquire the finest goods at every turn. Capricorn, poor thing, also loves high-quality merchandise. But, more's the pity, he or she deplores the very idea of waste. It's tough to love prestigious brand-name clothes that lend that air of class you so crave-- heartbreaking to hanker after cashmere dressing gowns, when you feel guilty about paying full price. Look, Capricorn, when you find a cheap treasure at the consignment shop, why not display the garment's brand-name label by turning it inside out? Only kidding. But you and Taurus do differ on shopping issues.

Capricorns tend to worry a lot. It's hard to tell if they choose the Spartan way of life or if it's truly their preferred mode. Their manner of decorating is often Zen-like: sparsely furnished rooms, bare walls, no frills. Think about it.

Taurus loves overstuffed everything—armchairs, sandwiches, friends, restaurants, pets, life in general. Taureans are cozy people. How do you two ever hope to resolve your polarized approaches?

Control is a big issue—Capricorn is rigid and judgmental; Taurus, although stubborn, is more mellow and easygoing. Perhaps you will best solve your lifestyle differences by getting twin houses, twin bank accounts, two different living rooms, and a giant kitchen where you can occasionally eat together (when Capricorn deigns to come home from the moonlight shift at the office.).

You, Taurus, should be in the sexual driver's seat here. Use all the mushy hearts-and-flowers folderol you can gather to carefully seduce the, prudent, self-controlled Capricorn lover to your world of sexual delights. It's not that your sweetheart Capricorn can't be physical: after all, we are dealing with an earth sign. But for this bony, angular creature, once a week, every Sunday morning, might indeed do the trick. You must realize that your Capricorn mate yearns for caress but will never know enough to ask for it. You are the Bull. Take over. In any case, without your fetching, alluring insistence, Capricorn will not use the imagination God provided for such nonproductive toys as sex. For this terminally remote character, all sex time would be better spent striving. My advice? Cover up the clocks and turn off the phones. Wrestle your favorite Capricorn to the carpet and tickle hard. Then you might hope for some glimmer of passion. And one last bit of info—Caps are late bloomers. When finally they succeed after many long years of climbing, they tend to loosen up. Might I suggest you either find yourself an older Capricorn or hang on a while till yours gets ripe?

I do not advise you to have babies right away. If you must one day, choose to have one clean-spirited little Virgo dumpling. Perhaps, if you're really looking for excitement, you can hatch yourselves a genius Aquarius propeller-head brainchild. Life will become suddenly *very* interesting for both Mom and Dad when that little Aquarian drives a spaceship through the den.

Taurus with Aquarius

Taurus is a fixed earth sign. Aquarius is a fixed air sign. Here we are looking at the ultra-conservative preservationist and the irreverent radical reformer. A stockbroker and a New Age astrologer. Domesticity meets eccentricity. Now, how on earth did you two get together? Unless you have more compatible rising, Chinese, or Moon signs, there is not going to be much joy in this relationship for either of you. You couldn't be more different. The only thing that you have in common is the fact that you both can be intensely stubborn and fixed: Taurus about material possessions, Aquarius about ideas and ideologies.

Taurus is mainly concerned with the personal world. Aquarius operates in transpersonal realms. Taurus needs stability and routines. Aquarius thrives on change and innovation. Taurus is rooted in the physical body. Aquarius lives in the intellect. Taurus wants solid committed relationships. Aquarius demands freedom and wishes to maintain individuality at all costs.

Taureans want to improve their bank accounts. Aquarians mostly dream of improving the world. While Taurus almost enjoys going to a nine-to-five job, the Aquarius partner prefers to stay involved in some non-directed, nonspecific *freelance* project. Not that all Tauruses are rigid, inflexible, and bull-headed. And all the world's Aquarians are not erratic druggies who never work. There are a lot of hard-working Aquarius scientists out there who make a ton of money. The only problem is that they get so absorbed in their visionary project that they forget to come home for supper with the family. If you, Taurus, feel that you can handle the inconsistency and uniqueness of the Aquarian's enforced bohemian lifestyle, you will certainly appreciate status (not to mention the monetary rewards associated with being married to a Nobel Prize winner who occasionally puts out the grass and cuts the cat before emptying the dishwasher into the garbage and saying *good night* to you in the dawning light).

Mostly, the Aquarius mate will be tolerant enough (or indifferent enough) to let you, Taurus, decorate your shared digs. With your innate sense of beauty and comfort you will do your best to create the cozy nest you so desperately crave. Although it's not your first choice, I would highly recommend you arrange for separate bedrooms. Your Aquarius mate needs space to spread out a vast collection of eclectic memorabilia, a giant beanbag chair, a narrow daybed, and several large surfaces covered in wall to wall computerware. Oops, I see more trouble. Tauruses want privacy, and Aquarians love to have a lot of people over to exchange ideas with until the crack of dawn.

And then there's sex. Poor Taurus crawls between the sheets, all revved up for a hot, sensuous summer night full of passion and eroticism—while the brainchild Aquarius mate does overtime on the computer in the den. Chances are that by the time your flaky egghead lover shows up in the bedroom, you, Taurus, will be fast asleep with a hot romantic novel over his or her face. Aquarians often have a hard time being physical, and physicality is exactly what Taurus desperately needs. My advice to Taureans involved with Aquarians? Find yourself a romantic Pisces or a sexy Scorpio to play with while your genius Aquarius is busy inventing a new software program for instant cybersex.

Still hanging in there? Then crank up the VCR and treat yourself to a juicy soft-porn movie. Aquarians have a decided taste for the kinky and might even watch the flick with you all the way through. If you are lucky, you will have fallen asleep by the time your beloved starts expounding on the sexploitation of young actors and actresses in faraway countries (where Aquarians will never bother to go or do anything about it— because it might be too uncomfortable).

Please think long and hard before you bring any children into this world together. If you do stay married, you, Taurus, will have your hands full just trying to keep up with Aquarius's oddball daily desires and needs. A child or two would only confuse the already weighty issues present in the very fiber of this relationship.

💘💘💘 Taurus with Pisces

Well, well, what of the earthy old Taurus hitched to the dreamy, mutable; watery Fish sign? Not boring. No. Not in. the least. Here, we have a builder/muse or banker/artist relationship. Taurus, as we know, is duty bound to tie down whatever is safe and sure in life. Pisceans, to the contrary, have no limits. They have but one wish—to remain unbound, indecisive, and terminally creative. Piscean power lies in the subtle psychic and emotional areas of existence. Taurean force resides solely in the tangible or concrete and is often measured in property. In the right circumstances, this unusual couple can put both structure and boundlessness to work for them. But each of you must strive very hard over and over again to seek and find a common ground.

Don't be discouraged. This is a sweet and magical union. Chances are, despite the many little idiosyncrasies that can plague your couple's harmony, victory is in store. After all, the well-grounded Taurus offers a distracted Pisces partner much-needed stability, and Taurus also sets the example for endurance and grit. On the other hand, the intuitive, compassionate Pisces character will encourage the sometimes fearful Taurus to follow his or her own dream. Pisces is so metaphysically inclined that he or she will have long ago determined that you two have shared at least one past life. Of course, the very idea of having had any past life gives the conservative Taurus the heebie-jeebies. But never mind. Taureans can't always relate to Pisces' deep longing for the inexplicable experience of oneness with the universe. In the long run, however, they can benefit from Pisces' willingness to impart information from somewhere other than safe, sure terra firma. If these two are clever and play their hand skillfully, as Taurus grows and comprehends what Pisces has to bring to the relationship—the wisdom of other worlds—your love will gain both strength and credibility.

Taurus and Pisces each have a fine sense of beauty and harmony. When it comes to decorating your home, you go out tandem hunting for the best and most authentic of everything. Each cranny and nook of your abode must sing *good taste* and also *feel* especially right. Tauruses favor earthy tones, whereas Pisces' favorite colors lean toward the violet and rose. Naturally, a Pisces partner longs to live within earshot of the ocean. The soothing sound brings Pisces peace and solace. You, Taurus, prefer to hang out in a comfy couch, relax in a wood-paneled TV room or simply play in the mud in the garden. Pisces may also want a personal meditation room where he or she can retire to be away from the concrete realities of this planet, envision new universes, and build a better dream house on the tail of a rapidly passing comet.

Pisces enjoy partaking of all things refined and beautiful Fortunately, our mellow, good-natured Taureans don't mind going out into the world every day to make sure that there is money in the bank and will always provide a solid backdrop for the ingenious Pisces, whose many gifts may prove lucrative and provide masses of money as well.

Most times, the sensuous Taurus earthling would prefer a quiet dinner for two followed by a torrid lovemaking session to almost any other pursuit of any other common goal with a partner. But you, romantic Pisces, often shy away from hot, physical, and passionate sex. You think that you feel sexy enough just floating aimlessly in the swimming pool watching the sky through rose-colored glasses, dreaming of the perfect Mr. or Mrs. Right. But watch out, Pisces. What you see is what you get with your Taurus lover. Taurus is sincere, loyal, and always very real. So when he or she wants to make love, Pisces' languid display may be irritating to Taurus—who, granted, is not the most imaginative person in bed. But sex with Taureans does get "seen to" and "accomplished" like some kind of amusing chore. Pisces' sexual makeup is lunatic. For a Fish, waiting, dodging, and anticipating is half the fun. Unless Taurus is willing and able to perfect the complex game of seduction (going fishing, as it were) necessary to seduce Pisces into the sack, there may not be quite enough physical intimacy in this duo to please the Taurus partner's hearty appetite.

Lucky are the children who are born into your gracious home. Here, your bright little Scorpio or fascinatingly moody Cancerian child will build on an already very solid structure and be sure to learn essential values. As a couple, you are past masters at providing both emotional support and total devotion for your united family.

GEMINI

Taken to the extreme, all of our qualities can become frailties. Some of us are generous to a fault, which can be wasteful. Good communicators can also be blabbermouths. Nurturing parents can smother their children. Fortunately, free will allows us to balance the positive and negative sides of our character. The mercurial Gemini was born:

POSITIVE | NEGATIVE

articulate | verbose

dual | schizoid

charming | pretentious

easygoing | superficial

investigative | prying

forgiving | shallow

❤️❤️ *Gemini with Gemini*

Twitter, Chatter and Balk should be the names of the pets in the household of this pair of brainy communicators whose tongues and ideas often get ahead of their thinking processes. Essentially, what we have here are two sets of twins (the word *gemini* means twins, so each Gemini here is his or her own better half) getting together for an emotional gab orgy while trying to keep all four of their souls from flying off the face of the earth. Not only is there enormous charisma in the combining of these signs, but there is also a good bit of madness, chaos, and din. Don't think for a second that a Gemini married to a Gemini has finally settled down to a tranquil secure life. It's quite the other way around. Geminis would be insane to imagine their relationship as a sanctuary. It promises to be more like a circus.

Geminis are the world's most garrulous communicators. So talking things out is not an obstacle. But when there is a difference of opinion, the rap session can rapidly become bickering, the bickering arguing, and the whole schmear turns into an elephant of a row. You said! I did not! You *did!* I did *not!* Yawn. Like little kids or politicians, they yammer away—and they enjoy the yammering, too. Not that these rows ever amount to much in the way of early divorce or split-ups. Gemini tensions evaporate quickly. And until there is a true loss of love or a resounding humungous grownup disappointment, Geminis often stick together.

This couple basically suffers from over-idealizing. Each is "just like me!"—and will naturally be the best lifelong companion ever, make a lot of money, provide security for life, and never be boring. But this is precisely why twinship relationships are frequently iffy frequently only lend themselves to the youthful period of one's life, where a like partner is preferable to an unlike one because there is so little about us that we want to face up to. As we mature, we often seek somebody different who mirrors our character back to us so that we can learn about ourselves. The more mature we are, the more we seek to balance our faults with our qualities and prefer to be equalized by a counterweight partner whose strengths are our weaknesses and vice versa. Gemini couples, like certain wines, often remain in the bubbly, youthful twinship stage too long and do not age well.

Geminis make excellent fibbers and can even become big-time liars and self-deluders as they grow older. Geminis are remarkably talented in fooling themselves (read, denial). They are rampantly intelligent, but they are also a tiny bit flea-brained (read: flaky) in the truth department.

Also, Geminis hate to be thought of as lightweights and frequently adopt serious social poses, trying to appear more bourgeois than the burgomasters themselves: buying expansive properties in chic locales and raising Arabian horses, Persian cats, or prize pedigreed dogs. Geminis who wish us to believe in their solid citizen image are forever frequenting posh spas or buying an elegant Montana ranch. This sort of Gemini needs to appear to be *grandly normal*.

Your sex life will be delicious—so long as you are *in love*. But when suddenly you are no longer getting along in the head department, there is little you can do to get yourselves back into the mood for love. This is one relationship that has potential for enormous bitterness. So long as you agree on everything, sex and snuggling and nuzzling and long nights of talk and love ensue. But when truth starts to creep between those sheets and you are forced to face facts about each other, ugly opinions often rise to the surface and exit Gemini mouths far faster than they can be withdrawn.

Money? Well, you are both good at making money but you are knuckleheaded about keeping it. I'd say you should hire somebody to apportion out and invest your mutual moneys so you will be sure to have enough to pay for your divorce.

Children? Nope.

Gemini with Cancer

My initial opinion of Gemini/Cancer as a relationship was, "Uh, oh!" On the face of it, these folks are not only different but at variance with each other's life plans. Then I reconsidered. Gemini and Cancer *might* be happy together, but it will take some very heavy soul-searching on both sides—plus a combined will to succeed at the relationship that surpasses its natural resistance to lasting long-term.

Little Geminis, we know, have a tendency not to hang on tightly enough to the iron railings at the fair. So loosely do they connect that sometimes they end up falling into the manure pile. Cancer has the opposite tendency. Crabs hang on for dear life—to everything. They want to take the iron railing at the fair home and parents end up having to pry little white-knuckled fingers loose. Geminis change moods the way lightning flashes and self-release from loss by taking things more lightly than other people. Cancers take everything to heart, are super vulnerable to loss, and change moods the way thunder rolls unpredictably closer, causing the air to grow dense and thick with its soggy cargo.

At first you are not much attracted to each other. Gemini senses that Cancer might be stodgy, slow, and dark. Cancer senses that Gemini is ready to split out the door at the first opportunity. Careful Cancer, who hates to be separated from what he or she loves, at first recoils in self-defense. Gemini, of course, fears being forced to sit still and peer into the labyrinths of gloom for which Cancer is so famous. But one thing about Gemini is that he or she rarely resists contact of any type, and eventually engages Cancer with characteristic ready charm and twinkle.

Each of these signs has much to learn from the other. A happy Cancer will joyfully put up with the flibbertigibbet side of Gemini. And Gemini will be curious enough to appreciate and even imitate Cancer caution, to value depth, and to accept being cared for by a real expert caring machine—the

Cancer mate. Cancer might benefit by absorbing some spontaneity and sparkle by opening the gummy clamshell of a somber nature.

Between you, there can grow a healthy love and admiration. But I am not certain there can ever be true coalescence of spirit—the details of which never quite get worked out and frustrations mount because of endless misunderstandings. Gemini is perpetually baffled by Cancer's murkiness and unwillingness to come out of the cellar. Cancer weeps alone, awaiting the return of the ever-gallivanting Gemini, whose refusal to hold still long enough to be cosseted and loved to death by the smothering Crab drives the poor, lunatic Cancer loonier.

If you choose to stay together, there is no question that Cancer will manage the finances and the household while Gemini covers the outside world. Gemini loves to be out and about. Cancer will provide amply as well, but always dreams of home, of tending and sweeping up after both family and possessions, and pondering insights into those never-ending waves of moodiness.

The house you share will be decorated in shades of blue and green, pleasing both tastes. There will be dark blue and green for Cancer and turquoise and electric blues and lemony greens for Gemini. The furniture will be cozy and cramped where Cancer treads, lightweight and spaced far apart in Gemini's favorite spots.

Your Gemini/Cancer sex life promises to be erratic but intense. Cancer's sexual motivations emanate from the viscera and *feel* best when they are met with heartfelt emotional response. Gemini's sex life evolves through the mind and during the actual act may dart aimlessly about from fantasy to fantasy, playing hide and seek with any errant emotion that is trying to seep through. Admittedly, there is not much enduring passion in this out-of-.phase sexual partnership, yet a solid, intimate friendship will survive.

If this relationship does endure long enough for children to become a possibility, these kids might just serve as the cement you both need to help you understand each other's true nature. Try to have kids in the balanced sign of Libra. Or get yourselves a genius Aquarian to hug and be perplexed about. You might also aim for a dusky Scorpio or a balmy Piscean genius artist type. These challenging little ones keep you both intensely busy and perhaps even put your mind (Gemini) and heart (Cancer) in synch, enabling smoother-sailing for the future of your not-so-compatible compatibility.

½ Gemini with Leo

The Gemini/Leo match, it seems to me, only works when the Lion part of the Leo's character is pre-tamed (maybe previously married to a Scorpio). If Gemini is to be hitched to Leo, then Leo had better practice being a damned good listener, be humble enough to step gracefully out of the spotlight, and know how-to jack up the applause meter to the max so Gemini gets his or her jokes laughed at and feats of magic oohed and aaahed over as they occur. Otherwise, Gemini—who does not have the most sterling of reputations for fidelity—may find Leo's native magnificence too haughty and start flirting with the chambermaids or footmen.

There is a certain kind of Leo person (I am sure you know at least one of this sort of Leo) who was literally born to marry a Gemini. Such a person is my legendary Monkey friend, Kathryn, who always calls herself a "failed Leo." Kathryn is actually as imperious as the next Leo, but she appears meek and likes to imagine herself unobtrusive. She's an "I'll stay out of your way" Leo. Kathryn could, have married a Gemini because Geminis take over in public situations, and the modest-seeming Leo that Kathryn is would not have minded that insurgence.

Most Leos are generous of spirit but closed about their own feelings. Geminis like to probe the depths of behavior of everyone around and may invade Leo's privacy. Gemini doesn't always remember to praise Leo's accomplishments. This negligence is very naughty on Gemini's part and may cause Leo to feel hurt, yet not be able to show it. Frustration may set in over the difficulty in sharing glory equally.

Also, Gemini, who darts here and there like a lizard on amphetamines, may find a sultry Leo mate a tad on the indolent side for his or tastes. Gemini can forgive the Leo that languid side so long as Leo lies about listening and paying attention to Gem's newest plans and exploits and doesn't get too absorbed in a book or a TV show. A Gemini who feels ignored may pull a neurotic fit, throw a tantrum, or make an outrageous cutting remark to redirect Leo's wandering focus.

Stalwart Leo may also be confused by this mercurial mate's dithering and altering of behavior, but will probably be fascinated by Gemini's excellent memory for facts, appreciate Gemini's adaptability, and admire Gemini's hearty sense of humor. The above are traits that Leo doesn't always own, as Leo takes Leo very seriously and doesn't laugh easily at his or her own foibles. Leo is a mite rigid by nature and confesses to having a poor memory. Leos write things down incessantly, recalling their dates and names through the stealthy use of pen and paper. Gemini simply recalls information—all of it, in context and in order. Leo is truly knocked out by a Gem partner's sparkling intelligence.

As for career, Gemini is gifted at professions that ask for communication skills and shrewdness. Sales, public relations, administration, and politics can make a Gemini rich and keep them sassy. As for Leo, well, Leo is somewhat more lethargic and doesn't enjoy moving about much. Leos make excellent monarchs, CEOs, purchasing officers, or museum curators. If they can keep their shirts on and not fly off too many handles, Leos can fit into hierarchies better than Geminis and so might work in offices or banks.

Money? Leo is probably the better money manager in your house. But if you put your heads together, you could become a wily team of stock market investors. Together, you should earn enough money to have a glamorous home, where Leo's taste for little cupboards and drawers will blend rather inappropriately with Gemini's taste for comfy disorder. Since you both like antiques and shopping for treasures, however, such a house can work very well.

The sex will be sensational. Gemini's airiness will be cozied up by Leo's fire. Gemini's sexual imagination is as fertile as the rest of his or her brain. All in all, I think that this relationship works jolly well and that you can expect to have a long and interesting life together. You will have to learn to adapt to each other's style at first, but you will long be passionate enough about each other for the adjustments to be worth the trouble they cause.

Plan the kids carefully. A smiley Libra child or a soldierly little Aries would be a welcome addition. You will be good parents—amusing and warm, bright and caring. Happy trails!

Gemini with Virgo

Air and earth might make a dusty combination in a relationship. But you two often prove to be the exception to that rule. Luckily, both of your Sun signs share Mercury as their ruling planet. Mercury is associated with communication and adaptability, so mental exchange is a part of your interaction. The bubbly Gemini has a quick, agile mind and is constantly picking up new data and grabbing at new information. Gemini, however, is not outrageously interested in processing or evaluating what is picked up. Like a butterfly, Gemini tastes a little here, then checks out the buds over there. Gem's main motivations are change, excitement, stimulation. And when Gemini tries to swoop down and share data with a Virgo lover, he or she may encounter an impenetrable wall of resistance.

What? Can't you see I'm busy? I am not available just now." The meticulous Virgo can't just open wide, zero in, and snatch your news. Virgo needs time to sort out details and analyze facts in a systematic way. Virgo may even blame Gemini for excessive superficial speed. Meanwhile, Gemini stands by, tapping both foot and fingers and growing more impatient and bored by the second.

Geminis are the networkers of the zodiac and have immense talent for sensing new business opportunities. Money flows easily in and out of the average Gemini's life. However, rainy day savings projects and planning for the future is not Gemini's domain. Gemini's money motto is: "Spend and you shall receive." Since they are such experts at gathering and dealing with instant information, Gemini might be a newspaper reporter; bookstore owner, writer, or sales representative. And Virgo tends to fret a lot about money and nearly goes mad with anxiety when a Gemini partner wants to invest funds that you have set aside, week after meticulous week in some aggressive-growth mutual fund or other speculative venture. Virgos prefer to shop around until they find the bargains. With their eye for detail, Virgos are definitely better suited to managing the couple's monetary affairs. Virgo usually has a steady job (and income) and can often be found working as an administrator, teacher, cook, health professional or skilled craftsperson.

Because you both so adore communication, your relationship will be built on the steady exchange of words and ideas. If the union endures, your Gemini/Virgo home will be filled with books and magazines, radios and stereos, and at least one TV in every room. The kitchen should be laboratory slick and easy to work in. Virgo likes to cook and may also have to take charge of the rest of the household chores. Gemini will be too busy talking on the phone. The scattier the Gemini, the more irritated he or she will become with fussy Virgo's obsession with order and cleanliness. "My coat is not thrown on the couch," Gemini insists. "My coat lives on that couch. It is there because it feels comfortable there and will be readily accessible next time I need to go out." Virgo reacts to this by freaking and stomping around, hanging up coats and pairing up boots and finding matching gloves and behaving in a positively militaristic fashion. Gemini should not try to make excuses for his sloppiness. Instead, Gemini should load on appreciation for the things Virgo does around the house. Virgo is shy about this trait but needs praise and attention. If you really lay it on, Gem, you may never have to do the dishes as long as you both live together.

Since both of you are intellectuals, you may have read every book about sex and intimacy. But when it comes to putting yours into practice, I am not certain of the outcome. I suggest that seduction be left up to Gemini, who instinctively knows how to make Virgo laugh and lighten up. If left up to Virgo to take the sexual initiative, the romantic advances will be limited to practical suggestions like "Shall we do it?" or "Feel like getting it on tonight, dear?"

You two make wonderful parents. You will both see to it that your children (a bright Aquarius or a diplomatic Libra) have plenty of encouragement to read, learn, and express themselves, from a very early age.

❤️❤️❤️❤️ *Gemini with Libra*

When the lively, articulate Gemini and the charming, refined Libra fall in love with each other, it feels to them like a match made in heaven. You two air signs flow harmoniously together, placing a healthy emphasis on communication and mental stimulation. Such intense social intercourse is very important in any relationship—and most especially in this one. You will endure as a couple because you will communicate—all the time. And, God knows, you both *love* to talk!

After the initial "honeymoon" stage, Gemini may exhibit signs of boredom and grow weary of hashing over "relationship stuff." Libra, remember, is a coupling sign who evaluates everything in terms of "we." A harmoniously balanced relationship is Libra's lifeblood. Gemini is more purely intellectual and has individualized, multifaceted, varied interests. While Libra focuses on the love relationship, Gemini is all over the place, bopping around the neighborhood, hanging out reading the paper in the local coffee shop, connecting with people from dawn to dusk. Ultimately, it will make Gemini uncomfortable if a Libra partner expects him or her to do everything as a couple. To avoid conflict, Libra will have to give Gemini lots of space. As for you, Gem, you must tune in more often to Libra's couple station, sit through the brainstorming sessions on how to make the relationship work better, and even provide some intelligent feedback.

You two could work together on a writing, theatrical, or teaching project. Gemini will be in charge of collecting data and turning clever phrases, while Libra does the program design and applies savvy Libra know-how to evaluating pros and cons. As each would be assigned a particular task, ego would be all but eliminated and the show would go brilliantly on. Typical Gemini careers are journalist, broadcaster, linguist, commentator, or public relations expert. Libra is gifted for working as a relationship counselor, mediator, color consultant, or interior decorator. Both of you are very generous with your money. You, Libra, like to spend it on clothes, cosmetics, and art, while Gemini buys a lot of books and fast cars. Who would manage your joint account? I advise hiring an expert, as you will get each other into hot water if you try your mutual hand at accounting.

As long as Gemini has access to a cordless phone, a computer, and a fax machine, he or she won't mind if the Libra partner takes charge of decorating your elegantly beautiful home. You are both very social--entertainment is your middle name. You have an easy time sharing the same friends, with whom you hold many lively discussions far into the night. You both enjoy expanding your knowledge through reading, writing, and attending growth workshops and seminars. You also love to go off on romantic hideaway weekends together. In short, you know how to be serious as well as to have fun together. What could be better?

Although you will both probably have demanding careers, you'll still manage to be responsible, loving parents who inspire and instill thirst for knowledge and excellence in their smart little kids. A jovial Sagittarius or a confident Leo would make an excellent addition to this wordy family.

You are a romantic's romantic, Libra, and may at times complain that Gemini is not affectionate or attentive enough. I suggest you curb the fantasizing and learn to accept your head-trippy Gemini partner for who he or she is. Otherwise your sex life will suffer. Gemini needs to talk his or her way in and out of sex. If Libra tries hard not to mourn low lights and champagne every single time they make love, this couple can have an exceptionally interesting and ever-evolving sexual rapport.

Gemini with Scorpio

Believe it or not, a Scorpio/Gemini marriage can actually work—if the chemistry between these two people is overwhelming *and* their intellectual goals and tastes are shared. Similar family backgrounds and religious beliefs would also help. But without this foundation, this complex coupling is good for about three solid weeks of intellectual sparring, occasional heady stabs at sexual intercourse, and the ultimate promise of dismal dissatisfaction. In order for this relationship to pass muster, you two will need to develop a strong foundation of mutual humility.

Gemini is initially attracted to Scorpio because of the latter's intangibly beautiful way of expressing emotion. Scorpio's hidden emotional life seems a jewel and a prize that Gemini longs to possess. But Gemini, poor dear, cannot hold an emotional state for long. Unlike Scorpios, who dig in their stingers for the duration, Geminis watch their feelings waft around like dandelion fluff, escaping their grasp and eventually disappearing into the ether.

Scorpio enjoys the love game. The more Gemini talks, the more Scorpio pretends to listen. The faster Gemini flits away, the broader Scorpio casts his or her net of wiles. Scorpio longs to entice, to seduce, and finally to enmesh her jittery Gemini in a tangled web of complex emotional commitment. Gemini beware! This mysterious creature about whom nobody—even themselves—knows much is after your soul.

Scorpio, fascinated by the theatrical mannerisms and invasiveness of freedom-mongering Gemini, must also take care. Scorpio wants everything Gemini is. Clever Scorpions first locate their prey's vulnerability, then plunge their stinger deeply enough to draw what they need from the well.

Geminis speak a lot—about everything and nothing at once. Scorpios have tongues as sharp as meat cleavers and don't hesitate to chop Gem's offhand remarks into tiny little pieces. Even the foxiest of Gems can be diminished by Scorpio's repeated attempts at stealing his or her thunder. Then, when Gemini shrinks in the face of Scorpio's stinging attacks, Scorpio loses respect for Gemini, which quashes all desire to share the bedroom. Woeful though it may be, Scorpio may be the source of Gemini's loss of self-esteem. The sex will be exciting only as long as Scorpio remains loving and limits the underhanded attacks. Gemini, after all, is only a twin human.

As you can see, marriage between these two characters may well end in bitterness and confusion. However, if the physical attraction is sufficiently powerful, the intellectual sparring stimulating—and the counseling effective enough—this couple may be able to set aside individual needs for the benefit of the collective effort. If properly nurtured, the Gemini/Scorpio relationship can gain wisdom from compromise. Negotiation is key.

A Scorpio/Gemini couple should try to have Pisces or Aries babies. Libra children will fare well too. Don't bring any saucy Leos into the world or birth a rigid Capricorn. Capricorns need more than you have to offer.

Scorpio/Gemini is quite zany enough. No need to create further chaos by adding a bundle of extra-lucid Aquarian joy.

❤️❤️❤️ *Gemini with Sagittarius*

This union strikes me as half perfect. That's an odd description, but let me explain: First, these are two very verbal people, each of whom has a gift for getting a point across. Sag, of course, brandishes revolutionary ideals and speaks of them with zeal and conviction. Gemini possesses a multitude of strategic ideas and voices them as cleverly and convincingly as two used-car salesmen at once. So, as a team, these two have a facility for expression that is unmatched. With all that oral acumen they should be able to talk through their problems and find solutions together.

Which brings me to the reason I think of Gemini/Sagittarius as half-perfect. They have polarized ideals. Sagittarius wants to make the world a better place, while Gemini usually wants to enhance Gemini's lifestyle off the backs of rich fools who will give up their money in return for some half-baked Geminian promise. At best, you two will suffer each other's points of view for the good of the future of your life together and your family's well-being. But underneath it all, a simmering cauldron of dissension bubbles nearer the surface than either of you wants to admit. Yet, if your Moon signs and other planetary aspects are in accord or you have utterly complementary Chinese signs, something very harmonious may come of your union.

If you can learn from each other, you will form a mighty effective team and would be excellent at owning a business, sharing a medical practice, or having a radio call-in show. You will undoubtedly also get involved in the typically Sagittarian activity of lavishing food and drink on any and all comers. Gemini adores holding forth, telling tales, making jokes, amusing everyone with antics, and sharing uproarious giggles. The synergy created by your two gregarious personalities promises that a memorable experience will be had by all. No doubt about it, together you make excellent hosts. Why not run a restaurant or start your own dinner theater?

The generous Sagittarius is profligate with money. Gemini is better at sticking to budgets, but not by much. If you do have business together—or even for the purposes of running a household—you ought to hire a stern accountant as consultant who forces you to manage rather than deplete your capital.

If you share a home, the decoration will be sparse but handsome. You tend to agree on styles, and both display a taste for the latest in sleek, modern design. The pair of you are out and about a lot, so you won't be needing too many cozy couches in front of the fireplace. If you have the money to spare, you will want to have a large master bedroom suite in your home with two separate bathrooms. Both of you delight in having your own private space within a shared space, as you have very different grooming patterns. Gemini is a quicker fixer-upper than Sag, who enjoys the process of primping before a mirror. Not that Gemini isn't vain, but Sagittarius is more finicky about appearances.

How is the sex? Well, it is really fabulous. The fiery Sagittarius really knows how to push the right buttons and turn Gemini on. Something about Sags' flash and verve causes Gemini's twin hearts to go pitty-pitty pat-pat. Sagittarians are very clever at keeping Gemini guessing, and there is nothing a Gemini likes better than surprises. The unexpected causes Gem to have to do a lot of instantaneous adaptation, which Gemini excels at. Sagittarius is not noted for eternal fidelity, and is such a blurtmeister that he or she will probably come home from a naughty weekend and confess. Not always having behaved in an exemplary fashion either, Gemini is usually quite accepting of this sort of announcement. After blathering on about some disloyalty and exacting some impossible new promises from Sag, Gem wipes the slate clean and life goes on.

Kids? Yes. You two could have one or two children. It will be a noisy household anyway, so get yourselves a pushy little Aries or a loquaciously loving Libra child. You will all adore talking to each other-- incessantly.

Gemini with Capricorn

One look at this couple's life and you will deduce that nothing short of flight will solve their basic problems. Capricorns dwell in the on-the-ground reality of ambition. They spend their lives stoically clambering upward to win the unattainable prize, reach the top of the heap, or catch the rarest of brass rings. Striving and making it is what Capricorns are about. To my way of thinking, no addle-brained, fast-talking Gemini has a hope in hell of making off with this determined, serious earth person's heart. Oh, the odd Gemini might occasionally surface in a Capricorn's love life, but only to satisfy some curiosity or urge that the Capricorn is temporarily unable to squelch.

Capricorn is simply too tradition-bound, family-oriented, and desirous of getting places the hard way to dally for long with the likes of the fun-loving, manipulative, gabby, lighthearted Gemini, who one day wants to be an Italian movie star and the next has decided to open a stand in Alaska. Geminis actually scare Capricorns with their outrageously flit-witted manner of endlessly jabbering, delving, and probing. I see the angular, ungainly Capricorn clumsily escaping out the window in the dead of night, discreetly fleeing the pressure of Gemini's electric energy. "Phew!" thinks Capricorn, stealing off into the dark. "I hope I didn't leave my phone number back there, or else that Gemini person will call me and talk at me again until I cannot put one thought behind the other."

And what of Gemini in all of this? How is a star-studded Gemini to feel when he or she is summarily dumped on by the austere and haughty Capricorn? Well, truth to tell, Gemini feels slightly ill. At best, disappointed. At worst, suicidal. You see, Geminis need an audience. And at first meeting with the rather stolid and reserved Capricorn, Gemini must think, "Yipppeee! I can prattle to my heart's content, throw ideas all around the room, and this baby will be quietly and gratefully entertained." But unfortunately for Gemini, Capricorn has little patience with Gem's need for applause and indeed very little time away from striving for goals to pat the Gem on the head.

Even if Gemini is a genius at making a living, unless he or she is a socially prominent *monstre sacré,* Cap will tend to consider the twin talker a loose cannon and a lightweight. Gemini/Capricorn is metaphoric: Springtime pitted against the glacial blue ice of Winter—and in this instance, I fear Springtime is the loser. No clever Gemini tap-dance routines or virtuoso juggling acts will melt that wintry Capricorn resistance.

Should you two, by some miracle or trick of fate, actually find yourselves living together under the same roof, I suggest (of course) that Capricorn handle all funds, organize the household, and make decisions regarding the future. Whatever planning needs to be done in the present—for the moment and for the general entertainment of the troops—Gemini will handle brilliantly.

Your decorating scheme had best be eclectic. Capricorn will want to drape everything in velvets and satins, and purchase traditional styles in sofas and chairs, antique chests and desks, and Old Masters paintings. Gemini will be happy with one great piece of exquisitely designed trendy furniture plunked right in the middle of the living room like an *objet d'art*. Any house you share promises to be a patchwork of Victorian and Louis XV period pieces mixed pell-mell with fifties' pole lamps and Naugahyde leather-look divans designed by the most famous contemporary furniture genius on earth. Capricorn will undoubtedly work in a bank, an advertising agency, or some law or dental or medical office as either head honcho or head honcho-to-be. Count on Gemini to make a living as a newspaper reporter, an entertainer, a used car dealer, or a fabulous teacher. Gemini needs to move about in a job, so nothing too staid will do.

Your sex life? Not so hot. Minimalist and eclectic. Capricorn is so rigid and Gemini so airy that when you do get together your seem awkward and nothing wants to fit quite the way it is supposed to. Think of elbows and knees getting in the way of the other areas of interest. After all, we are trying here to mix air and earth. So what do you get? A dust storm.

Children? Probably not. At least not in this marriage.

Gemini with Aquarius

This relationship may initially appear to be a grand passion. There is such a meeting of the minds between Aquarius and Gemini that when they are seen together, chatting amiably, whispering conspiratorially at parties, one imagines them to be the sort of joined-at-the-hip couple who allow for no distractions, do *everything* together, and seem to have the secret to happiness. But beneath the surface, idealistic Aquarius and prevaricating Gemini are shooting off in different and mutually misunderstood directions. Will it last?

Probably not. Aquarians are the most open-minded people any of us will ever meet. Aquarians are also truth-seekers, so they will encounter huge muddles when dealing with a Gemini partner who is perfectly content with half truths. Gemini bas a brilliant brain attached to an even cleverer mouth but, in between, there is fog in the channel. Gemini can remember only what it suits Gemini to recall. Aquarius, on the other hand, remembers everything.

If Gemini lets Aquarius do the thinking in this relationship, a lot more would get accomplished. But it doesn't always work that way. Every morning, Aquarius thinks before breathing. And every morning, Gemini speaks before breathing—and before thinking. As Gem spins out one fantastic tale after another, embroidering entertainingly on a thin veil of truth, Aquarius accuses Gemini of fibbing. Gemini feels attacked. Unfair? You be the judge.

Geminis are charming, convivial, talented communicators—which is more than I'll say for some weirdo Aquarians, whose towering intelligence seems to inhibit their stooping to small talk. Aquarians can be for Geminis, though. They inspire their partners to perceive aspects of life from new angles. Aquarians enrich the shallow side of a Gemini. But Aquarians take themselves so seriously that sometimes Gemini (and the rest of us) feels bogged down and bored. Why not try to balance your talents so that progress gets made and neither feels held in check by the other? You both enjoy entertaining friends and holding forth far into the night. Aquarius has ideals about improving society and saving the world. Gemini (when he or she stops blabbing for a minute) can be a marvelous implementer of an Aquarius's bright ideas. You might work well as a team. Gemini is gifted for professions such as law, the theater, teaching, and journalism. Aquarius is better at science, banking, espionage, and languages (especially codes).

Money will flow in buckets to Gemini, then will leak right out of the bottoms. Forget Aquarius with money. Why not just live life limiting yourselves to minimum needs—or else hire a proficient accountant to hoard your money for you? As a couple, you could live on an allowance, or could you?

You are terrific friends. You carry on inspiration conversations, dream up marvelous schemes together, and even manage your houses without too much yelling and screaming. Aquarius is more minimalist than Gemini, who adores trendy clutter. But you are compromisers by nature and unafraid to push the boat out in the communications department. So projects get done through your remarkable co-abilities to adapt. That is admirable.

But sex is not a thing you can think up ways to compromise about and then simply *do*. Mr. Chemistry enters the bedchamber and refuses to budge except when he *feels* like it. When passion is not here, it cannot be created. I fear we have that problem here. Aquarius and Gemini each need a more earthy or watery partner to snuggle up to in order to engender that oozey good feeling we call *lust*. In your marriage, the sex will be okay. But unless your planets are in some way aligned so that Moons and Venuses are simply awash in each other's rays, I dare not give this good friendship, kinship, fellowship relationship an A in the bedroom. You will have to try techniques and take seminars and courses to improve your rapport.

Kids? Sure—if you have a decent roof to put over their heads and a couple of rich grandparents to send them through college. You two can be a very marginal couple who live with little concern for the material things in life. That's all right for some children, but not for all. Unless you have some financial security, don't have kids. If you do have some shekels, make yourselves a Pisces or Sagittarius baby to start with. Then call me in the morning.

Gemini with Pisces

At first glance, this couple appears to share a similar turn of mind, enjoy a certain reciprocal style, and benefit from a not bad sense of humor about themselves. But I am afraid that this time, image is not the reality. What you see, with Pisces and Gemini, is not what you get. Unless these people are blessed with some very harmonious shared planetary aspects or perfectly aligned Chinese signs, after a few months of attempted cohabitation they may be seen slinking in opposite directions. Disappointment and basic incomprehension are the results of giddy air attempting to fathom introverted emotional water. It won't take long before Gemini will go under for the third time, kicking and screaming. Pisces, oddly enough, is the true force in this couple.

Gemini, we know, is usually a chatterbox dynamo with a short attention span and a dual nature. Surprise incarnate. One day's Gemini is a hard-driving, ambitions go-getter who smiles a lot. The next day (or even the next minute) that same Gemini unexpectedly becomes a slothful grouchy meanie. Gemini is all over the map—doing projects, then undoing other projects, undertaking new enterprises, and dropping them in favor of something newer and more exciting. Gemini is all mind, loving in an intense yet fleeting manner. Now you see Gemini, now you don't.

Pisces, although sometimes defensively argumentative, is consistently sweet-natured and tries, whenever possible, to give conflict the slip. A Pisces may disagree with you, but this peace-loving person will back off from waxing outright grumpy over something so piddling as an opinion. Pisces are more interested in sensation. They like to feel things as they happen, let experience ooze over them, and watch ideas develop through a series of emotional rather than intellectual events. Pisces stays put a lot, ruminating or just being in their heads. Pisces do not fancy being hammered at by excessive talking, disturbed by too much activity, or made love to in a snack-like hurry-up bumblebee fashion. Pisces combines sensitivity with intuition to make slow, deliberate decisions based very often on esthetics rather than on reason.

Could two types of people be less alike? Well, these two are not only different, they are ill-suited to achieve reciprocal growth by being a couple. Gemini gets easily bored waiting around for Pisces to connect. Pisces grows anxious and nervous, aware of never measuring up to Gemini's hectic pace and losing self-esteem by the bucket in the process. The Pisces half of this pair is always bringing up the rear in conversation and activity. The Gemini partner, instead of finding Pisces' snail's pace adorable, grows impatient and begins snapping at the poor embarrassed Fish, who wants nothing more than to swim under a rock and stay there. There are no two ways about it (except in Gem's head where the *always* two ways about everything): Gemini and Pisces would do better staying single friends than marrying up with each other.

If ever you did live together, your finances would probably be a mess. Your priorities being so diverse, you wouldn't be able to agree on what to buy and when.

Your decor would be all over the board, at least initially. Pisces would be content to be draped in gossamer fabrics and live in elegant, creatively designed furnishings with a tinge of the cozy in muted moody blues and greens. Gemini wants freshly picked trendy stuff or sterling examples of the latest antiques craze dotting the living room. In fact, Gemini may even be perfectly content with large, airy rooms full of nothing. Eventually, so as not to cause a fuss, Pisces would lose identity altogether in favor of Gem's tastes, schedules, and habits. Pisces is a lover. Not a fighter.

Bed? Sex? Oh, boy. I just don't see this one working. Sorry if you are madly in love and can't keep your hands off each other, but I see two very separate characters who will not be attracted to each other in the first place. Gemini, not understanding or caring a fig about what Pisces' real slow wisdom represents, may consider Pisces. adorable, but will also deem him or her weak and inconsequential. Pisces will spot an action-packed Gemini approaching and be instantly overcome by a dizzy spell. I will not give sexual advice here because I don't think it will be necessary.

Procreation between Pisces and Gemini would be folly. And should be avoided. Your couple is not likely to have the staying power to raise kids together. If it does, please send me some photos.

CANCER

Taken to the extreme, all of our qualities can become frailties. Some of us are generous to a fault, which can be wasteful. Good communicators can also be blabbermouths. Nurturing parents can smother their children. Fortunately, free will allows us to balance the positive and negative sides of our character. Cancer, the moon-ruled emotional sign, was born:

POSITIVE | NEGATIVE

considerate | self-sacrificing

persistent | unrelenting

emotional | moody

protective | stifling

intuitive | suspicious

nurturing | patronizing

Cancer with Cancer

At first, you will each be exceedingly strong-willed and a tad unapproachable. But having the same Sun sign means that you are essentially in tune with each other. The human compassion you are both so gifted for at will become your couple's trademark. You have the same objectives in life: family, a stable home and mate, financial and emotional security, and a relatively stimulating employ. Marriage is your ally. Therefore, marriage to each other makes sense.

Cancer is associated with nurturing, giving and receiving emotional support. Most of the time you are warmhearted and loving to those you love-especially to each other. But Cancers react emotionally to everything in life, and sudden mood swings are not in the least uncommon. Cancers also have a secretive side, which often prevents them from expressing their own needs and desires openly. Characteristic Cancer brooding and depressive sulking may stem from this frustration about saying what they feel. Cancer somehow expects a partner to intuit thoughts. Fortunately, with a pair of Cancers, mind-reading works. Two Cancers can actually peek into each other's ideas.

Problems will arise when you both need attention at the same time. Who will do the nurturing then? It's a toss-up. Moreover, as you are a couple of moon-ruled Cancers, one or both of you may play mind games or use manipulative tactics to get the care you want in times of great emotional need. Watch for tantrums disguised as pouting, moping, grouchiness, and woe-is-meism. Run reality checks to see if one or the other of you is not pulling an act just to get more than his or her share of affection.

Both of you long to be needed. If your relationship is working well and your intense need for affection and support is being satisfied, then life chugs along without a hitch. In most times of crisis, you console and comfort each other. When you are pleased content you hug and spoon and compliment each other on your looks. For a couple of intelligent Cancers, life as a married couple can be pure bliss.

You also delight in taking care of other people, especially children. Either one of you could be a teacher, a cook, a nurse, hotelier, or caterer. You might open a bed and breakfast or start a homecare service. As a team or on your own, you might launch a successful career as an antique dealer, archeological researcher, or as author of historical texts.

Obviously, you are both perfect homemakers and true homebodies. Cancers love to collect "stuff." Together you create a cozy place to live, filled with all sorts of treasures, sentimental knickknacks, and every variety of memorabilia. Another homey aspect of the double-Cancer life is that you both enjoy feeding others almost as much as you enjoy feeding yourselves. You may throw fabulous dinner parties or spend romantic evenings dining in front of the fireplace listening to opera or hearing your favorite rock songs over and over again. You are both incurable romantics and adore being in love—if only for the sake of being in love. Love really feels good. And God knows, Cancers like to feel good.

Thanks to your shrewd business sense, you usually make lots of money. Cancers are known for their thriftiness and knowledge of investments. You will probably be equally clever at knowing how to balance the family's budget, save for a rainy day, and still keep enough money aside for family fun and generous gift-giving. You will want to share the responsibility for managing joint finances.

Affectionate and tender, Cancers are usually very accomplished at sex. Holding, kissing, and caressing are not only allowed, but encouraged, in every room of the house. You are a nonstop touchy-feely sort of couple whose need for physical contact is strong and often urgent. In the beginning of your affair you may each be slightly timid toward the actual act of making love. But as you get to know each other's pleasure spots and test out new and different lovemaking techniques; you will make an admirable sexual team whose passion will endure.

You both long to have children and will become devoted, sometimes even smothering, parents. Cancers will get along best with another water sign in the family, a Scorpio, or particularly a dreamy, compassionate Pisces child. But a down-to-earth Taurus or an earthbound Virgo child would also thrive in the security and safety of your family-oriented home.

Cancer with Leo

Unless this Cancer has a Leo rising sign or a Cancer ascendant, or your Chinese signs harmonize like crazy, I would highly recommend this you end this relationship before it begins. There is no future in bickering, back-biting, tearful scenes, and angry misunderstandings. Sulking and blame are the name of this game. Forget it. Unless of course you are already wed and trying desperately to make a go of it. In that case, read on.

As a couple, you are fire and water. Cancer craves emotional nurturing but the Crab's edgy moods drive the fiery Leo crazy. Leo's ego-driven need to be admired and courted make quiet, introverted Cancer's skin crawl. Cancer, with a wave of the magic mood wand, can dampen Leo's naturally high spirits in a trice. The giant Leo ego is very fragile. Cancer takes delight in quietly teasing the Leo, hence slowly extinguishing his fire. Leo finds a Cancer partner's deeply sentimental nature preposterous and will actively and vocally deride Cancer's needs—which only makes a sad little Cancer want to shrivel up and die sooner. Then the cold war sets in. Cancer broods for days. Leo leaves the house and only comes home to change clothes. The war persists until some major event breaks the silence and once again Leo and Cancer are back on shaky speaking terms. But is this fun? Does life have to be a series of battles followed by long periods of emptiness? I don't think so.

Let us imagine that you have some intensely reasonable reason to want to stay together, and have decided to work on your basic differences. You are going to try to blend into a harmonious couple. With the proper counseling and effort, you, Cancer, might learn from your Leo partner to be more congenial, expressive, and playful. And you, Leo, to allow your Cancer mate to pamper you, to bring out your warmth, and to pique your sweet affectionate side. The key is to honor and accept who each of you is and not to continually put each other down for not measuring up to your individual expectations. Also, if you see yourselves falling back into the silence and weeping pattern, have a good look at what you are doing to each other—and then try to laugh at yourselves.

If it does work for any length of time and you do live together, maternal Cancer wouldn't mind staying at home playing homemaker. Cancer adores things old and collectible. He or she could own an antique shop, repair antique furniture, run a fancy consignment shop, or open a costume rental shop—the cozy sort of shop where you would have a freshly brewed cup of coffee ready for your customers. You, Leo, need to express yourself creatively. Your creations will net you the appreciation you so desperately long for. Any position carrying a promise of publicity and fame appeals to you, but you may also be an inspiring teacher or a business manager with great leadership qualities.

Your mutual spending habits may be a source of conflict. Leo is extravagant and loves luxury. "What are credit cards for, after all?" is Leo's happy-go-lucky motto. This upsets budget-minded Cancer, who tends to frugality and concern about preservation and survival. My advice: Keep separate bank accounts. And Cancer, do not lead Leo into temptation by giving him or her access to your credit cards.

Cancer will, of course, want heaps of recognition from a Leo mate—and this is quite a challenge. Leo should take notice of a Cancer mate's achievements. Praise the Crab for all the good he or she does, and give that sensitive partner a pat on the head or a kiss on the neck every time you pass him by.

In the privacy of your bedroom you, Leo, will have to ignite your sometimes reticent Cancer's fire by being gentle, affectionate and spontaneous. Again, you should heap Cancer with praise. This will bring out the receptive and responsive side of Cancer. Sexually, you can complement each other by cleverly combining Cancer softness with Leo intensity. Both of you are very romantic and -strong-willed. A well-designed sex life might prove to be the cement that keeps you two together.

I cannot advise you to have children, as you will probably have a stormy, uneven relationship to look after. But if you do insist, have yourselves one child. Choose a chatty Gemini or a loquacious Libra to add balance and intellectual perspective to your emotionally charged marriage.

💘💘💘 Cancer with Virgo

This may not be the most glamorous, sex-crazed, or outwardly demonstrative union, but many of your friends probably wish they had such a solid relationship. Bottom line, the warm lovebug Cancer and the conscientious, cerebral Virgo are good for each other. Both of you are somewhat timid and reclusive, appreciate financial security, and are family-oriented. Virgo's earthy sense of practical reality has a comforting effect on the vulnerable Cancer cuddler, making the Crab feel snug and protected in Virgo's reasonable presence.

You have much to learn from each other. The intuitive, receptive Cancer will teach you, Virgo, to get in touch with your feelings, so as to grow more self-assured and be less timid. Also, Virgos often commit slow suicide through overwork. They are forever trying too hard to live up to their own unrealistic work ethic. Cancer knows how to pamper a weary Virgo with gentle back-rubs, sweet nothings, plenty of comforting foodstuffs and praise galore. Virgo, being Virgo, may at first resist this treatment, thinking of it as spoiling or indulgence. But a Virgo who gets used to Cancer's special coddling will sink right into a pleasant routine of wanting more and more all the time.

One major drawback in this relationship might be the basic water and earth sign disparity. The touchy Cancer is prone to sudden mood swings.

When Cancer feels emotionally malnourished, a kind of mute despondency comes into the room and hovers there like a menacing frost. Poor Virgo is at a total loss, and may try to "fix" Cancer with unsolicited free advice. When that doesn't do the trick, Virgo may give up, leave Cancer alone in the gloomy house, and go off somewhere alone. What works best with a testy Cancer mood is unadulterated syrupy sweet romance. Next time the black cloud appears, pick up a red or white rose or write a sweet love note for your Cancer love. Like magic, Cancer will snap out of it and reward you with a hug—at least until the bad mood comes around again. The best medicine is not logic, it's good old-fashioned romance.

And speaking of romance, a Cancer who feels emotionally appreciated can be a hotly devoted lover who will awaken Virgo's hidden passionate side. Stop worrying, Virgo. Let go of your inhibition. Expose your innermost fantasias and bare your soul to the Cancer who so admires and adores you. Trust in Cancer's ability to draw out the best in you. Maybe you are the cleverest analyst and the smartest critic around, but nobody ever accused you of being the world's greatest lover. But Cancer? Yes. Frequently, Cancers make the best lovers of all. Why? Because Cancers are in love with love and make a fine art out of doing it right.

Finances should work themselves out because both of you spend your money only when necessary. Neither of you would ever dream of investing in risky projects or foolhardy schemes. As you are both good at sharing, I expect you will figure out how to manage the finances of your marriage with dexterity and common sense. Take turns balancing the checkbook and paying household bills. There should be no ego- based competition between you on this subject.

Your tastes are quite different, however. You, Virgo, hate it when your Cancer messes up your neatly structured and squeaky-clean home with those flea market bargains he or she drags home every weekend. Poor Cancers. They just cling to everything old and can never let go. Over time, they fill up their houses with cluttery antiques, knicknacks, china plates, plants, ruffles, wreaths and fluffy pillows. Cancer's ideas of a cozy, comfortable home is that more is better, while Virgo loves clean lines and spare design. But you will no doubt compromise in the decor department so that both of you can enjoy a warm, nurturing yet orderly home.

You are obviously very dependable, dutiful, and loving parents. Virgo might be a bit too picky and critical of a sensitive child, but Cancer can always be counted on to comfort and croon. If they are lucky enough to absorb the best of both your characters, your children (a Pisces, Libra, and Taurus would make a sweet trio) will grow up to be well-rounded, caring and sympathetic, as well as clever and down-to-earth.

Cancer with Libra

Although water and air are not traditionally considered compatible, with a bit of enlightened therapy and effort on both parts, you two are able to establish a sound lifetime relationship. Of all the air signs, only you, Libra, have the kinds of heartfelt qualities that can promise a fulfilling relationship with a Cancer partner. Your considerate and refined behavior is very reassuring for the timid, sentimental Cancer.

Both of you have always dreamed of being half of a felicitous twosome who, together, might eliminate everything coarse and ugly. The softhearted Cancer needs to feel a special glow of true affinity with a partner in order to feel emotionally comfortable. The esthetic Libra is so of his or her surroundings that anything short of perfect harmony makes them physically ill. Naturally, Libra will do almost anything to please a darling Cancer partner—anything, that is, that helps Libra's equilibrium. Fairness and the desire to cooperate are positive Libra traits. But come what may, Libras needs balance.

One of the major peculiarities in this union is that Librans are other-directed. They extend themselves to people, think about their needs, and sincerely wish to be of help. Libra is neither a loner nor a moody, impenetrable type. Cancers, on the other hand, are basically self-oriented. Yes, they do much for those who are close to them. But the major reason Cancers desire to foster and protect loved ones is to keep them near—not only to cherish them, but also to own them. When it comes to people, Cancer is the most possessive of signs. And self-preoccupation is one of Cancer's most disturbing blind spots.

Despite all of your well-intentioned efforts, Libra, you may never be fully able to understand the complexity of your Cancer mate. Remember, Cancer is a deeply responsive, emotional water sign, while Libra looks at life from an intellectual point of view. In order to blend your somewhat disparate characters into a thriving couple with its own particular identity, you must accept to practice the three Cs: communication, compromise, and compassion. Cancer, come out of yourself and *talk* to your Libra mate about why you feel hurt or frustrated. Do not pout, go silent, and expect Your Libra mate to read your mind. As for you, Libra, you will need to be careful of what you say and how you phrase your opinions. You are dealing with a very fragile set of Moon-ruled emotions whose first response to any hint of criticism is denial. Don't be upset by Cancer's reactions. Use your noggin. Pick your way more gingerly around the frail Cancerian soul. Once you learn how, it becomes easier and easier not to wound the tender creature—and all the devotion and nurturing you receive in return will make it plenty worth your while.

Here, the introvert meets the extrovert. The outgoing, artistic and beauty-conscious Libra may have a successful career in the field of public relations, as a motivational speaker, a fundraiser, or as sales director in a large firm. Cancer might be a youth counselor, a teacher, an antique shop owner, a gardener, or a floral designer. Cancer likes to hole up at home. Libra needs to mix with people. Why not give lots of parties together? Libra can take care of mingling, while Cancer enjoys the show from behind the scenes.

Due to an intense need for financial security, Cancer will often be thrifty or even stingy. Thrift doesn't correspond with Libra's lifestyle. Libras adore money. Time for compromise on both sides. Finances will be safer with Cancer, but a lot more fun with Libra.

Sex? Well, you are both very romantic and appreciate candle-lit rooms. But Cancer is less of the EverReady Battery than Libra, whose desire to team up and make whoopee is notorious. If Libra wants Cancer to be accessible, Libra should always remember that food and wine can make all the difference to a grumpy Crab day. As for Cancer getting Libra into the right frame of mind, well, it doesn't take much but—just in case there is resistance, Libras are pushovers for long, involved conversations in steamy tubs laced with aromatic oils.

You will be loving, inspiring parents to your kids. Have a sunny Leo, a solid Taurus, or an earthbound Virgo child or two. Following your fine blend of examples, your offspring should be friendly, creative, bright, and sympathetic.

Cancer with Scorpio

Classical astrologers contend that these two Sun signs get along because of their watery natures and harmonious placement in the zodiac. But I wonder. Are not both Cancer and Scorpio too emotionally permeable to cohabit without clashing? I worry. To advise a sensitive Cancer to take up with a samurai-tongued Scorpio has definite lamb-to-the-slaughter overtones. Nonetheless, this couple enjoys a reputation for knowing how to *love* each other. So I will go with the flow.

One thing is sure. Cancer and Scorpio are constantly offending each other. Slights and meaningless slurs turn into giant monster fights. An offended Cancer sulks, mopes, and chews his stomach lining. The poor creature lies there on its back, wounded, while the haughty Scorpio looks on, blasé, then observes with a shrug, "I think I need some air," and storms out.

The forsaken Cancer dreads these scenes, but knows the couple's incredibly intimate sex will always beckon Scorpio back.

Scorpio does love Cancer intensely. But Scorpio is proud and knows how to break Cancer's heart with that hard-nosed *attitude*. Cancers cannot easily control their emotions. They fall in love with love. And love, to Cancer, means live-in full-time ownership and adoration. Scorpios are flattered to be so desired, so sought after, so admired. But inevitably, they do something to infuriate the Cancer mate. Since both Cancer and Scorpio are secretive and moody, household tensions may rise to a fearsome pitch. Finally, Scorpio breaks the silence with a sharp-tongued remark that slices Cancer's soul in half. Cancer pouts, steams, and generally skulks about, searching for some desperately needed warmth. And Scorpio can be cruel and lay on the extra helpings of disdain—big time!

Once these two acknowledge the destructive side to their repeated rows, they may be able to build a very solid relationship. Complicity rising out of a true passion will help a lot. But lots of compromise will be required to turn this heady relationship into a lasting marriage.

Were you two able to stay together as a couple for a long time, the question of who does what with whose money would, no doubt, arise.

Here (at last!) is one element that does not threaten to cause undue stress between you. Scorpio is reasonably generous with money and definitely believes in providing for mates and offspring. Cancer, we know, can be slightly tightfisted. But miserliness is not the cause of this anomaly. Rather, Cancer's budget-mindedness comes from a need to be sure of security. Scorpio and Cancer work well together to earn, invest and even to enjoy their wealth.

If marriage were a pastime based entirely on sex, I'd give this couple a hundred hearts. Cancer/Scorpio amour is intense and *délicieux* in bed. If you are up to one of these titillating adventures, first invest in a giant swoop-curtain four-poster. Before retiring each evening, shoo children, pets (unless you have some erotic use for them), and nannies to the other wing of the house. To avert explosion, unplug all appliances. Then, hit the sack. Brushing teeth and the like will have to wait—the business of the Cancer/Scorpio day is at hand. Cancer inspires Scorpio to those sizzling heights for which the sign is famous. Likewise, Cancer finds sex with Scorpio addictive, because it allows for such an electrifying emotional outlet as to keep Cancer in a good frame of mind all day.

Kids? Maybe. But wait at least five years until the first blush of passion wears off and you can at least find time to speak to without wanting to jump in bed together. Have a Capricorn and a Pisces. They get along and help you to do likewise.

Cancer with Sagittarius

Sagittarius is freedom-loving, adventurous, and outgoing while Cancer is clingy, security-oriented, and withdrawn. Not only are there no points of real harmony between you two, but there is no reason to try. Because at the end of whatever therapy or counseling or intimacy seminars you attend, you will still only be one soulful Cancer trying to make a marriage to a firebrand Sagittarius run smoothly—square-peg-round-hole-City.

You can never really hope to merge as one and create a sweet, loving and compassionate team because you are so thoroughly unalike as to not be able to share a railroad compartment without having a difference of opinion. If, by some miracle, you are getting along fine, count your blessings and thank the harmonious aspects of the rest of your charts. Your Chinese signs may actually be doing the work for you as well. You see, for example, a Sagittarius/Goat married to a Cancer/Pig. There might still be rows. But they would be mitigated by the fact that Pigs of all stripes adore Goats of any nature—no matter what. Also, the Sagittarius/Goat is the only Sag who needs a cozy home first and independence second. So that Pig/Goat/Sag/Cancer match could work. There may be others. Read up on the various possible matches in the section on Chinese signs.

The symbol for the water sign Cancer is the self-protective, fearful Crab, who prefers to walk cautiously sideways rather than to take direct forward steps. The bodacious Archer Sagittarius is famous for spontaneous, sometimes even rash, actions. The intuitive and reflective Cancer is riveted to the past. Sagittarius always aims for the future. While Cancer yearns for a stable marriage and a big, loving family, Sagittarius is planning a trekking trip to the Himalayas—alone! In fact, Sag rarely commits exclusively to one relationship. What could be more distressing for the soft-shelled Crab than a freewheeling lover or mate who runs off every second day into the sunset on endless adventurous missions and errands designed to be experienced solo?

Marriage is really not a good idea, but sex might work fine—providing you don't discuss much in between frolics. Sagittarius is full of inspiring sex ideas and has a finely tuned sense of humor. Cancer may have to be seduced and coaxed out of a safe hiding place in the kitchen or garden, but making love with a restless and sometimes sexually blunt Sagittarius can be a sensual challenge. To make it work, Cancer, you will have to learn to communicate your need for tenderness. And you, Sag, must try to be more caring and receptive.

Being optimistic, truth-seeking, and jovial, Sagittarius can make a fine philosopher, teacher, lawyer, or travel agent. Sagittarians hate dull routine and thrive in exciting, hair-raising careers where they get to be either alone or boss. Sag is generous, sometimes wasteful, and loves to spend money on fast cars, long trips, and electronic gadgets. Cancer, however, is exactly the opposite. Cancer is money-conscious to a fault and has a strong urge to save everything and often choose careers as kindergarten teachers, antique dealers, chefs, or homemakers.

Cancer really ought to be the financial director for this couple. Sagittarians literally hate to be regulated by anyone but themselves. No matter how much he or she loves a mate, Sag won't hear of allowing his or her money to fall into the greedy little claws of our friend the Crab.

Sagittarius wants a big, bright home on a hillside. Sag hates to be boxed in, enjoys flowing, casual clothes, and freedom-loving sports. The retiring Crab would rather live nestled in a cove by the ocean or near a river in a secluded old house that can be remodeled and filled with years of collectibles. How will you work that one out? Separate domiciles?

Moreover, Sagittarius might be a reluctant parent. The responsibility of directing someone else's life seems overwhelming to Sag. If you are to procreate together, Cancer, being born in the traditional sign of parenting, will want to make the decision to get pregnant or not. If Sag is the female half and resists the idea of kids, Cancer will simply have to live without. Were you to agree and have a kid or two, I think a Pisces child would fill the bill—giving plenty of emotional feedback to the Cancer parent and beguiling the heck out of the emotion-resistant Sag. On second thought ... leave the kids out of this mess. Okay?

❤️ ❤️ ❤️ *Cancer with Capricorn*

Here is an intriguingly *possible* relationship, requiring much hard and compassionate understanding. Your Sun signs are exactly opposing each other, yet you have much in common. Although your styles are very different, you are both goal-oriented and your aspirations are quite similar: Both Capricorns and Cancers spend their lives stalking a secure lifestyle. They both favor a serious, even pessimistic outlook. And both are reputable and dependable. And as Capricorn and Cancer are respectively made of hard work and understanding, I reckon this couple stands a good chance of making it all the way through the fires of marriage.

Cancer is a sensitive water sign and responds to life in a highly emotional manner. Cancer loves giving comfort, craves affection and must feel cherished and appreciated in a relationship. Capricorn, to the contrary, is a pragmatic and realistic earth sign. Emotion and sentiment are rather foreign to Capricorns. They find it very difficult to access their deepest feelings and talk about them much less. Capricorn simply cannot always respond to caring and be as sympathetic as Cancer would like.

But don't despair. By adding a heaping measure of generous altruism to these polarized ingredients, Capricorn and Cancer can concoct a very balanced and complementary home-cooked meal. Capricorn, you will be proud and happy to handle the practical matters of life, hence amply satisfying your partner's need for material security. As for you, Cancer, you can begin work right away schooling your ambitions, hardworking Goat in the ways and means of becoming more receptive to emotion. It will take time. You may need therapy. But this marriage can work very, very well indeed.

Now to the bedroom. You Cancers are unswervably romantic. You long to be eternally lost in the labyrinthine process of wooing and serenading, surrendering and languishing in the throes of *le grand amour.* Unfortunately, your realistic Capricorn may never quite be able to live up to this dream. With the exception of fine food—which is a Capricornian preoccupation tantamount to an obsession--- sensual pleasures are often considered a luxury. To be happy, Capricorns must be productive first. If they take time out for lascivious luxuries, it makes them feel guilty and useless. So, naturally, as you are the romantic in the family, it falls to you, Cancer, to seduce your hard-edged partner and convince him or her that lovemaking and intimacy are of dire importance to a truly providential life.

Capricorns are usually both disciplined and ambitious. A lot of Capricorns become business managers in the corporate world, slowly but steadily climbing to the top. Family life may suffer because Cap is out there working such long hours and focusing far too much on success and career. Cancer can also be very successful in the workplace. But for Cancer, family comes first. So whether this Cancer decides to be a devoted homebody or work outside the home, or both, he or she is likely to be involved in a career related to children and domestic affairs.

Money and its sundry uses are of the utmost importance to both of you. Neither of you wants to see it wasted. Little matter who handles the finances here—funds will be spent wisely and invested and saved for the future when necessary. Squandering is for hotheads—not for Cancer and Capricorn.

Cancer would put tons of energy into making the home a comfortable place to be. Although Capricorn might prefer spare lines and white walls, chances are Cancer will insist on cozy terra cotta or tatty leather armchair decorating schemes. You may do the cooking together. Cancer will probably bake up excellent comfort foods such as cakes and breads while Capricorn whips together delectable gourmet dishes requiring exotic or hard-to-come-by ingredients. Cancer reads *House Beautiful* and *Parents* while Capricorn settles down with Money magazine.

You are both very loving parents. But Cancer will do the nurturing and indulging, while Capricorn takes care of the structure and discipline of the children's lives. Capricorn, try to spend more time playing with your kids. It will help to lighten you up. If you can choose what sorts of babies you will eventually hatch, why not try to stay in your own elements and have yourselves a huggable Taurus or a creative little Pisces baby?

Cancer with Aquarius

You have to be kidding. Cancer taking up with Aquarius? Or worse, Aquarius taking up with Cancer? As my friend Marsha the Cancer would say in her lilting East Coast voice, *I don't think so.* If you are already in this unlikely couple and wish to stay there, you are welcome to it. But unless there are enormously mitigating ascendants and the most harmonious of Chinese signs to balance it out, Aquarius and Cancer seemed doomed to dance around each other with hot pokers for most of their mutual hell of a life together. But ... harmony could happen.

The elements that influence this couple make the pairing less than fun from the start. Fixed air and cardinal water: It seems like a born dead washout. Your motives and methods are so different that no matter how hard you try, you may never really be able to understand each other. Cancer, of course, wants to feel loved, nurtured, and protected by a partner. A stable marriage, family, and sheltered home situation are Cancer's main goals in life. Cancer's emotions run from feverishly low to abysmally low, yet he or she has a hard time communicating them. Cancer dreams of an ideal mate who will know how to read his or her mind—intuitively. Aquarius is absolutely terrible at mind-reading. In fact moodiness and hypersensitivity scare Aquarius into next week. As friendly and tolerant as Aquarians seem, they live in the cool, abstract realm of the logical mind. Freedom and individuality are Aquarius's highest values. Aquarius is progressive and humanitarian and actively involved in many groups and causes attempting to change the status quo—often with unorthodox methods. Cancers are often adorable, but at their worst they can be opinionated, stubborn, and conservative in the extreme.

How does this all fit with intimacy and marriage (something that you, Cancer, crave so badly)? Well, it doesn't. And that's the point. You, Aquarius, want space and independence, and you, Cancer, want closeness and security. Of course, once Aquarians have decided to do "the relationship thing," they can learn to be quite loyal and committed to one person. But they still hate to be smothered and mothered and told what to do and when to take their cough syrup.

The biggest challenge for an Aquarius who wanted to live with a Cancer would be to quit his or her permanent head trip and try to connect with the body and the senses. If an Aquarian can allow a Cancer partner to relax and be open to physical joys and lascivious pleasures; then Aquarius does stand to gain a great deal. Of course, if Cancer wants all this to happen at all, he or she must cease clinging to his or her mate. Otherwise, Aquarius will take off in the other direction and will not listen. And what does Cancer stand to gain? Not a heck of a whole lot.

Aquarius is a born genius. You hate boring routines and need change and stimulation every single day. You should have some sort of exotic career. Cancers have a great talent for counseling people, making them feel good by comforting and feeding them. Therefore Cancer may have a career in any of the caring fields. But Cancer, try not to rely too much on your Aquarius partner for a regular income. You, Cancer, can satisfy your own intense security needs by being self-reliant. Aquarius is not, by nature, a provider of much more than fascinating schemes and grandiose ideas of great genius or artistic value.

If you do stay together and there is a home to be run, Cancer will be stuck with the job. Cancers have a strong urge for nesting and need to be able to-snuggle up in a safe haven. Since you can't relate to all this stuff, Aquarius, do your Cancer a favor and go along with his or her style. Be gentle and appreciative and he or she will remain your devoted companion forever. But if you are not sweet and understanding and leave poor Cancer to stew in his or her own juice, you will be cultivating one hell of a vindictive enemy. Cancers *never* forget.

If you decided to have kids (please don't!), Cancer would obviously be the more nurturing parent. Adult kids who can converse and reason with their weird visionary Aquarius Mom or Dad will eventually appreciate them. Either an ambitious Capricorn or a fiery Sagittarius kid could survive Cancer/Aquarius's unconventional and idealistic relationship.

❤❤❤❤ *Cancer with Pisces*

Congratulations! This couple is really a winner. When the nurturing Cancer and the compassionate Pisces unite, it feels like they are inside a match made in the glorious depths of the most beautiful undersea landscape of a tropical land made for pleasure. I should truly like to enjoy the liquid passion of the harmonious initial phase of your courtship. I know you both mused the whole time about how your prayers for the right person to come along had finally been answered. You are still doing a bit of musing even now about how amazing it is to both operate on the same wavelength. You are equally emotional, romantic, affectionate, intuitive, sensitive, and giving. As Cancer and a Pisces are tuned to the same frequency, even the worst rows you may have will feel somehow *right*.

How are you different? Well, Cancer is a personal sign, concerned solely about his or her private well-being and that of the loved ones in the immediate environment. Pisces, a universal sign, spends boatloads of energy caring about the world and the people in it in a selfless, charitable way. Pisces wants to help the down and out, succor and rescue society's rejects and misfits. Pisces' altruism may cause Cancer to feel emotionally neglected. If Pisces spends a lot of time in the homeless shelter when Cancer feels Pisces should be at home, sparks may fly. But since you are both so psychically attuned, these differences can (as can problems) be cleared up in a single conversation.

One caveat. Enjoy the deep rapport you have together but keep your feet on the ground. Each of you has a tendency to eradicate all boundaries in the presence of the other person. Between you lives a fierce and profound need to be needed by the other, and you may even encounter a tendency toward reciprocal clinging. Read a few of those codependency books and make sure that each of you spends some quality time alone once in a while.

Other than that, count your blessings and enjoy the good life!

Sexually, you flow and melt together. Intimacy and open sharing of feelings and vulnerabilities comes readily to both of you. You trust each other with your most private secrets. In fact, the act of lovemaking is probably not as important to you as the intense unity you experience when you are touching. You derive great satisfaction from the slightest caress or sweetest fondling as you lie together listening to soft, ecstatic music in anticipation of the act of love.

When it comes to making money, you, Cancer, are more enterprising. Your strong need for material security drives you to want to bring home a jumbo paycheck, and then to make the most out of it by being thrifty and budget-conscious. Pisces is a dreamer who does not share Cancer's disproportionate fear of poverty. Money comes to Pisces in the most arcane and mysterious ways, as it seems Pisces have an innate understanding that the universe will be supportive to them. Pisces may choose a glamorous career as a TV producer, a graphic designer, or an actor. Pisces are generous and spend lots of money on art, clothes, and beauty treatments. You might want to let Cancer handle the investments, but I don't believe Pisces could bear being given a meager allowance. Perhaps you can keep separate bank accounts so that Pisces can have the use of his or her own funds.

Your home is a safe haven, tastefully decorated with art objects and cozy, comfortable furniture. Pisces as well as Cancer people love to live by the ocean. You spend many quiet evenings alone together, enjoying home-cooked meals, watching sunsets, meditating, listening and absorbing that unique sense of connectedness that only two water signs can appreciate.

Having kids? Make yourselves a loquacious Libra, an analytical Virgo, or another sweet-natured Pisces child. All three will to be fortunate indeed to be born into your lighthearted, nourishing, supportive environment. Like you, your kids promise to be compassionate, creative, and kind.

LEO

Taken to the extreme, all of our qualities can become frailties. Some of us are generous to a fault, which can be wasteful. Good communicators can also be blabbermouths. Nurturing parents can smother their children. Fortunately, free will allows us to balance the positive and negative sides of our character. The magnificent sunny Leo was born:

POSITIVE | NEGATIVE

virtuous | sanctimonious

audacious | intrusive

loyal | clinging

majestic | overbearing

theatrical | melodramatic

self-assured | overconfident

Leo with Leo

Here is a felicitous yang family portrait if I ever saw one. When two self-assured Lions decide to join themselves in matrimony, it makes for an intensely powerful union. You are an affectionate, enthusiastic, cheerful, optimistic couple. Each of you radiates confidence. Leos have a natural ability to bring joy and sunshine into our lives. You are the soul center of every party. Men and women alike are drawn to your exceptional magnetism. People are truly inspired by your animated, playful disposition. You carry a regal air of flamboyance about with you. To Leos, life is one big movie set that is just waiting to be filled by their illustrious presence. You want to express yourself creatively and long to be cherished and noticed by others. Life can become a tad testy, of course, when one of you suddenly appears to be more successful than the other. The Lion rules the jungle, remember. Lions do not like to share the limelight - not even with their beloved mate.

With a pronounced flair for the dramatic, you will commit almost any social crime to get to be the center of attention, especially when a third person is involved and the green-eyed monster of jealousy peeks through the curtain to leer at you. Egotism, arrogance, vanity, and stubborn competitiveness are the downsides of Leo. Since you were both born under the same sign, it is important that you recognize and treat each other as equals. Otherwise, you will surely waste valuable time and energy in a futile fight for supremacy. Instead of competing, try to celebrate your imperial life together. You may look around, but you will never find anybody more capable of satisfying your seemingly insatiable hunger for romance, fun, appreciation, and grandiose gestures than your Leo twin lover.

Sex, love, and intimacy are all part of the wonderful game of life that you play so masterfully. Leo is seductive and sensuous and knows how to bring out another Leo's noble, protective side. Watch out in this relationship for displays of false pride and sudden attacks of jealousy and possessiveness that threaten to cloud your happiness—for no good reason except that you are both equally vain and jealous by nature. Squish those two ugly Leo qualities into a ball and hurl them out the window of your love nest. Without their interference, life will continue as passionately and playfully as it was in the courtship phase.

You both need to be known for having created something special and unique. That natural Leo exuberance is reflected in your work. A lot of Leos become famous artists, actors, dancers, and painters. Your love for children makes you great teachers, especially in the art and drama department.

Both of you spend your money generously and often excessively. Since you do everything on a large scale, and demand the best of everything, money slips through your hands easily. If you find you are overspending, hire yourselves a manger to keep spending in check and make wise investments so your old age will feel like a dessert instead of a desert.

Your extravagant home will probably be chockablock with huge plants, overstuffed chairs to accommodate your many visitors, and exquisite pieces of art. You Leos love scarlet and tones of gold and ochre yellow, shades that reflect your regal, impressive self-image. You entertain lavishly and are marvelous hosts. You like to keep an open house or even hold *salons*. Kids and animals (especially cats) are just as welcome as any influential art dealer and avant-garde artist from the capitals of Europe.

You are wonderful, loving, and caring parents. You two are probably best suited for parenting another fire sign, like a strong-willed Aries boy, or a jovial, visionary Sag girl.

Leo with Virgo

Although your friends may eventually wonder what attracted a high-spirited, gregarious Leo to a timid, analytical Virgo, with a bit of work and compassionate understanding, you two can make your extreme differences work positively for you. In the zodiac, it is thought that each sign is a response to the sign that came before. In your case, this theory makes very good sense. If Leo is associated with spontaneous partying and overindulgence, Virgo comes loping along right after you, efficiently cleaning up after your messes and teaching you about a healthier, more orderly lifestyle.

Virgos are so competent that they don't really even mind being of service to others. They do want appreciation for their selfless efforts; but even if they don't get plaudits and kudos all the livelong day, Virgos will still help people out, try to clean up the world, and wish for more order and analysis in every human endeavor. Leo wants to have fun in life: to play, laugh, flirt, attract, and boss people with inimitable, radiant charm. Can't you just envision how appealing that sunshiny, buoyant, self-assured Leo style must appear to that serious, organized, scowling Virgo? You, Leo, have the ability to erase the worry lines from a too-serious Virgo's fraught brow, inspiring him or her to try to be more relaxed, self-confident, outgoing, and pleasure-seeking.

If you decide to work together, you two will form a championship team. Leo is a natural startup person. He or she wants to become an artist, a performer, a designer, or an entrepreneur. Leo has no trouble conceiving of grandiose ideas, but may have a difficult time sticking to a disciplined routine when the chips are down. In order to convert a vision into something tangible, discipline is essential. That's where the bright, methodical Virgo comes into the picture. From behind the scenes, Virgo will take care of the day-to-day business by balancing the checkbook, paying the bills, answering mail, keeping track of appointments, and so on.

Money issues often cause disagreements in your relationship, and probably need the most compromise. Virgos are frugal, hate wastefulness, and like to shop around for bargains. Leos love to spend money generously, excessively, and often well beyond their means. My advice? Sign a prenuptial agreement and get yourselves separate bank accounts. As for investments and pension plans, leave that part up to Virgo. Virgos just about never die poor.

You, Virgo, may be a perfectionist when it comes to managing your neat, squeaky-clean home, but I fear that messy Leo will attempt to sabotage your efforts. Interestingly, messy Leos are tidy people—they keep neat closets and shipshape dresser drawers, clothes and goods neatly stacked and stored in little compartments. Yet their immediate surroundings, where they live and work, can be hugely disorderly and even pretty dirty without it getting to them. But then what Leo has time to clean and tidy up when he or she has a house full of fun-loving people sleeping over? Or a party in the making or one just finished last evening? Leos like to keep an inviting and stylish home but it is usually far from impeccable. My advice? Hire somebody to clean up after Leo and Leo's thousands of guests so that Virgo doesn't go raving mad trying to keep a cool bead in a topsy-turvy house.

Sexually, Leo's fire ignites the somewhat prudishly shy Virgo partner and brings out his or her passionate side. Leo would be wise to take lovemaking slow, always being careful to create the right ambiance, laying on the silk sheets for special occasions, and in short, trying to drive Virgo straight out of his or her critically analytical head. If Leo plays the sexual power trip for which that sign is so famous, Virgo will soon be melting like a dropped ice cream cone on a hot sidewalk.

Leos are kids at heart, and make enthusiastic parents. In this partnership, it's Leo who tends to spoil your kids blue. But never mind, the second parental figure is a rigorous self-controlled Virgo who can handle all manner of chaos through the use of discipline and elbow grease. No matter if Leo gets the kids off schedule with some outrageous form of play. Virgo will always be there to make sure that they take their vitamins and finish their homework on time. Your couple provides a healthy and balanced structure for kids to grow up in. You should try to schedule your kids for either Libra or Taurus.

Leo with Libra

Fire and air signs are inclined to be supportive of each other. And to my mind, the combination of Leo and Libra is a particularly salutary one. You are both remarkably romantic, idealistic people who make no secret of the fact that you yearn for a loving relationship. Your goals are the same. But your methods of getting what you want are not identical. Leo considers that being *in love* is the inherited right of the fiery, gregarious, leonine nature. "Love," declares Leo, "is what gives one vigor." You are turned on by the dating game. You live to flirt, to seduce, to woo, and to be wooed back. Leo is also a personal sign. You expect to get a lot of ego gratification from being with another person. As a royal Leo, you want to be made to feel special, pampered, and you always want to receive the bulk of the attention.

Libra is a social sign, much concerned about interaction with other people and seeing to it that everybody gets a fair shake. Libra believes in cooperation as a means to every end, and wants to create harmony in relationships. So, Libra doesn't mind compromising. This is especially useful when Libra is confronted by an inflexibly egotistical Leo partner. Libra is considerate, tactful, charming, and very aware of people's feelings. Although the overbearing, self-centered Leo can drive Libra crazy at times, these two basically form a fun-loving, outgoing couple. You two know how to have a good time together.

Professionally, you are both on the same wavelength and could very well work together in the field of creative arts. You, Libra, don't mind stepping back and to letting your Leo get more attention than you, as long as the relationship remains balanced and happy. Both of you are excel in the performing arts, interior design, teaching, and public relations. Being a diplomat and mediator, you, Libra, might also make a great lawyer, counselor, politician, or judge.

Whatever happens, you two will make enough money to keep Libra in silken luxury and Leo in ermine robes. I cannot think which of you is the best squanderer, but I have a feeling it's Leo. So what if you have more credit cards than any of your friends. Your motto is easy come, easy go. Keep your books together and try a system of checks and balances to maintain some order in your financial picture.

Your refined, tasteful home will reflect your mutual talent for designing and decorating, Together you can create an amazing showplace full of art, comfy with fine furnishings and lavish with luxurious accessories. You love to entertain your many friends and business partners at elegant dinner parties. Money (of course) is no object. You attract it easily and spend it generously on each other, your home, your kids, and even on those in need.

For Libra, sexual intimacy comes to the body via the head. Being born in an intellectual air sign, you, Libra, may need a little help from both atmosphere and your impassioned Leo partner to be able to connect with your own very delicate sensuality. To set the mood, you should light all the candles in the bedroom, pop the champagne cork, and relax into physical ecstasy with your lusty, sensuous Leo mate. As sexual adventures go, yours will be a very passionate long-term mutual discovery trip.

Once you have established a satisfactory sexual pattern, Libra will want to be married. Leo too likes having a full-time mate and family to boss around. So feel free to make your engagement short and get down to the bearing of children whenever you feel ready. Loving, optimistic, intelligent, and inspirational parents, you bring out the best in your offspring. I advise an adventurous Sagittarius or a witty Gemini for your firstborn. Then you might want to round things out by adding a Capricorn, and then a third child to spoil—such as a loving Pisces or a needy, huggable Cancer who will stay at home as long as you can stand it.

½ Leo with Scorpio

I *love* the idea of this match. I also fear it. As a Scorpio, I suspect that if I ever took seriously up with a Leo mate, a new definition of murder and mayhem might result. To me, the sensation of two imperious hotshot types—one a giant cat who pads about seeking prey, tearing it to shreds, and bloodily consuming it, and the other a sultry, stinging insect who hides under rocks waiting for victims, stunning them into submission, and leaving them for dead—well, it doesn't sound very cozy, does it? Truth is, you Leos and Scorpios do get along in many ways. In love, of course, the Leo/Scorpio plot thickens. Passion reigns side by side with unbearable spates of quibbling conflict. Put on your Sunday best armored suit or dress. The battles will go down in history as epic, and the war will go on forever.

At first glance, you won't have to face the problem about who will wear the pants. You will both be running your own personal shows at all times, as you did before you got together. After about a week of cohabitation, however, it may indeed come as a surprise that you have to play couplehood by the rules.

As long as the demands on your couple concern major issues—such as whether or not to have children or move house or change jobs, you get along just fine. When it comes to the big stuff you are a supremely reasonable couple. But you are dreadfully inadequate where the petty stuff is concerned. Neither of you wants to feed the cat, take out the trash, close up the house at night, or call the plumber. And neither of you wants to follow any rules that you didn't make. You niggle over who will perform the scut work, passing the buck and blaming each other for minor slipups all the day long. If you can afford it, by all means hire help.

When it comes to decorating, you will differ over such details as which color couches to buy. Scorpio dreams of burgundy. Leo has decided on beige. You each know that you are not only *right* but you are doing what is *best* for the communal you. The more Leo seethes, boils, and rages, the faster

Scorpio sticks to the wine-colored loveseat dream. What to do? Leo may be more of a sharer and a giver than Scorpio, still that imperious ego hate compromise. So, Leo, to save your marriage (and your imperial face), you call in an expert, hire a top-notch designer, or get out the latest issue of *Architectural Digest* to prove your point. "Beige, sweetheart," you announce to your Scorpio skeptic, "is definitely *in*. Burgundy, however, has not been seen in this since Queen Victoria's time." Scorpio *hates* to be thought tasteless), and so takes the bait. Besides, thinks the secretly vengeful Scorpio, *I'll get my own back when we do the bedroom.*

If it seems, so far, as if money is no object in this couple's existence, it's because money is indeed not much of an issue. Leo gets to keep the accounts. Scorpio gets to make the money. Or vice versa. Little matter as you are both competent with numbers. Of course, either or both of you can indeed make skillions because you're equally go-ahead, hard-working folks and know how to go after what you want in life.

As for the sex, it's damn satisfying between Leos and Scorpios. Both of these signs enjoy meeting head-on with their sexual partners. Domination is never a problem because you each feel safe in the knowledge that if one of you tried to become dominant in the bedroom, the other might trounce you in your sleep. Equal power makes for appetites and an intense, but sane sex life.

Having children makes you realize for the first time in your lives that *neither* of you comes first. Although the shock of "baby makes three" hits Scorpio/Leo hard at first, you both warm to the idea and find that the more offspring you produce, the more mitigating factors there are to teach your royal selves how to make deals with each other instead of considering divorce. I suggest a pair of Gemini babies for entertainment value. A Capricorn kid will serve as a balance between you two and will find his or her wintry self enjoying every minute of the special warmth from Leo and the passion infusion from Scorpio. Or why not have yourselves a sweet Pisces or a warm, cuddly Cancer baby?

❤️❤️❤️❤️ *Leo with Sagittarius*

You are an appealing, self-confident couple. Your positive, optimistic outlook on life is both stimulating and encouraging to others. Luckily, you are both extremely idealistic and can easily satisfy each other's needs for a fairy-tale romance. Being born with the Sun in action-oriented fire signs, you are outgoing and high-spirited. You know how to have a good time. Your fights are epic, too. Neither of you hesitates to speak your mind. But never mind. You know how to process information in a healthy garbage-in/garbage-out sort of way, which keeps you from living one of those awful lives of quiet desperation about which we hear so much.

Both of you may be competitive sportsmen or sportswomen. Sagittarius is a born daredevil, for whom no mountain is too high and no race car too speedy. Sag is constantly looking for new physical challenges—climbing mountains or trekking through Tibet or hang-gliding over Bolivia, smiling all the way to the emergency room. Seriously, although Sags may overextend themselves at times, they usually land on their feet. Their upbeat, adventurous, "No risk, no gain" attitude makes them more than just *very* attractive to a Leo partner. Not exactly a timid milquetoast either, Leo likes to stand up in the crowd and disclaim, "Hey, look at me, I'm the greatest. I deserve the very best!" Leo, you are a natural performer who thrives on attention-getting drama, exciting storytelling, and grandiose gestures. Introspection and modesty may not be your strongest attributes, but if you have found the right Sagittarius you may have found your perfect match. Together, a Leo/Sagittarius couple is able to create a colorful, never-a-dull-moment lifestyle.

The sexual fireworks aim high into the sky when you two passionate, charming people get together in bed. Sagittarius is a zealous lover whose fanciful, adventurous notions carry over into all aspects of lovemaking. And Leo is so playful and flirtatious that no matter what happens, he or she will know how to accommodate this delightful sex partner. Besides, Leo is a hot number. He or she will do anything in his or her power to keep the flame of love burning—even after many years of marriage.

Sagittarius needs a career where he or she can be boss or at least choose a work schedule. Most of all, Sag craves stimulation and change. Since Sag enjoys foreign countries and speed, he or she might choose to be an airline pilot, or a travel or sports guide, a forest ranger or a gliding instructor. You, Leo, want a career where you can express yourself creatively and get a lot of attention Choose something as glamorous as being an actor or an actress, a filmmaker, or a jewelry or clothing designer.

You two better make sure that you have a ton of money, because you both adore spending it on generous gifts, adventurous trips, scintillating entertainment, fast cars, clothes, beauty products, help at home and even (especially in Sag's case) on gambling. You are the original Mr. and Mrs. Buyout the town.

Think big, think flashy, think expansive!" says Sag to Leo as they head out for their third European shopping and châteaux tour this year. This motto is also reflected in the way you design and decorate your spacious, opulent home. You two are noteworthy among your friends for your outrageously fancy parties. Of course, because neither one of you is very much into householding or cooking, you will have to be catered. Even during the week, instead of slaving in the kitchen, you either go out to restaurants or order take-out.

Should you decide to have kids, things might shift to nuked dinners and maybe an occasional chicken you would throw in the oven. But then again, you have so much more important stuff to offer your kids: a great experimental life with two unusual, loving, openhearted parents. Have yourselves a willful, innocent Aries child or a funny-faced Gemini who will team up with the Leo parent and make all of you laugh yourselves silly. I don't advise a Pisces or even a Cancer child, as they are fragile and might be shaken up by all the changes your exciting marriage will put them through.

❤️❤️❤️❤️ Leo with Capricorn

A couple to love and even to copy. Capricorn provides a constant, replenishing fuel for majestic Leo's uneven fire, while Leo gives Capricorn respect and stature. With a Leo lover or mate, the Capricorn shines more naturally, achieves more readily, and learns how not to struggle so hard for the dream of success. The sedate Capricorn lover sympathizes with Leo's role as ruler of the world and allows the Lion to roar— while ably attending to the details of their interesting life together. All in all, this is an unusually harmonious relationship in which Cap takes care of the nuts and bolts and Leo sings his or her praises.

My affection for this particular couple derives from personal experience. I am neither Capricorn nor Leo myself. But for some reason, I have many Leo and Capricorn friends, and luckily, a lot of them are married to each other. Moreover, they have been married to each other for absolute ever! Something very positive happens when Capricorn falls in love with a Leo.

What I have noticed about these Leo/Capricorn people who marry and keep on being married is that Leo somehow doesn't mind being subservient to Capricorn. Perhaps the word *subservient* is too strong, but let's say that in this marriage, Leo allows Capricorn free reign to correct him or her in company, to interrupt a story Leo is telling, and even order/advise Leo to "Get the salmon mousse, darling. It's on the buffet. Bring it to the table. Thanks," without Leo going ballistic or storming away from the table. There is something regal about Capricorn that Leo respects. Is it a superior attitude? Or just a kindly insistence? I am not certain. But I do know that I have seen great big towering difficult Leo men dwarfed by their diminutive Capricorn wives with a split second's remark, "Mark! Your fork!" or "Fritz! I said no." I have seen shrewd Capricorns turned to concave-chested jellyfish by masterful but loving Leo mates. "Martha, forgive me, my dear, but I did say Chardonnay. Go get the Chardonnay. Now. There's a good girl." And

Martha—of whom even I am dismally afraid for fear she'll scold me—trots obediently back down to the wine cellar without a word.

Capricorn is rigid. Leo is not. Leo is sunny. Capricorn is winter personified. Leo is self-centered. Capricorn is self-propelled. These people are very different from each other. But somehow the Leo's sunshine melts the Capricorn's steely heart and Capricorn's ambitious do-it-right approach appeals to the laid-back Leo who also finds Capricorn irresistibly fetching.

You make fabulous business partners. Capricorn stays at the office, minding the slaves, doing the books, and counting the gold whilst Leo goes out selling, seducing the world, and being charming and effective in a social way. Money will always be an issue you, because Leo is so much more spendthrift than the careful Capricorn. But so long as Capricorn agrees to keep tabs on these credit card balances, Leo will be content to live within their means. Remember, Capricorn's built-in severity makes sense to the big Cat, who looks up to a mountain goat mate with gratitude for saving him or her from ruin. In a Cap/Leo marriage, Leo can feel free to goof off a bit or at least let go once in a while because Capricorn will always be there to pick up the slack.

Your home will be adorably appointed in a bohemian, countrified style. You will favor cushy couches with velvets and brocades in patterns from exotic lands where you have traveled or about which you have read many books. Every item of decoration will have personal significance. You will enjoy having guests. Capricorn is the cook. Leo pours the champagne, puts on the music, and greets people at the door. Your home is a haven for your friends, who feel comfortable in its nonaggressive atmosphere.

Best of all, the sex is excellent—as long as the Capricorn isn't miffed or hurt, this couple's epic bedtime romps will be frequent and passionate. Still, Capricorn may sometimes need a bit of prodding. Not to worry. Leo knows how to make a Capricorn swoon. And does that Capricorn ever know how to put on a good show for the Leo's lusty ego!

You may want children. But not many. If you have one, make it a Leo, a Capricorn, or a Scorpio.

Leo with Aquarius

You two can make a good team by working with the fact that your signs are exactly opposing each other. Each of you has a lot to give and each has something to learn. And what's that? Through constant contact with a philanthropic Aquarian partner, the almost too-proud Leo will begin to shelve his or her ego, to become more socially-involved with groups and friends, and to develop a taste for selfless humanitarian service. With a Leo around to lead the way, the eccentric Aquarius partner can learn the skills of creative self-expression, develop some of that special leonine strength, gain confidence, and adopt a more playful attitude to life. This relationship will never run smoothly all the time—you are, after all, completely opposite and have a great many incongruities between you. But as you are both very principles, upstanding citizens with a well-honed conscience, you are capable of ironing out any wrinkles as they come off the wash line of your life.

Aquarians are forever getting absorbed in heavy intellectual pursuits and spend far too much energy swimming around neck deep in dense complexities of altruistic group involvement. A conscientious Aquarian lover must try not to neglect an emotionally demanding, buoyant Leo partner by spending too many hours saving the planet or hanging out with brainy friends. Otherwise, Leo might develop one of his or her notorious fits of dramatics designed to impress upon you how necessary it is to dedicate more time and energy to your private life.

Aquarius may work in the field of science, communication art, or electronics. Whatever the job, Aquarius keeps odd hours. Leo wants to have an exciting career that brings plenty of recognition. Typical careers include running a fashion house, becoming a respected drama teacher, setting up as an artist, or trying politics or the law.

As for your tastes, they are very different. Leos love lavish decor, especially in red and gold. They favor paisley prints and flamboyant displays of sculpture and paintings. Everything around Leos—the parties they give, the jewelry they wear, even their opinions—seems bigger than life. You, Aquarius, like chrome-and-black high-tech design and may not always agree with the fancy way Leo decorates. You will probably have to find a compromise by each having your own personal room where you are able to entertain your very different sets of friends.

You are lucky, Leo, that your friendly, open-minded Aquarius is extremely tolerant of your financial extravagance. Of course, Aquarius prefers to spend money on computers, books, and records, or may even donate it to a worthy cause—especially one that Leo thinks of as asininely remote, like dog food for the bears in the Australian outback. Aquarians are like that. They are always more wrenchingly upset about things far away than they are when their baby gets whooping cough and almost chokes itself to death right under their nose.

Warm and affectionate, Leos are the expert masters of the love and sex department in this couple. Aquarians are so often emotionally detached, residing mostly in their heads and sincerely believing the emotional or feeling side of an issue to be both unattainable and even a bit silly. Aquarian aloofness can be quite painful to Leo, who is lolling out there in the sunshine and nature, craving some good old-fashioned attention and romance. But how to go about prying Aquarius air-brain off his or her mountaintop long enough to enjoy some quality time together? Take my advice. Befriend your Aquarius. Be your own person and make very sure that your partner knows that you accept the Aquarian need for freedom and individuality. Then, when you have gained trust, slowly and deliberately increase the degree of intimacy in your relationship. Use those magnificent acting talents of yours, Leo. Set the stage for a night of passion: Candles, gossamer fabrics, music that blends, favorite foods, and wines—the lot! Make it an Arabian night or a night in medieval England or even an Indian wedding feast—your progressively more intrigued Aquarius (who adores the unconventional) will spontaneously combust with delight.

If you do have any children, you might want to choose Aries or Librans. They are intelligent, confident, creative, and loving children who will know instinctively how to extract the best of both of their parents' interesting and very different worlds.

½ *Leo with Pisces*

Although combining the elements of water and fire is commonly considered dicey, you two have a better than average chance to be happy together. For starters, both of you are romantic, creative, and love-hungry—and you both enjoy lots of sex. So ... if ever you have problems of differences, your terrific sexual rapport will be inclined to hold your couple together.

Not that your relationship will be without challenges. Leo is gregarious, outgoing, confident, and sometimes self-centered and arrogant. The playful, magnanimous Leo charm makes it easy for the Lion member of this duo to attract all sorts of people and possessions. I daresay, however, that this fiery Leo activity may grate just a bit on the fragile sensitivities of the shyer, more retiring Pisces partner.

Pisces are okay with people—some of the time. But Pisces is a dreamer, a plotter, and a schemer with creative ideals who needs quiet time and room to think. Rather than being dragged around the party circuit night after luminous night, Pisces might rather spend some time alone with (or without) his or her Leo lover. Pisces is a humbler social sort than Leo, yet he or she is a visionary and a highly spiritual character. Pisces is immensely compassionate and sympathetic to human suffering—sometimes too much so for proud Leo, who is aghast to come home and find the strays Pisces has brought in off the street sitting on the velvet couch and drinking out of the Limoges teacups.

As for Pisces, it's the selfish, overbearing side of Leo that gets under the Fish's scales. Of course, Pisces knows that he or she could use a dose or two of Leo's courage and valor in order to learn to be less passive and impractical. Pisces can learn from Leo and vice versa. But we are dealing here with very basic character differences—any change for the better will be a mere behavior modification and not a true character shift. Leo is too aggressive at times. Pisces is overly impressionable, gullible, and flagrantly indecisive.

With a little goodwill and mutual awareness, you two could pool your positive attributes. Leo the entrepreneur could go out and seduce the customers into buying Pisces' products, while the Fish could stay back at the workshop or *atelier* creating them. Providing Pisces doesn't get sidetracked or lose focus and forget to turn off the machines or the oven (hence enraging Leo into an early divorce), such a joint business venture could work very well.

Leo runs the money side of things because Pisces doesn't really want all those boring numbers flitting around in front of his or her eyes. Both of you are very generous and quite extravagant with your money. You like to use it on fancy clothes, art, and fun stuff, like theater visits, fashionable restaurants, and cruises. Watch that squander syndrome. You will need something to get you through old age, as neither of you suffers from bad health in this relationship, and, moreover, you may keep having children until very late as you will never really be able to keep your hands off each other in bed.

It is in the bedroom where you two get along best. Here, as in everyday life, Leo will be the initiator. Thanks to your fiery, passionate nature, Leo, you are a master at seduction and all that follows. Pisces, you don't mind being swept off your feet by your Leo partner as long as he or she continues to display those wonderful Leonine qualities of sunny warmth, rollicking humor, and cozy affection. Your Leo makes you feel *so* special. Once Pisces is in the groove of regular sex with a Leo mate, he or she may take the reins and lift the carnal act of lovemaking from a terrestrial toward a celestial or spiritual experience. Trust me, Leo. You haven't felt anything until you have spent long hours in bed with a loving Pisces sex partner. It's gorgeous!

VIRGO

Taken to the extreme, all of our qualities can become frailties. Some of us are generous to a fault, which can be wasteful. Good communicators can also be blabbermouths. Nurturing parents can smother their children. Fortunately, free will allows us to balance the positive and negative sides of our character. The analytically minded Virgo was born:

POSITIVE | NEGATIVE

discerning | judgmental

helpful | servile

factual | square

scrupulous | inflexible

sensible | preachy

modest | submissive

💘💘💘 Virgo with Virgo

Picky. Why does that word come immediately to mind when I consider the marriage of Virgo with Virgo? You are both critical souls, but surely one is more nitpicky than the other—and the least picky one will suffer the most. On the other hand, service becomes you—both of you. Hence each of you may want to help the other, to ensure the other's happiness. On lifestyle matters, you see eye-to-eye: a decent, secure existence of piles of money in the bank or well-invested, a decent home and children, good jobs for both of you, and some refreshing outdoor activity to distract you both from the humdrum you each are so capable of getting stuck in. You are practical people, none too hasty to judge or reject the good in each other, so all in all—despite the picking—this couple has a sound basis for success.

Trouble is, if success and relative order in your household and bank statements do not occur on cue, you are so alike that the tension will rise to peak levels and put your whole relationship in danger. Virgos, when not at their best, have a tendency to blame circumstances (and sometimes even others) for their mistakes. They can love life only if it is terrific, so they slide into a funk when it fails them. Virgos are professional worriers. If you ever feel you're too busy to continue carrying around the world on your shoulders, just hire a Virgo to do the carrying for you. Nobody is more qualified.

Virgos traditionally go overboard. They exaggerate the seriousness of their woes. They wax louder and more vehement whenever they think they are right or have been wronged. They are easily hurt and put down, and overly vindictive and insufferably self-pitying about both. When there is simply too much hurt or anxiety or woe, they will sometimes take drugs or drink to calm their nerves. As they tend toward excess anyway, addiction is a possibility to be carefully monitored. As a couple, you will surely try to keep an eye on each other's bad habits. But as you are so alike, you might eventually fall into a mutual bad habit, such as overeating or worse. This couple can and does often work well—especially if they make peace with each other's desire to overestimate every detail and steer clear of the tendency to be exactly alike. Maintaining individuality will be an important hurdle for each to grapple with in this twinlike couple.

Your sex life will probably have the character of an *entente* rather than of heavy passionate intimacy. You are both capable of exceptional heights of sexual performance, but your appetites are uneven and sometimes even shut down in favor of panic or fear, worry, or some negative event in your work. Virgo brains are very much connected to their sex organs, so sometimes you have to create romance, else your brain will continue to top the body's priority list. Without sufficient sex, frustration can lead to tensions, which can spoil a heap of birthdays and après ski slumber parties.

Why not have a bunch of children? Well, you may find their piping little voices intrusive, or you might want to maintain your maintain your couple's privacy, or perhaps you don't want anybody messing up your clean house. All of these possibilities do exist. You may resist having children until you are nearing the jaws of middle age. But birthing some little darlings might actually encourage the two of you to get off other's cases and begin mutually to serve the children. With kids to care for, the pressure should let up and your couple will benefit by becoming more relaxed. I suggest stolid Taureans, emotional, home-loving Cancers, and even Scorpios to add pizzazz in the feelings department. You could do worse than an ambitions baby Capricorn who shares the love of slow-but-sure handwork you are both so famous for. Whatever you do, don't hatch a Virgo—you would be triple tripping over each other for the right to be of service.

Virgo with Libra

Virgo is attracted to Libra for the same reasons we are all attracted to Libra. Librans are damned attractive. They are enticing, loquacious, flirtatious, and bodacious. They surround themselves with beauty and enjoy all the graces that society has to offer. Their manners are unusually impeccable. Plus which, Librans can charm the very fingers off a ladyfinger!

Virgos like order and deal straight with others. They are detail-oriented sorts whose sense of precision and keen eye for a flaw make them critical—even cranky or finicky at times. They can go too far trying to make others behave in a way they feel is proper. At times, this critical approach borders on nagging. Libra hears the Virgo's criticism, but it spills by like a rushing rapids. Libra cannot bear nagging. In fact, nagging makes Libra laugh—or leave.

Of course, Virgo is a pushover for Libra's gentle charm. Male or female, eventually the Virgo will succumb. But when these two are finally joined together in a live-in or near live-in situation, Virgo will definitely begin to chafe. Librans are very wafty about life. They don't like to be tied or hobbled by one relationship. Unless the Libra here is a stay-at home Pig in the Chinese zodiac, or perhaps a plodding dutiful Ox person, this relationship is doomed to make the Virgo suffer. Librans may be faithful—for a while—but loyalty to one partner is not their strongest suit.

Libra, so just and fair of mind, will not intentionally hurt a Virgo mate. But Virgo can always ferret out behind-the-scenes discomfort and never leaves Libra alone until he or she discovers what is bugging Libra. Then Virgo is devastated to find out that what he or she did not know *does* hurt. Libra is sorry, but only protests *c'est la vie*. Nothing can drive the Libra away faster than being lectured about frivolousness. Libra won't even consider defending himself about it. Nothing gets on Virgo's nerves more than people who don't take them seriously. Do we see a pattern developing here?

Libra spends a lot of time thinking up provocative comments that drive the straight-arrow Virgo into a simmering rage. If Libra thinks Virgo is uninformed, why doesn't Libra just come out and say it? But no. Librans don't want to take responsibility for possible reprisal or even a good old pitched battle. Librans are quarrelsome, not pugnacious. They taunt others with their loaded remarks. But when the other person—especially the reasonable Virgo—rises to the occasion and begins to actually blow the Libra away, Libra changes the subject or somehow ducks the issue. Libra doesn't like the fight. He just likes to pick 'em.

As you can easily see, you two are not fated for a peaceable destiny as mates. At best, you could hope for a long affair. But Virgos are not given to long affairs—they like permanence, a home they can feel safe in, and a rigorous life full of hard-earned security. Libras? I don't think so.

Worst-case scenario: Many couples with adjacent signs such as yours are initially attracted by the very differences they later cannot abide. Oftentimes, adjacent signs get to boring each other as well. The enemy of any marriage is boredom. I'm sorry to say that intolerance and boredom are synonymous with the Libra/Virgo couple.

Finances too will pose a threat to the harmony between these two. I mean, what is Libra to do? Libra loves to buy presents and invite friends in, enjoy the pool area, and entertain guests in the best possible fashion. Virgo likes to keep the books, enter figures in ledgers, and watch the bottom line rise. Libra couldn't care less. Making money is fun. But then so is spending it. Virgo becomes stressed at the very notion of a negative balance. Hence a tug-of-war ensues over who gets to spend what, and again the tension rises in the household, and Libra takes a walk.

Please, whatever you do, don't have children right away. If, by some miracle, you actually do get along, live together, and establish yourselves, after five years you might think about having kids. Individually, each of you would make a terrific parent. But kids need both parents living together in relative harmony, which you would be hard put to provide. If it comes to that, try to have jolly Geminis or independent Sagittarian kids. They will know best how to handle you.

Virgo with Scorpio

Rough road ahead! Though you each admire the ideals and actions of the other, laugh in tandem over identical jokes, and adore spending time together criticizing absolutely everything, this couple struggles more than it harmonizes. I would like to tell you that this relationship can work. But I have doubts.

I fear that the tough-minded Scorpio, by exerting a will that crushes Virgo's tenderhearted spirit, is bound to disappoint the faithful, loyal, prudent Virgo. Virgo may begin by admiring the endurance and grit of Scorpio at work, adoring the Scorpio's sexual passion, and enjoying occasional matches of wits and words. But in the end, Virgo finds that being married to a real Scorpio requires subjugation. Virgo, for good or bad, says it like it is. And Scorpio (unless Scorpio decides to agree) doesn't always want to hear how it really is.

Much of Scorpio's behavior issues arise from instinct. Scorpios sense thing about others, sniff out the solutions to their dilemmas, and intuit whether new situations are worth getting involved in. Virgos also look hard before they leap. But their method is to analyze the information before entering the fray. So both of you are cautious—and, very often, right!

Problems arise when one of you is wrong. Virgo, you don't mind being proven wrong because your decision came from your intellect and not from your gut feeling. You can put the problem back into your mental hopper and work on it some more. Scorpio, you trust your own judgment exclusively. You are so intricately and personally involved in your choices that being proven wrong is tantamount to being punched in the solar plexus. Virgo sometimes ends up *very* annoyed at this implacably immovable Scorpionic force who never wants to be called into question. Scorpios are spiky. Virgos are nitpickers. Here alone are grounds for divorce.

You, Virgo, are the more flexible of the two partners. You do get angry, but you also know how to find yourself guilty if you are. Moreover, you know how to put yourself in someone else's shoes. You are empathetic and gentle-hearted. Scorpio, you are a slam-the-door-behind-you, split-the-scene type of person, who firmly believes that if somebody else doesn't like your way of thinking then they can just get the hell out of your way. I suggest if you two have difficulty fighting productively, you ought to go to couples therapy. You will always need a capable referee.

Virgo is the more concise and insightful critic of the couple. Here, I must say, Virgo is often right. Although ... Virgo can sometimes wax sanctimonious. When Virgo does turn out to be right, Scorpio turns bright red and starts defending him or herself vociferously from a towering rage—or is it a smokescreen? Whatever it is, Scorpio must one day be taught how to accept responsibility for his or her share of the couple's troubles. Otherwise, Virgo will become embittered and disappear into an impenetrable pout.

Finances should not pose a problem in this partnership because your ways of looking at money are similar and compatible. You both need security and are not afraid of making sacrifices to get it. Virgo knows innately how to be economical, budget money, and still manage to appear generous and glad-handed. Scorpio appreciates Virgo's talent and usually doesn't attempt to take the financial reins away.

You, Scorpio, need sex. Lots of sex. Virgo, you like sex equally as much, and are also expert at performing the sex act. But your urges only come in spurts, and your approach to sex is invariably too analytical. You can actually leave sex alone for long periods of time in favor of improving your mind, feeling sorry for somebody else, or pursuing your career. And since you are so critical, if your partner doesn't look his or her best, behave in a charming and seductive fashion, and keep a squeaky clean and fit body, you are instantly turned off. Hence, you, Virgo, are often felt by your beloved Scorpio to be lagging behind, avoiding lovemaking, or even losing interest in him or her.

Children? Risky, unless you two iron out your difficulties before embarking on parenthood. If you have survived at least five years and have a nice home and some grounded ideals, I think you might allow yourselves the luxury of a pair of bambinos. Each of you will get to have a favorite if you choose to birth a feisty Sagittarius and a sweet-natured Pisces.

Virgo with Sagittarius

Here's my hunch: I feel there is a strong attraction between Sagittarius and Virgos. I don't find many astrologers who agree with me, so I cannot give you sound astrological reasons for my hunch. It's based on my experience of happily-in-love Sag/Virgo couples. You can still remember the first time you saw each other. Sagittarius, that bold flirt, came on strong, flirted, and lavished presents and favors on Virgo. Virgo, you felt almost as if a spell had been cast on you. You were simply not your normal analytical, check-out-the-details self. Sagittarius aimed the Archer's arrow at your heart, swept you off your pedestal, and brought you down to an earth sexier and more adventurous than the plain terra firma you had previously known and loved. With work, I think you two have a good chance of making it.

On the plus side, you two share a taste for adventure and travel and enjoy participating in outdoor activities. On the down side, Sagittarius is just as drawn to playing poker with friends or cronies, or heading for the track to try to land yet another windfall. This behavior does not amuse you, Virgo. So, after a few months of moping around the house alone while Sagittarius is hanging out with the clan and running through winnings as though tomorrow was not another day, you will grow impatient. Why is so much of the nuts-and-bolts responsibility heaped on you? And why do you have to spend so much time surrounded by Sag's clique? Why, you ask yourself, don't I have a Virgo clique?

Reason? You don't cultivate that many close associates in your Spartan Virgo existence. And you do nuts and bolts better than almost anybody alive.

You are serious-minded. You prefer order to chaos. You are amused when Sag comes home with a bucket of cash, but you are not happy when the cash gets dribbled away just as rapidly as it was earned. Divorce court? Not yet.

Even if you don't always approve of your Sagittarius's methods, you still love him or her. Why? Because of your totally different ways of life. You, the reasonable, intellectual Virgo, are continually thrilled by Sag's slightly ne'er-do-well attitude of easy come, easy go, living on the edge, devil-may-care, and let it all hang out. You're charmed by Sag's generosity with gifts and revel in the pleasure you derive from being in Sag's Presence. Perhaps, Virgo, you too should find an outside joy that thrills you and draws you out of the house. Maybe you don't want to play poker ... so go back to school and learn calculus.

Your sexual attraction seems to come out of nowhere, and by and large it stays there. But on-again-off-again Virgins must remember Sagittarians adore variety in their beds—sometimes a bit too much. Virgo, you will have to reckon with Sag's occasional sexual straying, but at heart you are not all that surprised at Sag's occasional change of scene in the bedroom. Don't worry. Sagittarians mean no harm. Be jealous if you must, but be cool too. The less you fuss and fume, the less the Sagittarius in your life will feel the need to find romance elsewhere. Try taking a course in romantic foreplay: Sagittarius weaken considerably in their resolve when truly sexually motivated.

If I were you, I'd chance having children. Sagittarians need kids to ground them. They have to be obliged to set examples and to participate in family activities rather than setting off for the race course or going hang gliding at 6 A.M. Children help their parents express their feelings, which softens up Virgo quite nicely. And they would help one to focus on others and relieve the rampant navel contemplation so rampant in today's world. All in all, they will help you to better cope with your marriage as well as with the outside world. Sagittarius and Virgo traditionally get along with very different signs. You can choose your offspring from all the following: earthy, solid Taurus, passionate little Scorpio, magnanimous Leo, or fair-minded Libra. Several kids would work best for your testy but interesting couple. They would force you to agree on what is important in life.

💘💘💘 Virgo with Capricorn

Here is a remarkably compatible pair whose love endurance is not contingent on their sexual rapport—except in the initial stages. When first you meet, the attraction between you is very strong. You love each other's style. Virgo is thin, sleek, and clean as a bean. Capricorn is tall, slender, smooth, and chic. Instantly, both of you see the possibility for harmony, if only in your similar flair for clean lines, subtle colors, and discreet behavior. You thought you were shy about your feelings. But when you are together, each of you feels more empowered to speak up and say what's in your heart.

If for no other reason, Virgo and Capricorn will be bound by matters of taste. They agree on everything from car styles to travel destinations. Their life together can best be described as routine and stable. Perhaps there are areas where dysfunction can set in, but these two are neither screamers nor warriors. They are both, by nature, reasonable people. Capricorns sometimes sink into mini-depressions that make them feel uneasy and overly vulnerable. And Virgos may be tempted to blame circumstances for their own mistakes. If Cap goes into a funk, Virgo can usually lift the veil by performing some loving favor or tolerating Capricorn's sudden need for a little private space. If Virgos start griping about how Momma force-fed them and claim that that's why they've gotten so fat lately, Capricorns can cure their Virgo's woe-is-meism in a trice with something caustic but true, like: "Your poor mother has been dead and buried for twenty years now. Don't you think it's about time you started eating less?"

The home environment will prove very important to both Virgo and Capricorn. High-ceilinged rooms, angular lines, beiges and off-whites, beautiful geometric wall hangings, raw silk drapes, classical music, a library, and a sparkling kitchen fit for Julia Child to cook in. Not much of a hands-in-the-bread-dough type, the Virgo will find it simple as pie to defer to the clever Capricorn in the food preparation department. Capricorn leaps to the occasion, aptly preparing delectable exotic as well as home-cooked dishes for the appreciative (discerning) Virgo palate. Virgos, you will recall, criticize every last lentil's flavor, analyze the *al dente* nature of pasta until the final strand is slurped in and basically just love enjoying the best bite of the best cuisine from the hands of the best cooks around.

Further bonding between Virgo and Capricorn comes from your shared common sense about money. You, Virgo, are happy to be of service to the ambitious Capricorn. In turn, Capricorn admires your Virgo management skills and is even happy to defer to you for advice regarding investment in everything from stocks and bonds to a solid house where you both can live. Your couple is thus grounded through an accord about no overboard sex—just plain intimacy with a minimum of hearts and flowers—and no joint funds stupidly squandered. Agreement on these very basic issues practically assures longevity of happiness.

Neither of you is famous for overdoing it in the passion department. In fact, you both display a somewhat puritanical demeanor, never shouting sensuality or losing that all-important dignified bearing. Your mutual reserve and bearing may only be a façade but it's impressive to outsiders. So when Virgo and Capricorn finally do get together, it's pure joy to find out that the other guy is not just some sex pistol or sex kitten from hell who only wants your bod and whenever it's most inconvenient to you. You may have sex less often than others, but in the final analysis you have a better time at it. Your harmonious effect on each other leaves you with very little to fuss at each other about.

Your stable life together deserves children. Might I suggest you give the world a devilishly independent Sagittarius or a spiffy Leo to love? Two kids would be better than one, so if because of calendrical restrictions you cannot manage a Sag *and* a Leo baby, you might want to give life to a comfy little

Taurus calf, or a nice hyper-emotional Scorpio. You can always get along with a Cancer or a Pisces bambino—your opposite signs may bring an excess of emotion into your home, and at least you won't be bored anymore! Whatever type of babies you have, they will be lucky indeed to grow up in your clean, well-run household where good sense and good cheer cohabit comfortably and in excellent taste.

💘💘 Virgo with Aquarius

I can see it all now: Virgo rushing about getting efficiently dressed and off to work, bowing and scraping and pleasing superiors at the office, then racing home to see to the methodical management of a severely Aquarianized (or should I say terminally creative?) household.

The Aquarius partner, not one for routine daytime tasks, is either under the eaves in an attic studio encased in a work-in-progress self-portrait made entirely of silly putty, in the garage building a land-cruising rocket that will take the two of you off to a much dreamed-of desert island that nobody has yet discovered, or is off serving as a volunteer ambulance driver in a faraway, war-torn land. I suppose even your best friends think of you two as the Odd Couple. This Virgo/Aquarius team is definitely not your everyday boring relationship. Yet, strange as it may be, it can and very often does work.

The secret? Friendship. Aquarians are so loopy that they actually need someone as sane as Virgo to keep them from flying into next week without a parachute. And they know it. Virgos are such driven, straight-arrow good people that they sometimes even bore themselves. Virgos get into ruts. Let's face it. There is nothing more rut-ejecting and challenging to the Virgo than that inspirational Aquarius mate whose shoes don't match half the time and whose hair forgot to get combed at birth. The Aquarian's otherworldliness initially frightens the Virgo half to death. But, little by little, Virgo will begin to enjoy the Water-bearer's eccentricities and wonder how he or she lived without it for so many dull, predictable years.

You are both intellectuals and share the joys of long and heated conversation. So much so that by the time you get around to hitting the sheets, you are often too wrung out to make love. It could even be that you, earthy Virgo, will have to entice the heady Aquarius into the tangible world of physical pleasures. Since the concept of sexual intercourse is more of a theoretical challenge than a rational act to the Aquarius, and as the slightly obsessive-compulsive Virgo doesn't fancy getting too messy and sweaty, you may end up making love only a stingy little once a week. Not to worry. The relationship was never really based on sex anyway.

As Virgo is nimble with numbers and the Aquarius just plain brilliant, whatever professions you choose, your relationship will be blessed with affluence. Money flows effortlessly into your coffers, usually spent on practical gadgets, all variety of nonfiction books, software, records, and the latest in hardware and technical gear.

Chances are, that you, Virgo, as well as being the chief cook and bottle washer, are also the family home design consultant. Your choice of decor will probably be no-nonsense and functional—shelves and cupboards abound. Your obsession with order and cleanliness may at first irritate the Aquarius and cramp that bohemian style. Why not just give Aquarius his or her own personal studio where reigns an arcane mixture of bizarre artifacts: at least one computer, several drawings, a statue of unclear origin and significance, yellowing papers, half-read books, and pieces of magazines everywhere. Shut the door and call pest control once a month.

The subject of having children ought never to come up between you. Although you, Virgo, might indeed make a perfectly responsible parent, your Aquarius partner in this combination is better suited to birthing mental creations. To survive as a couple for longer than a few weeks, Virgo should agree up front to take charge of infrastructure while Aquarius remains free to create his or her brainy whiz kid head off till death do you part.

💘💘 Virgo with Pisces

Virgo and Pisces are in exact polarity. Normally, we think of you as different as night is from day. Yet, there is a deep connection. Each of you love fervently and with deep devotion. Each of you needs the other's sort of talents and qualities to round out an otherwise lopsided existence. A creative person's life is amply enhanced by the presence of an analytical ally. An analyst or logic freak such as Virgo can find enormous comfort and pleasure hanging around a soft-spoken, gentle, lateral-thinking Pisces partner. Yours is not an easy match. It will take work for you to live together harmoniously. But as you love each other so passionately in the bedroom, the efforts you need to make seem somehow more worth it.

When first you met, you were certainly wildly attracted. But Virgo wondered why this sensitive, warm Pisces couldn't seem to decide between tea and coffee, blue and green, chocolate and butter pecan. And while Pisces was thinking how this organized, analytical person would be a good ally to have around, the phone rang and the absentminded Fish lost that thought. You have two vastly different methods of react to each other and to life's events. As a result, it is going to take some time to get a relationship together.

Where money is concerned, you two ought not to have many problems so long as Virgo is the keeper of the safe combination. Obviously, Virgo keeps a tight lid on spending. But then Pisces finds ways around any and all rules Virgo may make about how much a couch or a silk scarf can cost. Virgo can be stingy. But if he or she decides to be overly budget conscious, then Pisces should insist on keeping his or her own money in a separate account.

It will likely be the Virgo who brings home the bacon, but it could very well be that Pisces makes a million as an artist of some sort. This ought to free up Virgo to go into semiretirement and enjoy his leisure time. But chances are Virgo will stay tethered to his or her workaday job—just for the delicious structure it affords.

In order to put up with the vicissitudes of living with a nitpicky Virgo, you, Pisces, will need to be able to take a healthy dose of "Neptune time" per day. Create a quiet space to dream and float. Once you have made this deep connection with your inner voice, you will be better able to work in a structured environment. For best results, Pisces should always have a mission, a passion, or in some way be able to express an idealistic vision through the arts: painting, composing, writing, and acting. Theater suits you well as empathy comes easily to you

The key to finding peace and harmony between you lies in learning enjoy each other's oddities. You, Virgo, with your firm grip on reality, can teach the easygoing Pisces to focus. Organize the household. Feed everybody at regular hours. Make rules and stick to them. Tidy up and systematize. But whatever you do, don't be too tough on Pisces. The sensitive Fish person has a hard time understanding Virgo's obsession with work and efficiency. Pisces does everything at his or her own pace, swimming along through the waters of life, scarcely ever forcing anything, going with the flow. This way, Pisces gets all the time necessary to process his or her feelings and emotions, think up new and different ways to make Virgo smile, and blend in with the underwater landscape. Pisces motto? *Make no waves and no waves shall be made unto you.*

The worst kinks in your relationship should not take much longer than two to three years to work out. This done (providing you have planned ahead), you two should plan a small family for yourselves. Pisces is a loving, inspiring parent—a little too permissive at times. Virgo will once more be called on to play disciplinarian, which suits the Virgo nature. I see you best with a leveling Libra, a moody but cozy Cancer, or even a feisty little Scorpio child. If you want to have two, the best pair would be Scorpio and Cancer. Try to make the Scorpio youngest child so he or she doesn't eat the chubby Cancer baby.

LIBRA

Taken to the extreme, all of our qualities can become frailties. Some of us are generous to a fault, which can be wasteful. Good communicators can also be blabbermouths. Nurturing parents can smother their children. Fortunately, free will allows us to balance the positive and negative sides of our character. Libra, the zodiac's great leveler, was born:

POSITIVE | NEGATIVE

impartial | indecisive

thoughtful | meddlesome

gregarious | verbose

pleasant | unctuous

creative | utopian

mannerly | precious

💘💘💘 Libra with Libra

In theory, this relationship ought to work effortlessly. There is nothing a Libra needs and longs for more than a love partner. And who better to understand this aching need than another Libra? You have such a deep-seated desire for companionship and somebody to play with that finding another person who is exactly the same as you might be just the ticket you need to get on that lifetime train ride to paradise. It is no secret that in order to achieve that special Libra balance, and harmony, you need someone to bounce off. To your way of thinking, a bad relationship is better than none at all. So, in theory, a Libra/Libra relationship should be a hands-down winner.

Communication and cooperation are very important to both of you. "Where would you like to have dinner, dear?" asks one Libra of the other. "Well, whatever you choose is fine with me, honey," the other responds. Libras are born tactful and agreeable. They are basically peacekeepers. But Libra/Libra shouldn't get too boring because although these two hate confrontation, they love argument. Libras are the world's greatest starters of quarrels, but as soon as the tone rises, Libra smiles coyly and backs right out. Libra doesn't want conflict. You get the impression Libra is just testing you to see if you have any spunk. It's annoyingly predictable

A Libra/Libra couple has a great need for surface harmony and wants to maintain a pleasant environment. "Looking good" means everything to you, and you both put a lot of energy into preserving not just your physical appearance, but also your reputation as a "happily married couple." Arguments may be frequent. But they will be just as short. Each of you is so thoroughly dedicated to making your relationship work that you will both make all kinds of special compromises to keep your life running smoothly.

As you are both refined and beauty-conscious people, you will no doubt spend a lot of time decorating your elegant home. Everything wants to be perfectly balanced and matched: colors, paintings, furniture, and lighting.

Your artistic talent combined with your pleasing manners may lead you to a joint and successful career as counselors, designers, gallery owners, beauticians, painters, or musicians. Your highest ideals are fairness, justice, and equality, so you may also excel as mediators, or judges.

You both attract and spend money effortlessly. Do your accounts together, as the suggestions one will have for the other will always help to consolidate your bulging treasury.

Of course, heady Libras are always in love with love. To you, love is a beautiful mind game. You can spend bouts together discussing your ideas and visions of love, but you rarely make any active alterations. Delving into the risky world of genuine emotion or feelings is difficult for you. Sometimes, your joint concept of romantic love does not include much "hands-on" physicality. When it comes to the "messy" part of sex, you both may make a lot of excuses. Relax, you two. Stop talking, turn up the music, and take a walk on the wild side.

Being so preoccupied with each other, there may not be space for kids in your life. You prefer to deal with children as people and friends. Therefore they will not always receive the needed emotion from you, especially if they are born in a water sign. You would do best with a set of Gemini twins or a detached Aquarius whiz kid.

½ *Libra with Scorpio*

Although Libra and Scorpio are adjacent to each other, you two are different. Unless you possess mighty positive factors in your charts and harmonious Chinese signs to balance out the basic incompatibility between you two, this is not a match for sissies. Yet, yours can be an interesting couple experiment. Don't give up too easily.

Agreeable Libra goes about dealing with life's challenges in an airy, intellectual way, and tends to avoid emotional outburst. Everything in the Libra world wants to be harmoniously balanced. And Libra will do almost anything to keep it this way. Libra is easygoing, charming, and partner-oriented.

Scorpio is sarcastic, willful, and brooding, a deeply feeling water sign who hungers for passion and cathartic experience. "I'm so depressed!" shrieks Scorpio. "I hate that Rasputin of a boss of mine. I hate his ugly guts." The quick-thinking Libra peacekeeper responds, "We'll discuss that later, dear." But Scorpio's not buying that.

Not later!" screams Scorpio. "Can't you see that I am in pain? Don't you even care?"

It would take a lot of soul-searching and compromise for you two to make this partnership work. You, Libra, might indeed learn from your Scorpio mate to be more authentic and to trust in emotion rather than only in what you think. You might actually stop having to be so *nice* all the time and start taking a stand. And you, Scorpio, could learn to be detached, keep your mitts off the control panel, and peek out of your hiding place once in a while. You already know that your healing and inspirational powers are much needed in this world. Is there any better place to start using them than right in your own home?

The sex? Well, it too could get to be good. But it will take lots of adjusting. While you, Libra, would prefer to *talk* about love in a theoretical way, your Scorpio wants you to *act* about love in a real flesh-eating-get-down-to-business way. Forget everything your mother ever warned you about, Libra. Allow your sexy magnet of a Scorpio partner to whisk you away into a land governed exclusively by pleasures of the carnal variety. You finally have someone you can act out your sexual fantasies with, Libra. Especially the ones you never knew you had. I promise you, if you work on the sexual aspect of this unlikely relationship, you will not be disappointed. If you can stand the heat, your erotic Scorpio could be your loyal sex partner for life. I advise working on this aspect of this unlikely couple because it can become so terrific that it can bond the rest of the pieces together and create a more solid foundation.

When it comes to designing a home, Libra will want to be in charge. Living in a harmonious environment is as essential as oxygen to Libra. Libra actually feels physically ill when surrounded by too much clutter and imbalance. Librans favor pastel colors and a light, flowing atmosphere. Libra enjoys having a big, well-designed common space to entertain many friends and business partners. Scorpios prefer darker colors and cozy low-light settings. Your Scorpio partner will need a private, secluded space to withdraw from the outside action. You may have to coax him or her to join in the parties you love to throw.

In terms of work and career, you two could make a great team. Libra's social grace and interest in relationships, combined with Scorpio's talent for probing the hidden complexes of the mind, would make you the perfect team of marital counselors. Indeed, if ever you manage to work out your own differences, you two could make a true contribution to teaching people how to achieve fulfilling and loving relationships.

The money that Scorpio will undoubtedly make may be spent on books, workshops, and therapy sessions. Libra will want to buy lovely clothes, dine at elegant gourmet restaurants, indulge in romantic weekend getaways, and beautify both body and home. If I were you two, I would not even entertain the idea of a joint bank account. You will not agree on how to budget or spend or save. Just keep moneys separate.

It may be possible one day to create some little ones. Wait and see if your own problems get worked out. If you are lucky, your children will be a perfect cross between the two of you. You, Scorpio, will supply the emotional support. You, Libra, will inspire their intellect and teach them social graces and diplomacy. You would get along perfectly with a well-grounded Taurean child or even another Scorpio. But think about having yourselves a cheerful Gemini or an artistic Pisces too.

💘💘💘 Libra with Sagittarius

Libran air feeds the Sagittarius wildfire, and off you two go into the scorching sunset to enjoy a life of pleasure, travel, and not-so-harmonious noise. Of course, Libra wants a balanced harmonious life, while Sag loves to be passionately involved—but marriage? Perhaps not. Nonetheless, with a solid foundation and some mutual understanding, this is a match with a real chance at success.

For starters, both of you adore carrying on stimulating conversations with trendy friends and richly interesting acquaintances. But even though Libra acts happy and joins in all the fun and games, deep down she wants a commitment: a real down-home marriage with a family and a house and well—a life! Sagittarius, just the opposite, is the kind of person who leaves the room when they begin playing the wedding march. Confinement makes the Archer fidgety, edgy, and sometimes even downright nasty to be around.

The average Sagittarian's idea of even a halfway good time is always something thrilling, exhilarating, and breathtaking. This appeals not at all to Sag's poor, poor Libra love who sits at home worrying about the welfare of the breakneck daredevil to whom he or she has plighted troth. Oddly, Sagittarians still love their Librans and worship their frilly undies or their Ralph Lauren boxer shorts. But they cannot stay at home day after day, waiting for the milkman to show up. Uninterrupted routine makes Sagittarians crazier than they already are. And they hate to have anyone rule their lives. This problem in the Libra/Sag relationship has but one solution: Either Libra gets used to being left alone a lot, or Libra has to find a new partner.

The challenge for you, Libra, is to feel confident and relaxed enough to let your Sagittarius rush about chasing danger while you take up knitting or gourmet meal preparation. Of course, there's no need to stay at home alone. Librans need company. So invite your friends to come or chat or play bridge or jeopardy when Sagittarius is away. This is important: If Libra does not behave in an independent manner and appears to be becoming overly dependent on Sag for both time and attention, Sag may just bolt over that fence where the grass appears ever so much more verdant. Or, one fine day, a Libra who has been left alone once too often may take up with that interesting person he or she innocently invited around for a companionable game of canasta. This will be an ongoing issue, so gird yourselves for a right battle of wills. What binds you together finally is that you both enjoy a rollicking good time, and you are both very sexual and mutually sentimental. Sag's soft, gooey center isn't obvious, but you'll find it if you scratch a little.

Libra will definitely bear the brunt of whatever householding needs doing. And I am not certain either that Sagittarius will always provide his or her share of the expenses. The spirit is willing but proud. When Sagittarius is flush, the whole world eats at Maxims. But when Sagittarians are broke, they are nowhere to be found. Add bookkeeping and banking to the list of Libra's duties.

Still, because you are both so hotly passionate about each other, you two can indeed hope to create the perfect Valentine's Day couple. The secret to making it last is to keep things light. You both have a tendency to reside in your heads, forever contemplating what *could* be rather than what actually *is*. Play this card to the hilt. Steer clear of trying to be too concrete when you are together. Just try to enjoy the ride. Take as many trips as possible together. Have parties and go out dancing. Stop philosophizing, count your blessings, and sink into luxurious hotel beds for the most exciting game of all which is-- and you don't need me to tell you this one—the best sex either of you has ever had.

Is there room for kids in a relationship like this? Not really. You are too self-involved when together. Besides, when Sagittarius is out on the loose (which is often), there's nobody around to play the second parent. Instead of having your own, why not borrow other people's? You two make terrific aunt and uncle figures, providing all the pizzazz and adventure that kids so miss with stodgy old parents. Take other peoples' kids to Disneyland—or

Europe! You both love to do good deeds. Hie a flock of poor children to the countryside for a month. But whatever you do ... don't ever take yourselves too seriously.

Libra with Capricorn

Despite a strong initial sexual attraction, marital bliss doesn't exactly come stalking you two. In order for you to stay together, you will need to work at sticking to it, talking everything through, and learning to recognize and gain from each other's strengths.

Capricorns strive for status and prestige. Of course, no self-respecting Capricorn will admit to snootiness. But it's a fact. Capricorn (although often retiring and fearful of crowds) adores knowing the "right" people. Libra is less given to snobbery but is definitely more naturally outgoing than Capricorn. So one of the ways that Libra can help a rather stiff and nervous Capricorn partner is to accompany him or her absolutely everywhere that the ambitious Capricorn wants to be seen socially. Libra is almost never shy, so Capricorn has an excellent time being escorted about town by an attractive, gregarious partner. In this way, Libra effortlessly builds a sturdy bridge for a conservative Capricorn partner to exit from a state of anguished timidity to a headier outside world of fame and success.

One very crucial obstacle to your happiness is that the cautious, work-oriented Capricorn may hate the idea of committing to loving another person—much less getting married. But if anyone can, Libra will find a way to warm Capricorn's heart and gain his or her trust. Time, by the way, is a giant element in the slow-reacting Capricorn's modus vivendi. Anyone dealing with Capricorns must have immense patience. Just when the marriage-mongering Libra is about to give up altogether, Capricorn may well drop this surprise: "Hey, do you realize .that we have been together for over six years now? Don't you think we ought to get married?" It can happen just like that. And when it does, your Capricorn mate will be in your life forever, loyal and reliable till death do you part.

A brick in the foundation of this romance is that both Libra and Capricorn are doers. Jump up early on Saturdays and go swimming, get the marketing done, grab a bite of lunch, rush back out for a hike, and rush home to have a shower. Then it's off for drinks at the So-and-sos and race back home to cook up a big meal for some friends passing through town. The only difficulty here is that you, Capricorn, prefer to decide and act on your own—you are a natural-born loner and control freak. The partner-oriented Libra is just the opposite. Libra wants to do things in cooperation with a mate, involving family and bringing along friends all the time. Librans are so completely relationship-bound that they may even neglect their own personal needs in favor of doing something with or for the others. It may be painful for Libra to accept the solitary side of Capricorn. But if the relationship is to survive, Capricorn needs space. So enjoy carrying out some of your activities together and leave others for Capricorn to do alone.

In the sex department, Capricorns have tremendous restrictions on expressing their love and affection. Although they long for love (perhaps more than any other sign of the zodiac), Capricorn cannot easily say, "I love you. I need you. I feel like making love with you. I want to touch you all over." Libra definitely has to take charge in the romance department. The sex between you can be smashing. But if it is left up to Capricorn to start the proceedings, there might be a long time between rolls in the hay.

You, Capricorn, with your good business sense and executive power, are a successful manager in the corporate world, banking, insurance, medicine, or the law. And you, Libra, make a great public speaker, designer, artist, or counselor. Libras like to spend oodles of money on beautiful clothes, home design, and entertaining. This may create conflict with your frugal Capricorn partner, who is reluctant to spend on frivolities. Your tastes are very different. Libra wants to have a lavish but balanced environment, while Capricorn is more interested in a practical, less-is-more, high-quality design style. To avoid style clashes, keep separate bank accounts and only spend jointly when it's absolutely necessary.

You probably won't have any children before near middle age because Libra's first priority is balancing the harmony of the relationship. Capricorn may need time to experience professional success first. When you are ready, why not decide to have a sage little Taurean or a jolly Gemini?

♥ ♥ ♥ *Libra with Aquarius*

As a very airy pair of Sun signs, you two have an innate understanding of each other's motives and ideals. You probably also share a packet of common interests. With such a stimulating, inspiring, and challenging mental exchange going on in this relationship, it is almost a natural winner. Yet, despite your similarities, your life together will not be lived without a hitch. The graceful, romantic Libra strives to create a perfect picture of two like-minded people living in eternal (and conventional) harmony and bliss. Unfortunately, the Aquarius partner has an intense need for freedom of action and thought.

Libra, no matter what you do to try to tame your partner's restlessness, no matter how many lovely dinner parties you throw or how many camping trips you two go on with the old gang, your Aquarian soul mate will continue to appear haughty, aloof, and detached to your normal *entourage*. Aquarius, you see, is forever acting on erratic, eccentric impulses: washing dishes at three in the morning with the garden hose, or mowing the lawn with pinking shears—leaving no doubt in either yours or your neighbors' minds that you are all dealing with a bona fide weirdo.

Being your equitable self, Libra, you work extra hard and put all your energy into balancing this lopsided public picture. While your genius Aquarius is busy testing the efficacy of manicure scissors on holly bushes and claiming to be contemplating *the bigger picture,* you are out there on Sunday afternoon playing apple-pie A-okay citizen, sweating merrily away and mowing the rest of the lawn with the regular lawn mower. You want your marriage to seem non-threatening and, well, *average.* Aquarius really *wants* to be strange.

Libra loves refinement and hates to be forced to work in messy or unpleasant environments. Libra bas a strong need for balanced beauty and adores luxury. Libra loves to draw people together and entertains with ease and charm. Aquarius claims to be content to sit on plastic milk cartons and light the house with candles. The only thing that Aquarius cares about is that there is plenty of space in your home to invite in cronies. Obviously, Libra should be given carte blanche to decorate this couple's abode. Libra will make it so pretty that the friends will come in droves. You will enjoy a very eclectic circle of acquaintances. Plan lots of parties. Nothing short of permanent open house will fill this couple's need for intense social interaction.

But strangeness and oddball behaviors aside, Libra, you love your kinky Aquarius—who is, deep down, your very best friend. Ok, so you don't give a fig about saving sperm whales. But Aquarius most decidedly does. A wise Libra, who wants to be sure that an Aquarius lover always finds his or her way back to Libra's bed at night, will get right out there and join the cause, man the barricades, and dam the torpedoes, full speed ahead—if only to lead your gorgeously sexy Aquarian lover into B-E-D, where you two really found each other in the first place.

Once the two of you have re-entered Bedroom-land, everything seems to flow naturally. Your relentlessly busy minds relax into a delicious, mutually sexy embrace. It is so magical that both of you can actually imagine that you were born that way. Here is where a Libra/Aquarius couple can forget about the cares and worries of the world. Intimacy comes easily to you and may turn out to be the real secret behind your terrific longstanding relationship.

You will make fabulous (if oddball) parents. Try (if you can stand scheduling your passions) to hatch yourselves a sweet Virgo, an artistically talented Pisces, or a politically active Sagittarius. A family built by an Aquarian/Libra couple with such unusual and remarkable children may bring the pair of you a mite more social criticism, than you had bargained for. But you can be sure that your kids will be grateful to have such progressive parents, mentors, and friends as you.

Libra with Pisces

You are some couple! The alluring, beguiling Libra and the mysterious, emotion-driven Pisces are naturally fascinated by each other. Both adore prettiness, are attracted to the esthetic, and love arguing over nothing. Libra, who will always be surrounded with what is loveliest in life and is the most quarrelsome person in the zodiac, is the perfect lover for Pisces. Arguments between Libra and Pisces often go nowhere. But, they agree, at least they are arguing with each other. You *do* have a lot in common. And with a little discipline, definition, and a dose of real life *reality*, you'll make it big time.

Libra and Pisces are both partnership-oriented, romantic, idealistic, and artistic. You each seek in your own way to beautify, embellish, find the esthetic in all you do. On the downside, you also tend to be indecisive, procrastinating and vacillating. What your couple needs to survive is good solid habits, structure, and shape. Because you both tend to be so ethereal, you will want to make an occasional reality check. "Is this relationship really happening or are we in some kind of fantasy?" Without the occasional pinch to see if you are dreaming, you may live in a mutual, blissful La La Land—until one of you has a baby, loses a job, gets in trouble with a tax collector, or falls ill with a nasty disease. When reality drops in through the transom, then a Libra/Pisces marriage—unless it is well-girded in reality from the start—may crumble.

The classically cerebral Libra puts a lot of mental energy into creating the perfect marriage. But a Pisces partner craves a lot of emotional support that the Libra cannot always provide. Pisces is so poetic, so utopian, longing only to merge with the perfect partner in the deepest, *feelingest* way. Libra, who operates so much from the brain department, may be made uneasy by Pisces' accent on emotional sensitivity. But, bottom line, Pisces *is* more spiritually inclined and less interested in the mundane. And the suave, elegant Libra is a brilliant negotiating mediator. You have the tools to do the work. All you have to do is decide to stick it out and excavate until you see where the other person is really coming from.

In fact, you two could make a great team as color consultants, designers, or artists. Both of you like to spend money on jewelry, wardrobe, and all sorts of *objets d'art*. You share your money generously with each other and with people in need. Your home is very elegant and tasteful, masterfully styled by both of you.

Yet ... Libra likes the city, while Pisces would love to live close to the ocean, a river, or a lake. And while your gregarious Libran loves to throw lavish parties for his or her many friends, go to the theater, or attend concerts, you, reclusive Pisces, would rather spend some quiet time alone—time with your Libra mate, meditating, soaking in the hot tub or listening to tuneless New Age music. Luckily, Pisces and Libra both know how to compromise. *Cooperation* is a word invented for your style of couple. Why not have a city apartment on the water? Or how about putting a hot tub on the penthouse terrace? When you finally get rich one day, you might even have two homes—one in the city and one at the lake or the ocean or next to a bubbling brook. Once you learn how to blend your dreams together, life will in fact *be* that dream you have each been waiting for all these years.

Your dissimilar sensitivities can create occasional problems in your sex life. The watery Pisces is always in the mood for a mood. Libra is always ready to create one. However, Libra requires intellectual as well as physical stimulation to create the right vibes for good sex to happen. My advice is to practice long sessions of foreplay and petting until you see what best arouses your partner. Is it whispering sweet nothings? Champagne dinners? Flowers? Favors? Gifts? Or is it all those sweet caresses you bestow every day as you pass his or her chair? Sex between air and water takes a while to get started—but once the storm bas begun to blow up, it's nirvana. Buy huge bouquets of balloons, write each other love letters, make passion dates together, and take plenty of touching and cuddling to keep yourselves in the mood.

Having kids? Why not? May I suggest an artistic Taurus child to bring a welcome earthy quality to your bubbly liquid life? Or how about hatching a fiery Sagittarius, who might scare you both to death with his or her exciting escapades but who is sure to make the two of you laugh a riot

SCORPIO

Taken to the extreme, all of our qualities can become frailties. Some of us are generous to a fault, which can be wasteful. Good communicators can also be blabbermouths. Nurturing parents can smother their children. Fortunately, free will allows us to balance the positive and negative sides of our character. Scorpio, the sign of mystery and sex, was born:

POSITIVE | NEGATIVE

loving | jealous

transforming | meddling

incisive | trenchant

sensual | lascivious

passionate | obsessive

committed | vengeful

Scorpio with Scorpio

Scorpio with Scorpio can be very successful—especially when two of the right sorts of Scorpios get together. Here is where the Chinese signs of the two parties are of prime importance. A Scorpio/Goat or a Scorpio/Pig might very well marry a Scorpio/Ox or Scorpio/Dragon and find real contentment. Two Scorpios may be a tricky love experience. But it is also enriching and can grow into a durable, intensely positive marriage.

When two profoundly emotional and powerful people like you get together, the relationship is either an extremely positive one, or it is a total nightmare of manipulation and control. Scorpio is an "all or nothing" person. Either the pasta is mushy inedible or it's just right al dente. If something's no good, throw it in the garbage. But ... if something or someone is pleasing and life-enhancing, it must be invited for every night and become incorporated into Scorpio's panoply of wonderful things and people—to be cherished for life. Scorpios are unconditionally loyal. God help anyone who betrays one—the Scorpio kills with one sting—zap! The End.

Scorpio's life is often marked by painful and transformative experiences. Hair-raising ordeals are routine for Scorpios. The good news is that Scorpios are more resourceful, courageous, and capable of overcoming difficult situations than any other sign. Scorpio thrives on intensity.

Ultimately, Scorpios have a remarkable ability to respect others' opinions, to welcome each other's opinions and even to welcome each other's dictates. A healthy Scorpio is one who senses bravery in others, who reads intelligence on people's faces, and sees compassion in their eyes. Scorpios can be daring, heroic, and sometimes foolhardy people. But if they can manage to avoid the murkier parts of their minds and consciously cultivate the light humanistic side of their characters, two Scorpios can construct some of the best marriages ever. Maybe it's the double intuition. Maybe it's fate. Or perhaps it's sex ...

Double-Scorpio sex is magic. Yours will be a highly erotic, sexual relationship. You are drawn to each other in a magnetic, nonverbal, sometimes even hypnotic, way. Once you have reached a point where you can unconditionally trust each other, you will be able to surrender totally and merge with your partner in a veritable act of soul fusion.

Careers wherein you make a difference in the world—surgeon, psychiatrist, detective, writer, researcher, etc—are the only ones that really attract you. Money will not be a problem in this relationship. You are both rather sensible about spending and yet have a discerning eye for a bit of luxury here and there. You also enjoy helping a friend in need.

Both of you are extremely private and will feel most comfortable and secure snuggled up in your own dark but well-decorated home. You probably both love quality antiques or odds and ends from garage sales. Together you read books, give each other massages, or listen to music. Each will want to spend time alone as well. As your public life will be strewn with dissension, except for a few very stormy in-house fights, your double-Scorpio couple will choose to live a quiet life.

Your emotional depth, loyalty and truthfulness will help you become firm, loving, and responsible parents. You would adore giving birth to a serious Capricorn, or a sensitive, creative Pisces. Or you might prefer a talented Cancer or homebody Taurus.

½ Scorpio with Sagittarius

There is not much future in a relationship between Scorpio and Sagittarius. It is possible that you two intensely interesting souls will meet at a party and hit it off, make a date to have dinner, and end up in bed together. But I do not see you ending up in life together. Below are some of the reasons why I suggest that if you cannot resist being a couple, you keep it loose and light—no marriage, no common finances, no commitments.

Scorpios are quiet, subtle, and darkly private. When your jovial Sagittarius mate intuits this murkiness, it's a downer. But to be nice (which Sagittarius is famous for), Sag may attempt to cheer Scorpio. Wrong. Sagittarius always feels that a little sunny Sag therapy will make things better, but very often Scorpio simply will not come out and play. Pouting? Maybe. But sometimes Scorpio just shuts down and Sagittarius is left to fend alone.

Sag is always on the go. Born gamblers and fiercely independent, they take disastrous risks that land them in deep trouble. But somehow things always work out. Scorpio is a secretive, personal, difficult, emotional, controlling and jealous creature. Scorpio's friends had better be loyal to Scorpio. When crossed, Scorpio is ruthless, vindictive, and hardhearted. When loved properly, Scorpio is a peach, a pal, and an invaluable ally.

Put these two signs together and you get chaos. Sagittarius may be initially attracted to Scorpio because Scorpio is sexy. Scorpio may be attracted to Sagittarius because of that upbeat nature, and also because Scorpio is not above adventure, for its own sake. What's wrong with a little fun? Scorpio enjoys a spontaneous trip in a hang glider or a surprise parachute jump here and there just as much as the next guy. But in the long run, when Sag goes away for days at a time in a motorless glider plane, doesn't turn up for weeks, then comes sailing in all glowing to tell Scorpio about the trip—well, can you actually envision even a semi-responsible Scorpio hanging out with such a crazy fool? I can't. On the bright side, the optimistic Sagittarius mate does add a high-spirited, colorful dimension to Scorpio's somewhat murky life. But is all the worry and distress worth it?

The sex can be very special between Sag and Scorpio. Both are intensely passionate. You are equally attracted to all of the physical charms of life—food, wines, conviviality, and other pleasures of the flesh. Your methods of expression, however, are very different. You, Scorpio, are intensely emotional and long for deep intimacy and verbal relatedness with your mate. Sagittarians are openly flirtatious, charming, and famous for blurting out blunt commentary on almost anything. The direct approach offends Scorpio who far prefers romance with candles, low lights, and pretty lies.

Commitment is also difficult and scary for Sag. If it were between you, Scorpio might have to stop being so possessive and jealous. Sag needs a huge amount of open space in which to perambulate and breathe—alone! Archers will refuse to be told what to do or to be manipulated into doing anything they are not good at, and will bolt like lightning if Scorpio tries to hold them to any promise whatsoever.

Money issues will be a horror in this relationship. Sagittarians are big spenders who enjoy fast cars, risky investments, and gambling. They adore betting and will bankrupt themselves and ruin their health in the pursuit of the thrill of winning—or losing. This kind of wild extravagance terrifies Scorpio, who at least thinks before he or she throws money into the sewer. Money issues will abound between you two. So, if by some fluke, you do stay together; keep your bank accounts separate.

Living together will require compromise. The freedom-loving, outdoors-oriented Sag dreams of a big house on a hill with huge windows and plenty of space to roam. Scorpio might visit Sag often, but will probably choose to live under a rock someplace where ruminating gets done—solo. Sag doesn't visit Scorpio very often, as Sag finds the dark depressing.

I don't advise kids. You will both be professional people who won't want to stay home and take care of a family. (Scorpio may be a banker, a counselor, or even a chiropractor. Sag might prefer to be a salesman in Africa, a philosophy professor, a traveling nuclear physicist, a horse breeder, a writer, or a croupier in a casino in Baden Baden.) You would both get along with Virgo or Aquarius children. But who would look after them? The dog?

Scorpio with Capricorn

Believe it or not, the combination of the Scorpion and Mountain Goat usually works quite well. When the two of you meet, it often seems that neither of you has had much luck with romance. Usually, Scorpio will have barely recovered from a couple of painful betrayals. And very often Capricorn suffers from feelings of inadequacy in matters of the heart and also has had trouble getting relationships to last. This new love between you should evince a huge sigh of relief from both of you.

For starters, Scorpio/Capricorn is not the flamboyant, fiery kind of couple who come dancing into an expensive restaurant wanting only to be seen. Instead, the two of you prefer quietly pulling the strings of life from the sidelines. Some people might even deem you overly serious and claim that you don't know how to have a good time. Let them think whatever they want. You two know what you have in each other. At last: Here is a person who is just as loyal, dependable, and determined as you are, and who shares a similar outlook on life. Both of you are loners at heart, shy, reclusive, and cautious. Before you open up to each other and trust in the notion of a real relationship for life together, you will have waited a long time. Neither of you want a lighthearted, open-ended marriage where nobody commits and nothing gets accomplished. You can make a happy home for each other. So for heaven's sake— go for it!

Scorpio, you want to satisfy your intense desire for deep emotional rapport and passion. But your pragmatic earth sign Capricorn mate may have a hell of a stretch trying to supply you with the tenderness and sensitive response that you need. It is not that your lover doesn't enjoy sex and aspire to intimacy. But Capricorn lives with a deep fear of failure in all pursuits, which translates into a sort of shy hesitancy unfamiliar to Scorpio, whose second nature is sex. This reserve on Capricorn's part may make it appear as if he or she doesn't hanker to be close. To make this couple work, you, Scorpio, must sympathize with this fear, and in your compassion for

Capricorn try not to take what seems like distance between you as a personal affront. Most important of all, don't become resentful or shut your reticent partner out. Capricorn's limits are just as painful to him or her as they are to you. Down inside, your Capricorn mate is just dying to be deeply close to you. Be patient, Scorpio, and let your Capricorn surprise you with a slow-to-ignite sensuousness and devotion that you will ultimately agree is well worth waiting for.

Both of you are ambitions career people who are after power, success, and recognition. This common sense of purpose creates a bond between you. The hardworking Capricorn truly doesn't mind spending long hours in a corporate office as a business manager or banker. Scorpio will also work till all hours, starting a practice as a family therapist or opening an office as a medical doctor.

Although you two often make lots of money, you don't part with it easily. You'd rather buy old houses, fix them up, and deposit your cash in some smart investment plan. You both enjoy traveling and may spend quite a lot on trips and on gourmet restaurants. But you will always have a whopping great nest egg to draw on in the autumn of your life.

The Scorpio/Capricorn home is well organized, practical, and very neat. Since you are often both career-minded and spend much time in the workplace, you cherish your private time alone. Evenings, you might read to each other from favorite novels or discover new films together at home. You may also study foreign languages or learn to play duets on the piano. If you do entertain, you will prefer giving small dinner parties with close friends for special occasions and holiday times. Capricorn frequently adores cooking, but housekeeping is not either of your strongest suits. You will probably have household help and take many of your meals in cozy restaurants where the food and wines are of excellent quality.

I have a hard time fitting any children into this scenario. You are a couple so intensely involved in each other, your ambitions, your common interests, that I don't know where you would find time for raising babies. If ever you did decide to procreate, choose from Cancer, Pisces, and Virgo babies.

Scorpio with Aquarius

It's a stretch to imagine the emotionally intense Scorpio in a relationship with a coolheaded, logical Aquarius for more than about two or three hours without a parting of the ways. In other words, to work, this relationship will require heavy labor, intensive analysis, and years of compromise. If your rising signs are compatible or your Chinese signs match up well, there may be a way to keep you two together for more than an afternoon. But not without lots of TLC.

Your Sun signs make you truly very different sorts of people. Scorpio has a fierce need for profound involvement as well as for serious transformation. Aquarius doesn't hate the idea of romance and passion, but would choose the chance to be innovative and original over being in love any day. Even more, Aquarius dreams of the opportunity to create social change. In this spirit, the Water Bearer most always behaves toward lovers in a brotherly, tolerant, yet somewhat eccentric fashion. Aquarians are famous for leaving loved ones behind while marching mentally (and sometimes even physically) off to right some imagined or real universal wrong. Although Aquarians are open-minded and concerned about the well-being of humanity at large, they very rarely get too emotionally attached to another individual. The thought of messy emotional encounters is frightening. Aquarius prefers to play the role of unbiased observer.

This intellectual, nonaffectionate detachment drives the passionate, probing, *involved* Scorpio-in-love into a cathartic frenzy. Scorpio is not afraid to express powerful feelings and so longs to be with a partner who is also supportive of a complex, penetrating, hyper-emotive personality. Aquarius falls short here. And Scorpio doesn't hesitate to let him or her know it, spewing every manner of insult and accusation to remind Aquarius of just how repulsive Scorpio thinks it is to be so ... detached.

Building a real relationship complete with home and family seems only a remote possibility. Neither one of you wishes to hang around the house bringing up babies. Of course, if you have been given a very nurturing Chinese sign, or if your rising sign or Moon is in Cancer, you might possibly be more of a homebody. But on the surface, the chances for a happy Scorpio/Aquarius marriage that lasts are slim at best.

A satisfying career may help to counterbalance the domestic disharmony between you. Aquarius is likely to apply scientific talent and an unusually keen intellect to a job as a computer programmer, an engineer, or a spokesperson for a political cause. Aquarians also make magical artworks and write abstract music and poetry. They spend their money generously on education, technical gadgets, and friends in need. A Scorpio partner is more material-minded. Scorpio's desire for comfort and the purchasing of *things* for the sheer delight of owning them annoys the hell out of the ascetic Aquarius. Scorpio is always complaining that Aquarius should have a more seductive wardrobe. Aquarius wishes that Scorpio didn't care.

If you are a Scorpio/Aquarius couple, you probably have different sets of friends. One part of your unique home is filled with the many and varied scientific or nerdy buddies and acquaintances of Aquarius. Scorpio, a more private person, prefers to have a few very close friends with whom to be totally honest and share a murky interest in metaphysics and the occult.

It is no surprise that this discrepancy in expression and style may occasionally turn the bedroom into a battleground. Your conflicts seem to crop up at bedtime. Depending on how appreciated you feel by your overly independent Aquarius, a sensuous Scorpio will probably try to find a lusciously sneaky way to patiently introduce your left-brained Aquarius into the world of erotic pleasure. Or, failing said seduction, Scorpio will have an immediate affair with the mail carrier Aquarius's sexual needs are minimal by comparison to the sex-driven Scorpio. Besides, in the finite world of a

Scorpio, there is only love or hate, all or nothing. Aquarius's cool approach to things makes the evil part of Scorpio try to sting the Water Bearer into action, only to find that he or she has stung the poor dear to death.

Children between Scorpio and Aquarius? I don't think so. Have your children with someone else. Keep each other as friends and go about the business of serious marriage with somebody your own size.

Scorpio with Pisces

The fact that these two Sun signs share the same element (water) is a good indicator of a potentially happy relationship. Same element rhymes with same emotional values. And no matter how well you get along sexually or intellectually, when the roof blows off the house in a hurricane or the baby tumbles out of the carriage onto the sidewalk, a good emotional rapport is what keeps couples from murdering each other and helps them remain married no matter what.

You two are capable of understanding and supporting each other intuitively and often on a nonverbal level. This is highly significant, since you are both ultra-sensitive by nature, and heartfelt verbal expression always come trippingly off your tongues. Oh, Scorpio can be vile-tongued and sarcastic enough to slice the head off a pin. And Pisces can weep up a mean boo-hoo. But neither is particularly gifted at verbally processing feelings as they fly by. Scorpio might rather slam out of the house than openly deal with a nasty urge to kill, and Pisces might leap from a ground floor window for effect but not be able to explain why.

My guess is that the courageous and strong-willed Scorpio will be the one who gets to make most of the decisions affecting your life as a couple. Flexible, kindly Pisces, an introspective dreamer if there was one, usually doesn't mind Scorpio playing head honcho. Pisces often has a hard time dealing with the harsher aspects of the world anyway, and prefers to be guided than to have to lead the pack. For a Pisces who knows his or her own limitations and is comfortable with both strengths and weaknesses, having a Scorpio lover really comes in handy. Scorpio is strong and steadfast in adversity, tried and true in devotion, and (being a closet control freak) doesn't really mind carrying his or her share of the responsibility in this type of union.

Trust is a big issue between you two - especially for Scorpio. By nature, Scorpio trusts absolutely nobody. But once he or she feels confident to fully rely on a Pisces partner's loyalty, these two subjects can merge in both a physical and spiritual sense. Scorpio/Pisces is a real soulmate connection. Although Scorpio plays the more passionate, erotic, sexual role in this union, he or she could certainly not attain the pitch of passion without you, sweet Pisces. Your contribution adds a tender, romantic, poetic touch to an already intensely torrid business. When you two perform the sex act together, it is as though you were redefining the words *love and affection.*

In terms of career, Scorpios always want the best, the most prestigious, the most lucrative profession. Their determination and self-discipline combined with a shrewd business sense helps them earn a handsome living and brings both public and private respect and esteem. Scorpio could be almost anything, which allows independence and freedom of decision-making—a lawyer, a surgeon, a detective, or a cracker-jack psychotherapist. More than money and social acclaim, the compassionate Pisces wants to commit to a dream or an ideal. Pisces' employment might span anything from volunteering in a homeless shelter to becoming a visionary artist.

Of course, none of these idealistic ventures is associated with income. Oh, yes, Pisces might be discovered as a famous sculptor. But until that lucky day, you both may need Scorpio's paycheck to buy yourselves the glorious lifestyle you so deserve.

Two watery creatures like yourselves would probably want to live close to the ocean or a river or stream. Because both of you need a lot of privacy and time alone, you might each need to have your own personal study room or studio. Pisces is the more spiritually inclined and may even want to retreat into an outdoor sanctuary to meditate. You are both fascinated by the occult and delve daily into all forms of metaphysics. I see you, spending your evenings reading, talking, listening to New Age music, and planning your next trip to South America to find the lost tribes who claim to know the meaning of life.

If you can possibly make time to be parents, you would be both loving and responsible. A jolly addition to your married life would come along in the form of a nurturing Cancer baby or a more practical Virgo or Taurus child.

SAGITTARIUS

Taken to the extreme, all of our qualities can become frailties. Some of us are generous to a fault, which can be wasteful. Good communicators can also be blabbermouths. Nurturing parents can smother their children. Fortunately, free will allows us to balance the positive and negative sides of our character. Sagittarius, the gambling adventurer, was born:

POSITIVE | NEGATIVE

open-handed | spendthrift

philosophical | idealistic

confident | pompous

festive | excessive

adventurous | gambling

broad-minded | permissive

Sagittarius with Sagittarius

You two lucky Sags form a rather frenzied, upbeat couple, whose jovial, optimistic outlook on life inspires those around you to buck up and look on the bright side. Your Sagittarius is a sign of great luck, associated with expansion, confidence, and abundance. If you can channel your common talents and dynamic energy, you are likely to be remarkably successful. There is little you cannot accomplish—if you want to. You are both fairly driven, eager to break ground in new realms, and take on the world—alone, if necessary. If you are not mutually motivated in the same direction, your couple may break apart. But when you are aiming in the same direction, doubling that luck of yours is a sure thing.

More than good fortune comes with the double-Sag package. Sagittarians are basically high-spirited. Their philosophy of life is not to take anything too seriously (neither of you plays victim), to keep involvements to a minimum, and to *keep moving.* You are a restless pair, and things go best when you take off on long trips (alone or together), especially to exotic, unexplored parts of the world that offer adventure. Your common ideal is often some kind of search for meaning or truth. You are avid readers, devoted to higher education, and often interested in spiritual subjects. Clearly, a double-Sag couple will never be bored.

There is a slight downside. Sagittarians can sometimes be annoying know-it-alls. One or the other (or, God forbid, both) of you could be dogmatic or even fanatical about certain subjects, always trying to impose his or her truth or religions belief system on others. This darker underside of your character might not show up at all in a well-balanced Sagittarius couple. But if it does, you might actually prove to be nothing more than a pair of rabble-rousers or religions proselytizers who will team up more for the sheer thrill of persuading others than for the love.

Since neither of you is born dreaming of the joys of commitment, you may agree to live together and never marry. Chances are, in fact, that you will have met late in your single lives and decide to stick together because neither of you wants to settle down in a classical sense.

You are likely to be a magpie couple who rarely, if ever, keeps quiet. You love to share heated conversation, chat the evening away, and can often be seen whispering to each other of private jokes or little secrets that amuse you both.

I wonder if you will stop talking long enough to enjoy a satisfying sex life. You are equally romantic: Gifts and little surprises are your way of showing your admiration and affection for your partner. Although you can both be loving and giving, sometimes one of you will be a mite sarcastic or sharp with the other. Tenderness and compassion improves the act of love immeasurably.

Astrologers often see Sagittarius as the eternal student, forever questing after new and different bits of knowledge and experience. Most likely, you two intelligent people have or want to have a college education. You may even continue to improve your skills and knowledge as adult students. Because you love to move about so, you could be a team of travel experts or archeologists. But one of you may also be a university professor, motivational speaker, interpreter, publisher, pilot or flight attendant, writer, or professional gambler. Whatever career you choose, you want it to be both exciting and stimulating.

Money and success do come to you easily. But beware of taking the final big risk. With two full blown Sagittarians working in tandem, there is always the danger that success may vanish just as fast as it arrived. You can lose just as rapidly as you won by dint of extravagance and even rank wastefulness.

Neither one of you is very much interested in the routine tasks of cooking and cleaning, yet you are probably fanatical about living in a well-tended home. Hire a meticulous Virgo housekeeper to care for your casual home, which is filled with books, artifacts from your travels, large wall maps, and plenty of space to entertain and just wander through.

It may be a good idea to wait a few years before you decide if you want to have children. You could be loving, supportive parents, but I fear you won't want to compromise your busy travel schedule to have kids. I would highly recommend an Aquarius whiz-kid, or a fun-loving bright-eyed, and bushy-tailed Leo child. Both are quite independent and could take the stress of being educated on the road.

½ *Sagittarius with Capricorn*

The optimistic, adventurous, risk-taking Sagittarius meets up with a pessimistic, cautious, mortally ambitious Capricorn, *and* they decide to call themselves a couple. I know that opposites attract, but there are limits to just how incompatible people can be and still stay together. Irreconcilable differences? Or simply boredom. I see frustration. I see sorrow and misapprehension of each other's goals and methods achieving them. And most of all, I see fights and flights—a seesaw marriage that does not really deserve that august appellation.

How did this peculiar pair even meet? Maybe you, my enthusiastic Sagittarius, felt that you needed more structure, discipline, and commitment in your life. Maybe you were in one of your prosperity slumps. So along comes an attractive, serious, organized Capricorn and you shoot your arrow into its heart, capture it, and take it home to try to love it properly. And you, my reserved, responsible Capricorn friend, have been weary of slogging through life and felt the need of some sparkle and fun. Sagittarius partners are expert at motivating lugubrious Capricorns to get the hell out of their ruts. And it works—for a while. Sagittarius invites Capricorn to go on a picnic. Capricorn accepts and forgets to be gloomy while listening to Sag's woolly tales of adventure. But soon, Capricorn's eyes glaze over and Cap worries about business or the overdraft at the bank or an unpaid Visa balance. Sag is highly motivated by the realization that this Capricorn can make money, organize a home, and even cook. As Capricorn packs the basket to head home early, Sag still hopes that life with Capricorn may finally make Sag get organized.

But it ain't gonna happen like that, Sagittarius. You're not going to change. You will still want to expand your mind, open your horizons, and seek thrills. The only way Capricorn might keep you home is to clip your wings, burn those perfumed arrows, and confiscate your quiver for life. And you can make the Mountain Goat pretty miserable too. Capricorn will quickly tire of a diet of roasted marshmallows on the run. Caps like well-prepared gourmet vittles. Picnics and thrilling rides in ultra-light aircraft are not Cap's idea of fun. Order and safety are Capricorn's friends. Work is Cap's religion. For a Capricorn, gain and accomplishment can even replace passion.

Capricorn wants a stable, successful career to achieve status and social acclaim (not to mention to earn a lot of money.) Cap makes an excellent accountant, banker, lawyer, or contractor. Financial security is essential to Capricorn. Sagittarius's bad habit of throwing money around will not do. Finance is a sore spot in your relationship. If you live together, Capricorn should watch closely or Sagittarius may succeed in filching a few bucks off the top of the grocery money.

As one would expect, your tastes are also quite opposite when it comes to choosing a residence. Capricorn wants to own a solid home and live in it happily ever after. The restless Sagittarius feels most comfortable out on the road traveling in a clapped-out RV. If you want this couple to work, compromise. Sagittarius, stay home and ride those exercise bikes together while watching TV. Or Capricorn, next time you go on a hike with your Sag lover, try to hang in there long enough for the lovemaking to get under way.

If this couple is to stay together for more than three and a half weeks, Capricorn will have to listen to the call of the bedroom. Learn to be more playful and take the initiative once in a while. Although Capricorn is said to be yearning to love and be loved, your inhibited emotional reserve makes it nigh unto impossible for your spontaneous, openhearted Sagittarius to ignite any passion in your body. Unlike quiet Capricorns, Sagittarians love to talk while having sex. To encourage the onset of tenderness and affection, you might want to try using accessories: rent a Tantra video, hire a sex coach, or simply snuggle up together for hours under a big feather quilt in some cozy bed-and-breakfast inn. Don't forget to eliminate those accessories: phones, faxes, computers, casinos, and game rooms.

Don't have kids. When Junior needs an angel costume for the Christmas pageant, Capricorn will be too busy at the office to take care of it and Sag will have left to save a rain forest in the Amazon. Your kids would have to be either self-cleaning, low maintenance Virgos or space cadet Aquarians, who wouldn't know if you were there or not.

❤ ❤ ❤ ½ *Sagittarius with Aquarius*

These two Sun signs share a basic understanding. Air (Aquarius) feeds fire (Sagittarius) but does not try to extinguish it. Fire graciously receives the nourishment of the air, which helps to keep the home fires burning for a long, long time. Whether you are talking, reading, studying, traveling or working together, you two get along.

There is a brother-sister quality to this relationship that, I believe, gives it an excellent chance for long-term survival. Friendship and reciprocal approval are redoubtable arms against adversity in marriage. To compound this, the rhythms are right. You never mind the sound of each other's voices. You are not annoyed by each other's making coffee or licking stamps. As friendly lovers, you treat each other as equals, with respect, and you both honor the other person's individuality and need for space and independence. Moreover, you are both open-minded, socially outgoing, freedom-loving, tolerant people who enjoy a good time.

Sagittarians and Aquarians are both truth seekers who have a great interest in philosophy, the occult, and metaphysics. The fiery, inspirational Sag will lead the intellectual, unconventional Aquarius partner into all kinds of exciting external adventures. Be it horseback riding in Montana or trekking through Nepal, Sag will want to turn Aquarius on to the fun and the thrill of it all. Otherwise, Aquarius might indeed spend too much time alone at the computer, workshop, or studio, tinkering with his or her latest invention, painting, or science fiction novel.

The liberal humanist Aquarius works best with like-minded people or as an activist within humanitarian organizations trying to create social change. He or she might also choose to be a fund-raiser, spokesperson, politician, a charity worker, scientist, or a revolutionary sociologist. Sagittarians are not as politically inclined as Aquarians. They prefer to stay out of the media fray. To Sag it is most important to have a career that challenges a need for intensity, speed, and stimulation. Sagittarius would make a terrific pilot, flight controller, explorer, or travel writer.

Both Aquarius and Sagittarius are generous with money. You, Aquarius, don't really need much in the way of material goods in order to be happy. But Sag, you do overextend yourself at times on carefree, almost manic, shopping sprees. You are not above taking a few little gambling trips to Vegas either. So watch out for the money in this marriage. It could leak through the cracks. Aquarius is so frugal about material things that he or she might be the best choice for finance manager here. Sag isn't sure.

When first you met, you probably had a very passionate, steamy hot love affair. But over time, you may have to struggle to keep the original passion burning. Sameness, routine, and taking the other person for granted will be detrimental to any relationship, but if this happens here it will be because Sagittarius feels neglected. Aquarius has this odd way of seeming not to love those he loves. Intellectually, one feels Aquarius's presence very strongly. But the physical Aquarius is distant and uneven. In light of this, the more vibrantly sexual Sag may soon start flirting with the idea of an invigorating little fling. Instead, Sagittarius should take more time just to *be* with an Aquarius partner. Sag will have to make the first move, create the whoopee surprise birthday party, or seduce Aquarius by serving yummy appetizers and champagne in the bedroom. Once Aquarius oozes down off his or her cloud and hits the mattress, things do improve. But because Aquarius lives at a huge remove from Earth anyway, Sag will be obliged to perform a lot of the romantic hoopla in this otherwise solid-state A-one relationship.

Your nontraditional, casual, but comfortable home will always be open to your many interesting friends from all over the world. Neither of you can be called a five-star cook or a perfect housekeeper. You have more important things to do. Besides, if Aquarius invented the microwave oven, he or she had good reason.

Kids? Sure. Ideally, they should be born in Leo or Libra. They may not learn how to sew on a button or iron a shirt, but they will sure grow up in a progressive, action-packed household.

Sagittarius with Pisces

Although you two are respectively ruled by fire and water—a combination that often does not work—you have a fighting chance at a very sound relationship. You will each need to work at making this couple function at a peak level. But you are both people of generous goodwill, and can surely create an admirable harmonious marriage of both mind and body.

Sagittarius and Pisces are idealists. You are tolerant, adaptable people with an intense common interest in spirituality and metaphysics. This shared concern for the spiritual in life will be a major link that can serve as the foundation in your relationship. Your approaches to these subjects are very different. Pisces, you are the mystical, dreamy character who carries a divine longing in your heart. You sincerely want to transcend physical boundaries and become one with the universe. Pisces lives and breathes spiritually. For more mundane creatures who plod along with their noses to the ground and the grindstone, Pisces sometimes seems ethereal.

Sagittarius is also a truth-seeker, but of a more vocal, participatory spiritual variety. Where Pisces might become a charming, soft-spoken minister or a gentle soothsayer, Sagittarius might aspire to pulpit evangelism or itinerant circuit riding. Where spirituality is concerned, Sag preaches, Pisces seeks. Sag is also interested in philosophical exploration of theology and belief systems. The idea of spending a silent weekend meditating in the lotus position next to an introspective Pisces lover in a Zen monastery does not appeal to the restless, intellectual Sagittarius. To a Sagittarius, an act of faith might be a long ride in nature on a spiffy new mountain bike—alone!

Despite your similar goals, polarized styles may mean that Pisces doesn't always get the sympathetic kind of response he or she needs from the outspoken Sagittarius mate. Pisces needs to be handled with kid gloves. It won't do to disturb Pisces' fragile system of nerves and feelings. Sags are not noted for their tact and can shoot right through the very soul of a Pisces with a thoughtless remark. On the other hand, the goal-oriented, outgoing, optimistic Sagittarius enthusiasm will, more than once, inspire a Pisces mate to get his or her act together. You can learn how to learn together, so that you can lean together. Pisces lends sweetness and light, while Sag serves up heaps of realistic, charge-ahead motivation. It's a match.

To improve your basic rapport, Sagittarius should tread softly at home. Your Pisces mate needs peace and quiet. As for Pisces, you should try to become more actively involved with the jovial, high-spirited Sagittarius. Unfortunately, this may mean learning to ride a motorcycle or even attending clanging rock concerts. Give it a try. Build and share some truly wondrous times together.

Sag, you will want a career that challenges your need for risk and excitement—perhaps a skydiving teacher, investment salesperson, or high-flying stockbroker. The creative or healing arts are Pisces' strongest talents, and serve as a channel for a vast imagination and spiritual vision. As for money is concerned, you will both earn it and spend it on materials to improve your image or on gossamer garments that make you feel gloriously otherworldly or beautiful to behold.

You are both charter members of the Big Spenders Guild. Worse off is the carefree Sagittarius, who too often overextends credit cards and hates to hear the word *budget* pronounced in his or her presence. I know, Sag, you play hard and you work hard. But why not try to save hard too? I don't know who should manage the money in this couple because neither of you is worth a dime in that department. A rich uncle, anyone?

Both of you are incredibly romantic, but again you behave in different ways. You, Sagittarius, are more the hot-blooded eager beaver who can give both sex and passion but may lack tenderness, intuition, and patience. You must learn to tune your subtle Pisces' sexual instrument so that love and affection can thrive. Pisces is nonaggressive and definitely turned off by shows of force. Go easy. But go together into the passionate act of love.

If they are anything like you two, your unusual kids (a witty Gemini or an unconventional Aquarius would work well), ought to be the spearhead weirdoes of the twenty-first century.

CAPRICORN

Taken to the extreme, all of our qualities can become frailties. Some of us are generous to a fault, which can be wasteful. Good communicators can also be blabbermouths. Nurturing parents can smother their children. Fortunately, free will allows us to balance the positive and negative sides of our character. Capricorn, the ambitious loner, was born :

POSITIVE | NEGATIVE

determined | stubborn

wise | pedantic

reflective | depressive

reliable | predictable

autonomous | lonely

diplomatic | disingenuous

Capricorn with Capricorn

Following a youthful attraction based on a feeling of twinship, wherein they find they share a lot of goals and ideals, these two long-suffering Mountain Goats will inevitably lock horns in some hairy dispute over whether or not *he* is more ambitious than *she*, whether *she* is more rigorous than *he*, or if *she* is ever going to let up her pickiness long enough to give *him* a chance to breathe. The word *rigid* comes to mind ...

Bounce will be absent from this household, and anxiety will leap out of the very cupboards. Their bookshelves will be crammed with books on how to find peace in relationships. I would venture that unless these two Capricorns have highly mitigating rising signs, planetary softeners, and quiescent Chinese astrological data to soften and render their personalities more yielding, they are doomed to implode from their sheer angst.

Both Capricorn wills are immensely strong and hugely tenacious. Both people desire success and aim for perfection, slogging dutifully up the mountainside without respite. Neither character possesses a sunny disposition and each will seek to overpower the other in the *meticulosity* department. Nonetheless, a double-Capricorn couple might find a meeting of the souls in their communal kitchen. They both adore food, would sooner expire on the spot than skip a meal, and are often excellent cooks. Trouble is, both Capricorns hate to share their toys.

My recipe calls for a quarter thimbleful of curry powder and not a smidgen more," says one.

Well, *my* instructions say to put in a whole thimbleful," says the other, summarily dumping the yellow pungent powder into the partner's saucepan.

The first Capricorn naturally takes umbrage, the second defends an untenable position, and the fight is on. What started out as a jolly *cuisine à deux* experiment in cooperative meal preparation may rapidly disintegrate into a battle royal fought deftly with finely honed European boning knives, sterling silver pickle forks, and classic wooden rolling pins. For best results, one Capricorn should be assigned the main dish and the other be asked to prepare the rest of the meal.

In fact, learning how to predict which situations increase the tension and which ones tend to slow its progress would be the sort of secret to making this relationship successful. Capricorns are stolid, security-conscious, and socially aware. If their love is sufficiently strong, they can ultimately triumph over the stodgy side of their marriage by making a mutual effort to relax more. They should establish patterns of leisure activities that they can enjoy together—hiking and skiing, jogging and swimming—anything they can engage in together to spend excess nervous energy and share an occasional giggle.

Giggles, by the way, are all important when we treat the malaise of a double-Capricorn couple. For best results these two should view as many funny movies as they can afford to rent or attend. A good belly laugh or two, a tickle fest, or a silly rollabout on the rug can lead to some of the best sex they will ever know. Otherwise, Capricorn foreplay threatens to remain in the realm of "getting some paperwork out of the way so we can have a bit of fun." This is a serious-minded pair whose effect on each other is anything but jolly.

If, after reaching all their ambitious social and financial goals, this couple finally does get around to having kids, they must plan them with great care. Ideally, they should fill up their angular house with round little Cancers and feisty little Leos. A performing Gemini kid could lighten them up, too. And a smart-assed little Scorpio or a loony-tune Aquarius wouldn't hurt either. As a pair of Capricorns who do get married will certainly "settle down" into a safe, secure, routine life before ever deciding to have kids, they should feel free to have as many offspring as health and time will permit. Such thoughtful and resolute souls as they will make exceptionally conscientious parents.

❤ *Capricorn with Aquarius*

There are probably not many married couples who have taken a lifetime subscription to this particular combination of signs. I mean, who would take on such a challenge? If a Capricorn and an Aquarius actually choose to marry, either their charts had better harmonize perfectly *and* their Chinese signs blend like a barbershop quartet, or they are in for a few hundred thousand surprises before they even get back from their honeymoon.

Let's examine my premise a bit. Capricorns are conservative, cautious, conventional realists. Aquarians are unconventional, idealistic, and gregarious. Capricorns are ambitious hard workers who adhere dutifully to both schedules and hierarchies and will commit almost any personal sacrifice to achieve their goals. They are earthbound climbers with a no-nonsense approach to almost everything they do. Capricorns are conformity experts. As for Aquarians, they couldn't care less about achieving anything conventional. Aquarians do not work well in groups, hate conformity, deplore the very existence of government, and despise all the repressive rules and programs it imposes on humanity. Aquarians are professional misfits. They *like* being different.

This couple is so mismatched that I would delight in making up stories about them for pages. But I will spare you those asides and get on with the business of what to do, if by some chance or emergency green card requirement, you find yourself embroiled in one of these messes.

For starters, the open-minded, tolerant Aquarius should try to motivate Capricorn to soften his or her rigid, often too judgmental attitudes. Aquarius wants to assure Capricorn that he likes him or her a lot, but that he feels disapproved-of in this relationship. Aquarius is deeply afflicted by too much Capricornian seriousness and emphasis on responsibility. Capricorn already knows that Aquarius is a free spirit who wants to break out of the status quo. But Capricorn cannot accept the Aquarius's need for condoning outrageous acts merely to create a more humane society. Capricorn has a hard time with weirdness. Aquarians are weird.

Although some accuse Capricorn of being a born stiff, he or she does not mind letting his or her hair down once in a while. Caps may even secretly envy Aquarians for their guilt-free eccentricity. If I were you, Capricorn, at the next Halloween party, I'd arrive late, in the nude, and with a bear's head mask (none of your bosses will recognize you) over my entire head. If you deign to take an occasional stroll on the wild side, Aquarius won't feel so outlandish and you may get along better for a minute or two.

You, Aquarius, are not only erratic and unpredictable, you also have the ability to be truthful, focused, kind, and determined. These are perhaps the qualities that made Capricorn fall in *like* with you in the first place. Neither one of you is very good at sharing your innermost feelings with your partner. But then again, too much intimacy and passion is not either of your cups of tea. You have such busy, productive, yet polarized lifestyles that sex is something you probably only get around to once in a while (post-Halloween party?)

In terms of career, the ambitious Capricorn would like to be a powerful executive, a shrewd real estate agent, a responsible teacher, or an administrator of some kind. This relationship will have a more solid foundation if Aquarius learns to appreciate Capricorn's need for material security. Aquarius could be a brilliant physicist, archaeologist, or union leader. But getting rich is not likely to be his or her goal.

As to who handles the money, there's no question. I suggest that Capricorn bind the family purse tightly to his or her ankle and wear it to work.

Your home will reflect the vast differences in your tastes. The style will be unorthodox. Furniture style? Eclectic bizarre with an occasional hint of solid, prestigious.

Kids? I wouldn't let any little kids near this outrageous household.

💘💘💘💘 Capricorn with Pisces

How sweet! The loyal, committed, practical Capricorn with a loving, caring, inspirational Pisces mate. In the case of this charming couple, water and earth exert a stabilizing, healing effect on each other. Therefore the impressionable, dreamy Pisces can greatly benefit from Capricorn's realism, gaining both structure and order. In turn, Capricorn can hope to enjoy the advantage of a softer, gentler Piscean lifestyle, which guaranteed to open wide the doors of awakening to the spiritual flip side of Capricorn's sometimes stodgy mind. Pisces is the dreamer, the visionary who brings to this marriage a dowry of golden opportunity for Capricorn to discover the vastness of the cosmic world outside of the confines of a large imposing oak desk. This relationship has real promise.

If you treat your Pisces well, Capricorn, you will behave in an emotionally available and supportive manner. It's a big order. But Pisces doesn't want material things from you the way a Leo or Cancer might. Pisces wants love, comprehension, complicity, an understanding shoulder to lean on, and a good audience for those New Age philosophies. In return for your kind favors, Pisces will stick by you, forever loyal—always adding a poetic, mystical touch to your otherwise conventional life. If you listen to Pisces, you may actually be able to stop worrying about recognition, status, and money. One of the greatest gifts your intuitive, highly spiritual Pisces has to offer you, O serious Capricorn, is to teach you to trust and have faith in the wisdom and sustenance of the universe. Let that sensitive Pisces mate of yours help you to heal your old childhood wounds. Forget about issues of deprivation and abandonment, Capricorn. And above all, be subtle and smooth. Don't crush your Pisces' delicate spirit with too much control and order. Instead, join forces with Pisces to celebrate a life full of wonder and miracles together.

If the above text sounds annoyingly *New Age* to you, Capricorn, that is exactly its purpose. To intentionally spur you to get off of your spiritual duff and go with the flow. Shorten your stride. Be more flexible. Accept certain nonscientifically proven notions. If you are to keep your little Pisces pleasure trove happy, you will have to lighten up. Moreover, unless you have a water sign ascendant, you probably feel overwhelmed by Pisces' uninhibited thirst for emotional reassurance. Don't panic. Don't let any lingering feelings of fear and inadequacy prevent you from giving as much love and affection as you desire to receive. Stop thinking you will look like a fool if suddenly you take Pisces by the waist and place a passionate kiss on his or her lips. Pisces will reward you for it in kind when you are least expecting it.

Of course, no matter how Capricorns try, they will never be quite as romantic and intuitive as Pisces. But Pisces' compassion and selfless devotion can actually melt Capricorn's armor-plated heart over time. With a little practice and good will, Capricorn and Pisces can build a richly satisfying sex life—sensuous, magical, and warm. You will learn how to take care for each other's needs and grow more and more passionate and frisky as you lose your inhibitions.

Money may be a big issue in this relationship. Pisces longs to live well. Unfortunately, Capricorn has a tight grip on the monetary assets and an annoying tendency to nip your shopping enthusiasm in the bud. Your only defense, Pisces, is to make your own money. It's easier than you think. Just focus on one of your many creative talents and stay determined to stick with your career choice, whether it be as an artist, a social worker, or a decorator. Capricorn will always provide security as an accountant, banker, administrator, attorney, doctor, or professor. So even if Pisces only earns pocket money, it will soothe the savage miser in Capricorn's anxious little heart.

Capricorn's conservative handling of money will enable you two to build your perfect dream house—the one with the white picket fence and the three-car garage. Pisces should be in charge of creating a cozy atmosphere in your home. Pisces is an excellent designer and householder. Home is not only Pisces' safe haven, but a place where a poor, beleaguered Capricorn can forget about the stock market for an evening, relax with a good bottle of wine, and play kissy face with a cuddly Pisces mate while bobbing in the hot tub.

Blessed are the kids (a sensuous Taurus or a graceful Libra) born to loving, idealistic and reliable parents like you!

AQUARIUS

Taken to the extreme, all of our qualities can become frailties. Some of us are generous to a fault, which can be wasteful. Good communicators can also be blabbermouths. Nurturing parents can smother their children. Fortunately, free will allows us to balance the positive and negative sides of our character. Aquarius, the oddball, was born:

POSITIVE | NEGATIVE

visionary | deluded

original | eccentric

charitable | profligate

broad-minded | permissive

genius | dilettante

independent | isolated

Aquarius with Aquarius

Aquarius is associated with brotherly love. And this may be how it felt when you two first met. Essentially, you share the same philosophical approach and are extremely comfortable and at ease with each other. We know you are alike. But what you need to know is just how different from each other you are so that we can break the stasis of immature twinship and infuse your relationship with some spice. Please check out your individual Moon signs and ascendants and verify the rapport between your Chinese signs to determine your chances at harmony. You are both equally fascinated by things intellectual and have remarkable facilities for working long, unscheduled (even non-fruitful) hours trying to discover or invent stuff nobody has ever dreamed of before—like radium or a new name for pizza or a boneless chicken.

One thing is sure. You both experience this relationship as a deep friendship—or a mission. You probably wake up in the morning having dreamed dreams of irrational proportions that nobody else but you two could imagine. All day, your brilliant intellectual minds challenge each other and test your tremendous common capacity for original thinking. Thank Zeus, you are not the least smidgen concerned with validation or approval. This, of course, saves you from going mad and allows you free reign to radically open to new levels of nonreasonable thought. Aquarius is known for his uniqueness of perspective, innovation, and eccentricity. Your main objective is to bring about some sort of progress or social change. You are concerned with the ideals and aspirations that characterize humanity as a whole. It is therefore not impossible that you two will spend many long winey evenings discussing and possibly fighting for your individual visions. You may be too opinionated, too erratic, fanatical and, destructive, and end up by tearing down the status quo without providing an alternative. But that's your lookout. I'm just telling you how (best-case scenario) life might go down at a double-Aquarius couple's house.

If you have not left each other by now, let's look at your chances for romance and passion. Lovebirds you are not. But, as you are each Aquarian and hence not overly zealous about sex in the first place, you may nevertheless be content. Could you breathe a mutual sigh of relief every night and sleep on both ears knowing you have finally found a partner who doesn't drive you crazy with mood swings, or make you feel uncomfortable or inadequate for not being more expressively loving and affectionate. You are both kind and friendly, but as Aquarians, you probably prefer to remain detached from excessive intimacy. This doesn't mean that you won't have a satisfying sex life. In fact, whatever it is that you do cook up to do to each other under those torn sheets could be ravishingly unique (and maybe even a bit kinky.)

Since you are both so dedicated to humanitarian causes, you would do well to work on a project together. This could range from getting involved with Amnesty International, to being a fundraiser for your local public television channel, to doing complex AIDS research, or running an idealistic school or youth hostel. Whatever you choose, making a difference and having some sort of impact on the world is always more important to you than making a lot of money.

For your own peace of mind, and particularly for your kids' (if the thought of procreation has ever crossed your collective mind), hire a warm, down-to-earth housekeeper to cook and care for you and your home. Domesticity is definitely not up your alley. The pair of you are always off on a lecturing circuit around the country or giving workshops on your favorite topics (from astrology to quantum physics, to spaceman pizza brainstorming seminars) in your living room. Nevertheless, I think you might have the ability to be quite remarkable parents. Just like you, your kids (an idealistic Sagittarius or a determined Aries) will be fearless, unorthodox, and very independent.

½ Aquarius with Pisces

When a coolly intellectual Aquarius gets together with a compassionate, emotional Pisces, sparks decidedly do not fly. Oh, you will undoubtedly have plenty to talk about. But I am afraid I do not see passionate vibrational currents flashing about to indicate that you two are going to fall irretrievably in love. Not right away. For this relationship to work at all, it will extract its price in enormous compromise from both sides. I daresay that making this Aquarius/Pisces couple stick will take guts.

Both of you are aware, idealistic people, interested in social causes and metaphysics. Many times, you share the same ideals and visions. You might actually have met because you were working on the same paranormal study project and found something mutually attractive or cute about the other person on the job site. Having a mutual mission or goal to accomplish together would create a strong bond here and help to balance some of the challenges that will surely arise between you.

An independent, progressive Aquarius, although he or she will surely try to dodge the issue, will be obliged to find a way to overcome a defensive fear of intimacy. The question is, can you learn to share your feelings with your sensitive Pisces partner? Pisces needs a lot of affection and devoted acknowledgment. A little handwritten "I love you" note left on the breakfast table or a red rose will work wonders. Aquarius, you are lucky. A Pisces who really loves you will ultimately be able to help you open up to your softer, more vulnerable and intuitive side. Let Pisces erase some of that opinionated, rebellious edge, and smooth your erratic ways. Don't be afraid. Pisces is not out to rob you of your precious uniqueness. But if you heed the wisdom of the plain-hearted, good-natured Piscean who cares more about you than you even do about yourself, you won't lose your freedom or your individuality. Instead, you will gain a new, more holistic outlook on life.

Pisces was born with a deep longing to merge with a partner in an empathetic, melting, nonverbal fashion. The restless, high-strung, and often too heady Aquarius manner may act as a turnoff to Pisces, as when it comes to giving passion and receiving physical love, Pisces is a master of sensual intimacy and shared tenderness. Pisces' sensual body will have nothing to do with intellectual sex. The imaginative, adaptable Pisces is happy to set the romantic mood with music and candles. But can Aquarius, who depends on mental titillation for excitement, be any match for Pisces here? Maybe. But it will only work if you are both patient and communicative. Learn to be playful, outrageous, seductive, and crazy. The rest will take care of itself.

Although Aquarius doesn't require much money to be satisfied, I cannot say the same for the spendy-pants Pisces. Except for the fact that Aquarius usually never has any money to give away, he or she will be tolerant and good-natured about a Pisces spouse's extravagant spending habits. Pisces have exquisite taste and a strong desire to be refined and evolve in tasteful and harmonious decors. Pisces may be a dedicated painter, designer, sculptor, astrologer, or musician. The humanitarian Aquarius may choose to be a scientist, a computer programmer, a lawyer, or a lobbyist for cancer research. Either way, unless they win the lottery, this couple doesn't threaten to crash the *Fortune 500* list. Neither or them is a huge earner and one is a huge spender.

Moreover, your tastes are entirely different. Aquarius, you like eclectic art, high-tech objects, chrome, gray, and black. But your Pisces partner may want to decorate a home in a more serene, mystical way with religious artifacts, wind chimes, fountains, and soft pastel colors. Pisces is very private and needs to spend time alone in contemplation and meditation to recharge spiritual batteries. Aquarius is more people-oriented and will delight in meeting friends in a restaurant or going to an astronomy lecture or a local book-signing. Remember I mentioned compromise?. You will be needing that—especially when it comes to socializing.

I don't recommend kids right away in this marriage. Too much disparity of feeling may end this relationship sooner rather than later. I suppose if you prove you can stay together for five years and make enough money to support the poor things, then you might want to have yourselves a Leo or a Virgo child. If they take after you, they will certainly grow up to be sensitive, bright, and bizarre.

PISCES

Taken to the extreme, all of our qualities can become frailties. Some of us are generous to a fault, which can be wasteful. Good communicators can also be blabbermouths. Nurturing parents can smother their children. Fortunately, free will allows us to balance the positive and negative sides of our character. Pisces, the emotional genius, was born:

POSITIVE | NEGATIVE

sensitive | self-pitying

creative | distracted

compassionate | laissez-faire

easygoing | indecisive

intuitive | superstitious

malleable | weak-willed

Pisces with Pisces

Here we confront the true romantic challenge—the passionless passion. First of all, when two Piscean subjects fall in love with each other, they probably won't take much notice. Though the tug on their heart strings may be major, the very chore of getting out of one's clothing to accomplish the necessary gestures incumbent on mad passionate affairs could keep this relationship from ever being consummated. Pisceans embody the very definition of laid-back and cool. They only move when pushed. Pisceans wish and they wash and they dilly and they dally until finally, one day, they simply forget to call each other. The danger of a Pisces/Pisces marriage or live-in long term relationship is that it may just engender one giant pile of inertia.

Unless they are subtly assisted by a feistier element in their individual charts (Aries or Sagittarius or Leo, for example), or propelled down life's rocky road by a lucky accident of birth in Ox, Rat, Tiger, or Dragon year, Piscean people may suffer some pretty mean tortures before the final *flup* to the top of the tank. Yes. They are excellent, strong swimmers. But as evidenced in the image of two fishes headed in totally opposite directions that symbolizes their sign, Pisceans don't really know where they're going. Nor do they mind. They live to be adaptable, flexible, openhearted, easygoing, gentle, intuitive, and spiritual. They are romantic in the extreme. Concrete they are not. And in this couple, who's going to make money, support kids and a household, make decisions? Who'd fill out the forms?

As you have noticed by now, I do not favor this combo. Pisces matched with Pisces strikes me as a giant gamble at best. If it happens—if you are a sweet-natured, kindhearted, pleasure-seeking Pisces type and along swims an even more lovable Pisces type and you simply cannot resist hooking up with him or her—allow me to give you some advice:

First, make sure one of you has a sound, income-producing profession into which you are firmly (read, *for life*) ensconced and committed. Pisceans who start young to pursue well-defined career paths are the most successful at sticking things out. Second, surround yourselves with parents, aunts, uncles, and the like, whose advice and guidance will keep your couple grounded and focused. Three, don't have children until you have lived together for at least three years. Build your nest soundly before imposing new strains on the relationship. Finally, share one or more creative activities in which you are both involved. You will need every last ounce of all this glue to keep you two Fish swimming in the same general direction.

There is at least one reward in this relationship: The sex will be extravagantly gorgeous. Pisces is essentially giving. You are both ultra-romantic and caring. Flowers, wine, music, and soft lights please and excite you both. There will never be any embarrassment or silly modesties between you two. Neither is afraid or shy about intimacy. Good physical exchange between partners can hold a couple together for life. Don't go looking for passive obsessive sex, à la Scorpio, between two Pisces. Rather, lie on your backs, hold hands, and float to ecstasy through waves of delight.

Watch out for excessive pleasure-seeking, incipient depression following failure, patterns of mutual gloom leading to self-pity, and a tendency to paranoia. If and when your couple starts to feel a bit shaky, openly consult friends, family, and professionals. You are not self-starters and will frequently require assistance from outsiders.

About your kids: Scorpios, Cancers, and Tauruses would be most harmonious with you two. But, in truth, there are not many signs with whom you cannot get along. Do watch for your own desire to please the tougher tots you may hatch. You may shrink from giving discipline because you so long to be their loving pal. Again, get advice from somebody who has more experience. Left to your own parental devices, you may be too permissive and laid back to raise those kids to be solid citizens.

ABOUT THE AUTHOR

Author/Astrologer Suzanne White is American, but she lives in France and Buenos Aires. She has been a college professor, a fashion model, a journalist, an interpreter, a novelist, a fireworks salesperson, director of a Parisian Couture boutique, an elevator operator, a shoe salesperson, a single mother of two and a simultaneous translator. In 1971, she began writing articles for women's magazines and by 1975 had written her first book about Chinese Astrology.

Suzanne has published four best-selling books on both western and Chinese Astrology. Her books are available for quick download at http://www.suzannewhite.com. Ms. White has been dubbed the "High Priestess" of both Chinese & Western Astrologies by her readers and critics from around the world. All of Suzanne White's books sell steadily and remain in print. Since 1995, White has been a continued presence on the Internet, at first working for both AOL and Disney sites. In 2001, she started her own web site . This most original and amusing web site has been an enormous success and given Suzanne White's name even more global recognition than she previously enjoyed. SUZANNE WHITE is available for consultations, chart readings and compatibility advice at http://www.suzannewhite.com.

###

Made in the USA
San Bernardino, CA
09 November 2016